The Rise of Asia and the Transformation of the World-System

THE RISE OF ASIA AND THE TRANSFORMATION OF THE WORLD-SYSTEM

edited by
Ganesh K. Trichur

Political Economy of the World-System Annuals, Volume XXX
Immanuel Wallerstein, Series Editor

LONDON AND NEW YORK

First published 2009 by Paradigm Publishers

Published 2016 by Routledge
2 Park Square, Milton Park, Abingdon, Oxon OX14 4RN
711 Third Avenue, New York, NY 10017, USA

Routledge is an imprint of the Taylor & Francis Group, an informa business

Copyright © 2009, Taylor & Francis.

All rights reserved. No part of this book may be reprinted or reproduced or utilised in any form or by any electronic, mechanical, or other means, now known or hereafter invented, including photocopying and recording, or in any information storage or retrieval system, without permission in writing from the publishers.

Notice:
Product or corporate names may be trademarks or registered trademarks, and are used only for identification and explanation without intent to infringe.

Library of Congress Cataloging-in-Publication Data

Trichur, Ganesh K.
   The rise of Asia and the transformation of the world-system / Ganesh K. Trichur, editor.
     p. cm. — (Political economy of the world-system annuals ; v. 30)
   Includes bibliographical references.
   ISBN 978-1-59451-741-9 (hardcover : alk. paper)
   1. Asia—Economic conditions—21st century. 2. Asia—Social conditions—21st century. 3. Asia—Politics and government—21st century. 4. Globalization—Asia. I. Title.
   HC412.T744 2009
   337.5—dc22
2009004020

Designed and Typeset by Straight Creek Bookmakers.

ISBN 13 : 978-1-59451-741-9 (hbk)
ISBN 13 : 978-1-59451-742-6 (pbk)

CONTENTS

PART I Asian Regionality and the Geopolitics of the World-System

1. East Asian Regional Dynamics in the Twenty-First Century
   World-System   3
   Ganesh K. Trichur

2. The Politics of Geopolitics: The Case of Northeast Asia   25
   Immanuel Wallerstein

3. Asia, Eurasia, Eurasianism: The Role of Russia in the Transition
   from U.S. Hegemony   39
   Boris Stremlin

4. China in Three Geographical Contexts   59
   Steven Sherman

5. The Roles of Central Asian Middlemen and Marcher States in
   Afro-Eurasian World-System Synchrony   69
   Thomas D. Hall, Christopher Chase-Dunn, and Richard Niemeyer

PART II Asian Struggles

6. Dictatorship and Development in China: Their Impact on the
   Workers of the World   85
   Robert K. Schaeffer

7. China, Asia, and Labor Standards After the 2005
   Multi-Fiber Arrangement   99
   Robert J. S. Ross

8. Aquaculture Commodity Chains and Threats to Food Security
   and Survival of Asian Fishing Households   117
   Wilma A. Dunaway and M. Cecilia Macabuac

9. Utopystics and the Asiatic Modes of Liberation: Gurdjieffian Contributions to the Sociological Imaginations of Inner and Global World-Systems 139
Mohammad H. Tamdgidi

Contributors 157

Acknowledgments 160

Series Page 161

PART 1

Asian Regionality and the Geopolitics of the World-System

1

EAST ASIAN REGIONAL DYNAMICS IN THE TWENTY-FIRST CENTURY WORLD-SYSTEM

Ganesh K. Trichur

Introduction

The rise and upward mobility of the East Asian region in the hierarchy of the interstate system is the other side of the long-drawn-out world-systemic crisis of transition (Wallerstein 1982), a transition that began in the late 1960s with the crisis of U.S. hegemony (Arrighi 1994; Wallerstein 2000) over the interstate system. In the course of this crisis the terms *globalization* and *neoliberalism* began to occupy increasing attention from left and right, largely following the disintegration of the Soviet empire in the late 1980s alongside U.S. claims to be the only remaining superpower on the planet. As Goran Therborn and Habibul Haque (2006: 1) observe, our "almost everyday use of the word 'globalization' has nearly robbed itself of any great theoretical import or empirical value." Globalization is nevertheless the name for a U.S.-led project in the 1980s that succeeded the failed global "development project" (McMichael 2008) that the United States had spearheaded during the two Cold War decades following the 1945 Peace of Yalta. What Gilbert Rozman (2004: 353) calls the "power of globalization" and what others call the pursuit of "open regionalism" (Hamilton-Hart 2006: 114, 126) is closely related to the U.S. neoliberal project in the

1970s and 1980s to supply financial, political, and redistributive fixes for the late 1960s–early 1970s crisis of ruling-class power emerging out of the more general crisis of overaccumulation of capital.

The overaccumulation crisis signaled the exhaustion of profitable opportunities and returns from further investments in the U.S.-led post-1945 "free world" developmental path organized through the Bretton Woods institutions (the World Bank and the International Monetary Fund [IMF]) and secured through far-flung U.S. military bases in Western Europe and East Asia. The fiscal and monetary crises in the United States that emerged out of U.S. military defeat in Southeast Asia created the conditions for the global stagflation (stagnant output and accelerating inflation) of the 1970s and the breakdown of the Bretton Woods institutions, alongside the serious erosion of the wealth and power of U.S. ruling classes. During most of the post-1945 period of strong world economic growth, the top 1 percent of income-earning U.S. households commanded a stable 8 percent share of national income. This share however, plunged precipitously in the 1970s (Harvey 2005: 44, 15–22). Between 1965 and 1973 the rate of profit fell by 30 percent in the U.S. private business sector and by 20 percent in the G-7 core group of nations (Brenner 2002: 22). It was in this conjuncture that neoliberal globalization—in both the United States and in the UK—dramatically consolidated itself in 1979 as a new orthodoxy regulating public policy in the capitalist core. In the 1980s the globalization project redefined development as successful "participation in the world market" (McMichael 2008: 117) and reconstituted class power in the core states by enabling ruling classes to switch from investments in material expansion to investments in an ongoing financial expansion (Arrighi 1994: 1–15).

"Neoliberalism has meant in short, the financialization of everything" (Harvey 2005: 31). In general it has meant the hypermobility of transnational capital since the mid-1980s. If in 1983 the combined foreign exchange reserves of the five largest central banks (in the United States, the UK, Germany, Switzerland, and Japan) dwarfed the average daily turnover of $39 billion circulating in major foreign exchange markets by more than 3:1, by 1986 they were about even in size; and by 1998 the volume of daily trading in foreign exchange markets ($1.8 trillion) was four times greater than the foreign exchange reserves of these five central banks (Pempel 1999b: 63). In particular, neoliberalism has meant the triumph of monetarist doctrines, extensive industrial and financial deregulation of national economies (although the United States, the European Union [EU], and Japan continue to protect agriculture through farm subsidies and tariffs), and widespread privatization of state-owned assets. If financial globalization has been the characteristic response of the world-system to historically recurring overaccumulation crises, the historical response to these system-wide crises has entailed the reconstitution of the world-system on entirely new structural foundations (Arrighi 1994: 74–84). What these newer structural foundations are and whether or not these foundations will be built on more socialist and egalitarian structures than the foundations organized under previous world hegemonies is part of the ongoing struggles in the current transition. The rise of East Asia is, however, an integral part of the structural crisis.

The turn toward neoliberalism has been accompanied by three interrelated developments. First, the neoliberal turn has produced a general crisis of the interstate system of sovereign states through the worldwide (although uneven) disempowerment and retreat of all (Keynesian) welfare states and national developmental states in most of the Third World. Second, neoliberal globalization is associated with generally uneven world economic growth: most of the growth of the world economy during the period of neoliberalism has taken place in nations and regions that have little to do with neoliberal doctrines. Third, the neoliberal turn has created the material circumstances for a strong regionally networked integration and economic expansion of East Asian states, thereby creating the distinct possibility of the recentering of world-scale processes of accumulation in East Asia. These three developments are closely related to the crisis and limits of the U.S. developmental path that unfolded in the late 1960s and early 1970s and accelerated in the course of the financial expansion of the 1980s.

The First Development was the crisis of the interstate system of nation-states that began with the global debt crisis and collapse of the Third World as a political entity in the aftermath of the U.S.-initiated Volcker monetary shock (1979–1982). By hiking up real interest rates, the Volcker monetary shock bankrupted most Third World nation-states in Africa and Latin America. It also put intense competitive pressure on East Asian states to restructure themselves. Third World states had borrowed extensively during the 1970s from U.S. and Western European transnational banks at a time when the world economy was afloat with excess liquidity and interest rates appeared to reach all time lows. When the United States raised interest rates to relieve the pressures on an oversubscribed dollar, it also astronomically raised the costs of servicing Third World loans. As a result, the direction of capital flows dramatically reversed in and after 1984 in the form of massive financial outflows from the Third World, mostly for servicing the inflated interest costs of monetary debt. In the 1980s the net extraction of financial resources from the Third World exceeded $400 billion (McMichael 2008: 138). The collapse of raw material and primary commodity prices in the early 1980s only worsened the capacity of indebted nations to repay their debts. In the process the former Bretton Woods institutions became part of a new global debt regime in which IMF-led structural adjustment programs (SAPs) complemented the World Bank's structural adjustment *policy* loans for rescheduling Third World debts. The demise of the Third World took place also because of the growing differentiation within the noncore regions of the world-system. Although nations in the world's periphery remained locked into the new debt regime, the oil-producing and -exporting Organization of Petroleum Exporting Countries (OPEC) nations in West Asia profited greatly from the oil price booms of the early and late 1970s (oil prices were to fall only in 1986); on the other hand, the newly industrializing countries (NICs)—primarily South Korea, Hong Kong, Taiwan, and Singapore—successfully launched export-oriented industrialization strategies in the 1970s and 1980s in relation to the transnational expansion of Japanese multilayered business networks in East Asia. The effect of this differentiation was to sharply polarize the world-system into affluent nations of the core (the global North) and their poorer counterparts (the global South). These divisions remained relatively stable during the myriad financial crises of the late twentieth century.

The Second Development relates to the geography of neoliberal economic growth in the context of recurring financial crises in the world economy. Two empirical observations stand out. The first is the dismal record of economic growth in the organic core (the United States, the UK, Western Europe (excluding West Germany), and Japan), especially among countries that championed the neoliberal path. Along with low growth, unemployment averaged 7.5 percent in the United States during the Reagan decade and was more than 10 percent in Thatcher's England. By the end of the 1980s, countries that had taken the neoliberal path continued to be in economic difficulties (Harvey 2005: 88–89). Among noncore nations, those that performed well (such as Poland) did so by flouting IMF advice, whereas those that did follow neoliberal prescriptions, such as Latin America, experienced the 1980s as a "lost decade." Africa experienced an economic meltdown by following the "dangerous and destructive illusion" of neoliberal panaceas of deregulation and privatization for economic stagnation: "Instead of economic recovery, the structural-adjustment era has seen the lowest rates of economic growth ever recorded in Africa (actually negative, in many cases), along with increasing inequality and marginalization" (Ferguson 2006: 11). And Russia nearly collapsed in the 1990s when per capita income declined at the rate of 3.5 percent annually (Harvey 2005:154).

The second empirical observation is that the engines of global growth in the 1980s were Japan, West Germany, and the four East Asian NICs. Asia's annual average growth rates stayed consistently above average annual world economic growth rates for every decade since the 1960s. If we follow World Bank statistics, average annual Asian growth rates were 4.5 percent in the 1970s (compared to corresponding world growth rates of 4 percent), 4.6 percent in the 1980s (compared to world growth rates of 3 percent), and 3.5 percent in the 1990s (compared to world growth rates of 2.8 percent). In 2008 the Asian economies grew at a rate of 4.1 percent compared to the average world growth rate of 3 percent. The Indian economy alone grew by close to 6 percent on average during the 1980s and 1990s and 6.4 percent in 2008. The Southeast Asian region (Malaysia, Indonesia, and Thailand) grew at annual average rates of 7.3 percent in the 1970s, 5.6 percent in the 1980s, and 5.3 percent in the 1990s and maintained a growth rate of 5 percent in 2008 (Siebert 2007: 35). According to a recent report in the *Financial Times*, Malaysia grew by 7.7 percent in 2007, although the report also notes that the spread of the U.S. subprime crisis and the inability to "decouple" from the U.S. economy, and U.S. markets in particular, may soon have an impact on Malaysia and East Asia more generally (Burton 2008: 4). Economic growth in the Northeast Asian region (China, Japan, and South Korea) was adversely affected by the poor performance in Japan in the 1990s—the entire 1990–2005 period ranks as Japan's "lost decade" (Pempel 2006: 38). Japan's growth rate fell from close to 4 percent in the 1980s to 1.7 percent in the 1990s. In 2008 Japan was expected to grow at the low rate of 1.5 percent (Siebert 2007: 35), and the *Financial Times* revealed that the contraction of the Japanese economy by 0.6 percent in the second quarter of 2008 was "its worst quarterly performance for seven years" (Giles 2008: 1). Growth rates in South Korea averaged 8.3 percent in the 1970s, 7.6 percent in the 1980s, 6.1 percent in the 1990s, and were projected to be 5.2 percent in 2008. The People's Republic of China (PRC) alone shows consistent and remarkably rising growth rates: from 7.3 percent in the 1970s to 9.7 percent in the 1980s and 9.9 percent in the 1990s (Siebert 2007: 35). The Chinese economy grew at the rate of 10.4 percent in 2008 (Anderlini 2008: 15). As the *Financial Times* recently observed, the "anemic performance" of both the EU and the United States "is not, however, matched by many of Asia's emerging economies and oil producers, where expansion has barely paused" (Giles 2008: 1). This robust economic expansion of East Asia since the 1970s is largely because the region's economies advanced by *not* implementing the wholesale neoliberal reforms that were supposed to be the palliative for economic stagnation and high unemployment. As Wallerstein (1999: 47–48) observes, East Asia's economic success during the world economic downswing (1970–1995) helps explain why antistatism has no significant purchase in the region.

The Third Development: The contrast between dismal neoliberal economic performance and robust East Asian growth needs some qualification. For one, the question of the rise of East Asia is the question of the East Asian *region* as a whole, so that a country-by-country breakdown of economic growth fails to capture the ways in which the different countries in the region cohere as elements in a densely structured region of growing interdependence. It is this *interdependence* of the parts that comprise the whole region rather than any one of the parts considered in isolation—as is entailed in breaking East Asia into component countries—that offers useful insights (Cumings 1984: 3–4; Hamilton 1999: 52) for understanding the contemporary centrality of the region in world-scale processes of capital accumulation. To borrow a metaphor from Katzenstein and Shiraishi (1997), the rise of East Asia is the emergence, interaction, and expansion of different kinds of "network power." Even though the leading agencies in spinning these regional networks of connectedness represented different combinations of governmental and business enterprises at different times, their cumulative effect has been to intensify the economic, political, social, and cultural interdependence of the region. Who are the agencies behind the networked expansion of East Asia? How have they constructed the East Asian miracle? The next section attempts to engage with these two interrelated questions.

East Asian Networks and the Rise of East Asia

Drawing upon Giovanni Arrighi (1994), I want to argue that the U.S.-led global financial expansion—along the tracks of what Marx calls "the abridged form" of capital accumulation, M-M`: M`>M—has unfolded concurrently with an East Asian-led material expansion—along the tracks of what Marx calls expanded reproduction of capital following the general form M-C-M`: M`>M (Marx 1976: 247–257). The economic success of the East Asian region is often represented as a "miracle" because it appears as the exception to the widespread failure of, and loss of credibility in, the post-1945 U.S.-led global development project that had offered the newly independent Third World nation-states the prospect and promise of linear convergence, through industrialization and modernization, to the living standards enjoyed by the First World. As anthropologist James Ferguson reminds us, the loss of credulity toward narratives of developmental convergence "has not occurred universally, but in specific ways and in specific *places*." In East Asia, to claim that development is over "would surely sound strange to many people" (Ferguson 2006: 182–183). If East Asia accounted for only 4–5 percent of world gross national product (GNP) in 1960 (compared with 37 percent for North America and Mexico), by the early 1990s, the East Asian share (comprising Japan, South Korea, greater China, Taiwan, and the Association of Southeast Asian Nations [ASEAN] group) was 30 percent of world GNP (the same as that contributed by North America on the one hand and Western Europe on the other). The region showed similar jumps in its shares of world trade, as well as per capita gross national product (GNPPC) and foreign direct investment (FDI) inflows (Pempel 2005: 12). Nevertheless, the East Asian miracle is a highly concentrated miracle. In the first place it applies primarily to Japan's emergence in the 1960s from a semi-peripheral position in the world hierarchy of wealth to the top position among the organic core group of nations in Western Europe (excluding Iberia, Ireland, Italy, and Greece), North America, Australia, and New Zealand. A period of high and stable growth (1976–1991) with real income increasing by 100 million yen every eight or nine years followed the period of extremely rapid growth (1955–1973). Japan's gross national income grew more than tenfold, from 48 trillion yen to more than 500 trillion yen between 1955 and 2001 (Ikeda 2004: 367). Second, the miracle of upward mobility was extended in the 1970s and 1980s to include South Korea and the city-states of Taiwan, Hong Kong, and Singapore: the combined GNPPC of these NICs in relation to the GNPPC of the organic core doubled between 1970 and 1980 (Arrighi, Ikeda, and Irwan

1993: 47). More recently, China's undiminished economic expansion appears as part of a general East Asian regional integration and expansion, although the economic success of China is quite different from that of the success of Japan and the other four "minidragons" in terms of growth of GNPPC and in terms of its implications for a more egalitarian global future. What are the conditions of possibility of these East Asian miracles? How have these miracles unfolded across the region?

The postwar trajectories of all the states in East Asia were shaped by the Cold War conflicts between the United States and the USSR. The post-1945 rise of Japan—and of South Korea and Taiwan as well—is directly related to the presence of U.S. military networks and bases in the East Asian project of containing communism in the region. In contrast to the multilateral military alliances forged between the United States and Europe (through NATO), U.S. links with its East Asian allies were predominantly bilateral and country-specific rather than region-wide. As frontline states in the Cold War, Japan, South Korea, and Taiwan served as U.S. military protectorates, and in exchange for a "semisovereign" status they were granted continuous access to U.S. markets. South Korea and Taiwan also nurtured bureaucratic authoritarian industrializing regimes (BAIR) that repressed labor struggles and democratization processes, protected domestic markets, and followed export-oriented industrialization strategies that geared production for export to U.S. markets (Cumings 1984: 28). Intraregional relationships were defined by vertical economic, political, social, and cultural ties between each of the three semisovereign states and the United States rather than horizontal ties between each of the dependent East Asian states (Selden 1997: 312). Unmediated links among the U.S.-East Asian allies were rare, since the United States resisted the creation of intra-Asian ties. Faced with overwhelming military and strategic forces pressing toward fragmentation, East Asian regionalism and integration were at best a dream (Pempel 1999b: 63–64). Although the Vietnam War sharpened collaborations between Thailand, Indonesia, Malaysia, the Philippines, and Singapore (through the formation of ASEAN in 1967) to minimize the effects of great power politics in Southeast Asia, and the Sino-U.S. détente in 1971–1972 led to the normalization of diplomatic relations among China, Japan, and South Korea, until the 1970s the gains in GNPCC from rapid state-promoted industrialization were confined to the U.S. militarized zone in East Asia. If the crisis of U.S. hegemony following its defeat in the Indo-China war precipitated a crisis of profitability for these regimes as well as for Japanese business enterprises, it also created the opportunity and the circumstances for the unfolding of an East Asian *regional* economic expansion through greater *integration* in three different but overlapping phases.

The **First Phase** of regional expansion spanned the period 1968 to 1985. It began with the late 1960s conjunctural crisis of corewide profitability following a corewide explosion of wages that intensified interenterprise competition within the general context of the breakdown of the dollar-gold fixed exchange rate standard in the early 1970s. The U.S.-induced sharp appreciation of national currencies (including especially the yen and the mark) compounded the squeeze on enterprise profitability, creating the circumstances for a general transnational business expansion and relocation of production (along with rising FDI and supply of bank credit) from high-income to low-income regions between 1973 and 1979. If the Volcker monetary shock (1979–1982) raised interest rates (from -2 percent in 1981 to an average of 7.5 percent between 1981 and 1985) and strengthened the dollar (the nominal value of the dollar rose by more than 46 percent and 15 percent against the mark and the yen respectively, between 1978 and 1985) to attract foreign capital inflows into the country, it did so at the cost of domestic U.S. manufacturing output (which declined by 10 percent between 1979 and 1982) and U.S. manufacturing profits (which declined by 43 percent between 1978 and 1982). At the same time, record tax cuts and quantum jumps in U.S. military spending generated unprecedented federal deficits: from a current account surplus of $5 billion in 1981, the U.S. current account faced a deficit of $119 billion in 1985. If the U.S. economy did not go into a tailspin in the 1980s it was because of huge Japanese advances to fund the U.S. deficits, despite the risks of future losses in the event of the dollar's devaluation. Japan and the four NICs also raised their shares of manufactured exports to U.S. markets: between 1979 and 1986 Japan's share increased from 12.5 percent to 22 percent of U.S. imports, and the four dragons' share rose from 7.6 percent to 15.3 percent (Brenner 2002: 54–56). The flip side of rising U.S. dependence on Japanese funding of the U.S. deficits was growing Japanese (and East Asian) dependence on U.S. markets. But the deepening of this relationship of economic dependence and "political exchange" (Arrighi 1994: 352–353) between the United States and Japan that emerged in the 1980s required the deepening of the transborder expansion of the Japanese system of multilayered subcontracting networks into the lower-wage regions of South Korea, Hong Kong, Taiwan, and Singapore.

The Japanese system of the 1970s was a decentralized production system comprising a large number of small and medium-sized firms in the domestic economy integrated through stable and long-term cooperative arrangements into a multilayered hierarchy (the lowest layer comprising a large mass of households) of subcontracting networks of large firms. Unequal wage structures reflected the hierarchy, with wages rising with the size of the enterprise and lower wages corresponding to the lower ends of the value-added chain. Although large firms controlled the upstream networks, the downstream activities were controlled by the *sogo shosha,* powerful trading companies who supplied financial, managerial, and marketing assistance as well as materials for downstream processing and distribution to their own small and medium-sized firms. The *sogo shosha* and small and medium-sized firms—along with large firms in the upper layers of upstream subcontracting networks—were the leading agencies in the transnational regional expansion of Japanese business in the late 1960s and early 1970s, a process in which the lower ends in the value-added chain of the Japanese manufacturing apparatus were transplanted to South Korea, Singapore, Hong Kong, and Taiwan (Arrighi, Ikeda, and Irwan 1993: 49–53). China became a growing export market and outlet for Japanese investment and bank loans following the Sino-Japanese rapprochement in 1972, and in the 1980s Japan became China's leading trade partner and had a balance of trade surplus with China until the early 1990s (Selden 1997: 316). Moreover, in contrast to other core-based business enterprises who swiftly slashed their FDI outflows to low-income regions in response to the effects of the Volcker monetary shock, Japanese FDI and capital continued to flow to the four minidragons throughout the1980s (Arrighi, Ikeda, and Irwan 1993: 62). In this sense the regional expansion of the Japanese multilayered subcontracting system became the basis for the East Asian economic miracle of the 1970s and 1980s organized around what is known as the "flying geese" pattern of Japan-led East Asian development.

The **Second Phase** of East Asian integration and expansion started in 1985 with the Plaza Accord and ended in 1996, the year before the onset of the Asian financial crisis of 1997–1998. It was shaped by two interrelated developments. The first was the September 1985 agreement imposed by the United States on its productive protectorates—in an attempt to bring under control Japan's enormous trade surpluses with the United States and other nations (Selden 1997: 323)—that entailed another round of currency appreciation and ten years of more or less continuous devaluation of the dollar with respect to the yen and the mark. The yen appreciated by 10.5 percent between 1985 and 1990 and 9 percent between 1990 and 1995 (Brenner 2002: 84–85), Taiwan's NT dollar rose by 28 percent (1985–1987), and the Korean won appreciated by 17 percent between 1986 and 1988 (Pempel 1999b: 68). The second was the Japanese response to the Plaza Accord. Japan renewed the flying geese model of regional expansion between1985 and 1994 by taking into its flight-path not only the four dragons but also Thailand, Indonesia, Malaysia, and the Philippines (Arrighi 1994: 351; MacIntyre and Naughton 2005: 78–85). As Japanese firms regionalized their previously national production networks, between 1992 and 1995 roughly 25 percent of Japanese capital was invested in the manufacturing of Southeast Asian–based consumer electronics and automobiles. By 1995 Japanese-owned companies were manufacturing more overseas (more than 41 trillion yen) than they were exporting from Japan. By the late 1980s Japanese direct investment outflows comprised 20 percent of international FDI, 25 percent of equities outflows, 55 percent of bond outflows, and 50 percent of short-term bank loans (Pempel 1999b: 67–68). Although these waves of Japanese FDI were concentrated in Southeast Asia and the NICs (and did not include Mainland China), an unintended consequence of this regional expansion was that it revitalized the Overseas Chinese business diaspora, who became significant intermediaries between Japanese investments and Southeast Asian environments (Arrighi et al. 2003: 312–313). The significant difference between this transborder expansion of Japanese multilayered subcontracting networks into Southeast Asia and the earlier 1970s expansion was that this time the regional expansion was led not by small and medium-sized firms but by large and powerful Japanese corporations (Arrighi, Ikeda, and Irwan 1993: 63–64). Large Japanese (*keiretsu*) and South Korean (*chaebol*) corporations "that had previously been almost exclusively domestic replicated their own vertically integrated systems in various parts of Southeast Asia" (Pempel 1999a: 7). These large corporate business networks, however, were not the only agency of regional expansion; neither were they the best fit, in the aftermath of the 1985 Plaza Accord, in Southeast Asian environments dominated by Overseas Chinese networks.

Far more important in the context of the general turn toward more profitable business strategies of "flexible accumulation" (and away from the large vertically integrated business form that dominated the organization of the most successful businesses in the Cold War period) as a means to overcome the rigidities of the U.S. Fordist regime were the predominantly small-firm environments of Hong Kong, Taiwan, and the PRC. These small firms dominated by ethnic Chinese entrepreneurs created myriad networks of buyer or demand-driven "reflexive manufacturing systems" within the PRC and ASEAN that became the best fit in the pursuit of opportunities for flexible accumulation (Hamilton 1999: 51). As Hamilton and Chang (2003: 202–204) point out, flexible distribution-driven commodity chains were in fact long characteristic of late Imperial Chinese business practices. The general revival of this form of business enterprise as a competitive alternative to vertically integrated business enterprises came at a time when U.S. businesses switched to strategies of vertical *dis*integration to compete with the expansion of large Japanese firms in East Asia. But both U.S. and Japanese networks had to rely upon the intermediation of the Overseas Chinese ethnic business communities who occupied commanding positions in Southeast Asian regional economies (Arrighi et al. 2003: 313). Overseas Chinese diaspora also served as crucial "bridge builders" between Mainland China's vast supplies of skilled and low-wage migrant labor flowing into the PRC's coastal provinces (Guangdong and Fujian) on the one hand, and small and medium-sized firms based in Hong Kong and Taiwan on the other. In this way they significantly expanded the "greater China circle" of trade and investments. Foreign investors in the PRC during the mid-1980s and especially after the 1989 Tiananmen crackdown were almost exclusively Overseas Chinese, the "critical group in providing the capital and expertise to fuel China's economic takeoff, ... adding wings to the China tiger" (Ong 1997: 175). The Plaza Accord reinforced these emerging linkages in a milieu of labor shortages, escalating land prices, and growing environmental protests in Hong Kong and Taiwan. If prior to the mid-1980s East Asia's foreign trade was dominated by *transpacific trade,* between 1986 and 1992 *intraregional trade* assumed greater importance: it surged from 32 percent to 44 percent while the region's trade with the United States dropped steeply from 37 percent to 24 percent (Selden 1997: 321). Between 1985 and 1995, the combined exports of the China Circle in world exports increased from 2.8 percent to 6.6 percent. Between 1987 and 1996 the U.S. trade deficits with the China Circle rose from $26 billion to $47 billion, with virtually the entire deficit recorded against the PRC (Naughton 1997: 7, 17). As the U.S. market share in the exports of Japan, Hong Kong, Taiwan, and other Asian countries dropped following the Plaza Accord, these nations and Japan invested heavily in Chinese and ASEAN industries, which then were credited with rising shares of exports to the United States. The United States thus entered into an endless process of accumulating trade deficits with the China Circle (Selden 1997: 319–320). Finally, FDI in the PRC grew from almost nothing to $5 billion in 1991, to $28 billion in 1993, and to more than $40 billion in 1996, with most of it concentrated in Guangdong and Fujian. This China Circle has emerged not only as a global workshop manufacturing labor-intensive toys and garments; especially since the mid-1980s it has become the world's third leading producer and exporter of electronics. In the process Mainland China has made itself indispensable as a regional market, a prime location for regional and global investments, as well as a technological collaborator in the newer electronics industries crucial for the long-term profitability of Japanese business (Ernst 2004: 25–28).

The **Final Phase** of East Asian integration and expansion starts with the regional financial crisis in 1997 and the region's response to the effects of that crisis continues into the new millennium. During the 1990s East Asia was fast becoming a prosperous region led by strong regional exports to the rest of the world, and its wealth and prosperity made it a magnet for deregulated flows of capital from Japan, the United States, and Europe. These capital inflows were largely composed of private capital flows of highly volatile "hot money" that could move in and out of the region without effective governmental restraints on their movements. From the 1990s on, huge inflows of Japanese money (after the official Japanese discount rate fell close to zero in order to bail out failed Japanese banks and financial institutions) flooded Southeast Asian economies with Japanese bank loans accounting for more than one-third of the total commercial bank debt in five ASEAN member countries (Pempel 1999a: 7–8). "Japanese banks were trying to outgrow problem loans at home and, given the lack of quality domestic borrowers, their only option was to focus on expanding overseas assets" (Hamilton-Hart 2006: 111). Low borrowing rates in Japan also facilitated extensive borrowing by U.S. and European banks which then lent out that money throughout Asia in the "carry trade" (Pempel 1999a: 8). By 1997 East Asia had received more than 60 percent of FDI flowing into developing nations and more than 50 percent of the FDI stock in developing nations. Short-term bank loans (equal to 70 percent of total capital inflows into the region in the mid-1990s) and portfolio investments dominated the capital inflows, most of which went into highly speculative stock and property investments, creating asset bubbles (Pempel 1999b: 73–74). It was in this context that U.S. policymakers sought in 1995 to enhance the value of the dollar by reversing the Plaza Accord (the 1985 accord had after all failed to reduce the staggering U.S. trade deficits with East Asia). The ensuing exchange rate shock triggered massive capital outflows from countries whose currencies were pegged to the dollar alongside an export slowdown (China's export competitiveness in relation to the rest of East Asia by contrast was enhanced when it devalued the yuan in 1994). In the absence of strong political and financial institutions that may have protected the region from swift surges of inflows and outflows of money, a financial meltdown gripped East Asia when its limited organizational capabilities to handle the effects of huge movements of liquid capital combined with the vagaries of capital outflows catalyzed by the U.S. revaluation of the dollar.

Although Brenner (2002: 131) argues that the United States "turned upside down what had appeared, up to that very moment, to be the cornerstone of a competitiveness-and export-oriented US foreign economic policy," he overstates the U.S. desire to restore manufacturing competitiveness. In fact, by the 1980s the ruling classes in the United States had the strongest stakes in the ongoing financial expansion and had given up on manufacturing and industry-based expansion as the route to endless accumulation. Although "East Asia slid from record boom ... to export impasse, speculative bubble, and regional depression, occasioned by a currency revaluation ignited by the reverse Plaza Accord" (Brenner 2002: 133), the impact of the crisis was highly uneven. Thailand, Indonesia, and South Korea (with extremely high debt leverage) were affected the worst, with strong political repercussions. Japan has yet to recover, although economic stagnation in Japan dates from the bursting of the bubble at the onset of the 1990s. China, Taiwan, Singapore, and Hong Kong, with high foreign exchange reserves, were less subject to speculative attacks and stock market collapses. Malaysia was also relatively unaffected because it kept strong capital market controls in place.

More remarkable than the course of the financial crisis is the course of the recovery from the regional crisis. Although Katzenstein (2003: 233) argues that contemporary Japanese enterprises are, for better or for worse, "replicating their domestic *keiretsu* structures in Asia" and promoting regional integration "through thousands of vertically organized quasi-integrated corporate networks," this appears to be only part of the story. At least in the leading electronics sector, Japanese business networks are actively restructuring themselves to compete better in the vibrant East Asian environment. This restructuring of Japanese production networks entails the "fine-tuning" of the division of labor between domestic and overseas production through a reduced reliance on *keiretsu*-type linkages with other Japanese firms. In this shift in business strategy (especially in electronics), it is small and-medium sized enterprises with their relatively greater flexibility who are "the main drivers behind the current expansion of production into East Asia" (Ernst 2004: 10, 12). In this sense Japanese businesses appear to be converging toward the general business form utilized by Overseas Chinese business firms in the greater China Circle.

Although Japan has yet to recover from its long "lost decade," Katzenstein (2003: 216) stresses that Japan is still a technological leader in East Asia. Japan has always sought to maintain (with increasing difficulty) its technological autonomy (considered essential for its security) and leadership in the region. Nevertheless there are growing signs that the technological distance between Japan and the rest of Asia is eroding, as is a Japan-led hierarchy in the East Asian technological order. This is because the economic future of Japan is inextricably intertwined with East Asian growth and prosperity and increasingly with the PRC. Mainland China (not the United States) is now Japan's largest export destination in the world-system (Nakamoto 2008: 4). As Dieter Ernst points out, in the current East Asian milieu, Japanese electronics firms "appear ready to accept that they are no longer capable of imposing an unequal 'flying geese' division of labor on East Asia." The PRC in fact has "the world's biggest market for telecommunications equipment (wired and wireless), the third largest market for semiconductors, and one of the largest and most sophisticated markets for digital consumer and computing devices." Greater technological collaboration between Japan and China on an equal footing—as illustrated in the partnership between Sanyo and Haier since 2002—is not only increasing but also appears to be the trend of the future (Ernst 2004: 25–26, 9, 26).

The other regional trend is the accumulating wealth of the region. In terms of holdings of foreign exchange reserves, by August 2006 Japan held $664 billion in U.S. Treasury securities, and China's holdings were $339 billion, which surpassed the $300 billion combined holdings of the UK, Germany, and Canada (Norris 2006). By 2002 net bank lending to East Asia had turned positive again, although China has been the major recipient of FDI inflows into the region. Large current account surpluses and huge accumulations of foreign exchange reserves (of more than $1 trillion compared to $171 billion held by the European Monetary Union and $29 billion held by the United States) have become strong financial buffers for the region. In general, the crisis has served to reinforce intraregional dependence. Intra–East Asian FDI flows excluding Japan rose from 37 percent of total FDI inflows to Asia in 1999 to 40 percent in 2001: "non-Japan East Asia gets more than half of its inward FDI from regional countries" (Hamilton-Hart 2006: 115). The financial crises in the region also appear to have strengthened the resolve of East Asian states to gain more leverage over the flows of capital and to create robust institutions for this purpose. Even though most East Asian financial markets are relatively more open now than they were before the crisis, this greater open regionalism appears to have been accompanied by a greater capacity for regional crisis management. Although an initial Japan-sponsored proposal for an Asian Monetary Fund was rejected by the United States in favor of IMF programs, the creation in 1999 of the ASEAN Plus Three (APT) group, which includes China, South Korea, and Japan, has been followed by regular meetings since 1999. In May 2000 the regional Chiang Mai Initiative (CMI) offered facilities for emergency foreign currency liquidity support, and an ASEAN Currency Swap Arrangement was enlarged from $200 million to $1 billion. Between 2000 and 2003 several bilateral swaps amounting to more than $30 billion were negotiated. These regional initiatives were devised following widespread regional distrust with the IMF, whose policies in the aftermath of the financial crisis only worsened the effects of the crisis on the region. Korea and Thailand announced intentions to complete repayments of IMF crisis loans in 2003; in February 2003 the Philippines announced its intention to withdraw from IMF supervision alongside demands within Indonesia for exit from its IMF program (Hamilton-Hart 2006: 115–121). Equally significant is the recent "explosion of bilateral trade pacts." "Hardly in existence as recently as 1998, these were extensive and expanding in number and inclusiveness by 2002" (Pempel 2005: 15). Utilizing informal policy networks and coalitions, East Asian governments remain committed not only to "open regionalism" but also to strengthening intraregional cooperation and stability (Solingen 2005: 46). East Asia's "outer limits" are no longer defined by U.S. hegemony: as Pempel (2005: 28) observes, the region's "outer boundaries" are varying constantly as "an undeniable core of countries is becoming more closely linked" without eroding or eliminating established territorial lines. This "remapping" is taking place even as the core countries in Northeast Asia (China, Japan, and South Korea) are cooperating more and more with each other and with Southeast Asia. If Japanese business networks in the late 1970s and early 1980s created a vibrant Northeast Asian "trade and investment corridor" (anchored at one end by Tokyo and at the other end by Hong Kong) running down coastal South Korea, Taiwan, and the PRC, a similar corridor of trade and investment emerged in the 1980s in Southeast Asia, extending from Chiang Mai in Thailand to Surabaya in Indonesia (Tachiki 2005: 165–166). Simultaneously, East Asia's material expansion has not only deepened its trade, commerce, and investment linkages with the oil-rich nations of West Asia but has also widened the trade and investment relations between China and Africa, China and Latin America, and East Asia and regional markets in South Asia. Partly as a consequence of these global networks of East Asian production relations and the growing competitiveness of the global South in the production of world exports, Arrighi (2007: 382) observes that the 1997–1998 crisis also marks a growing bifurcation between the current account balance-of-payments deficits in the global North and the current account balance-of-payments surpluses in the rest of the world. Even though much of the rest of the world's surplus continues to flow to U.S. financial markets, a growing proportion of that surplus is ending in southern destinations and being rerouted to build up currency reserves, thereby relaxing the hold of northern financial institutions on the global South. As the *Financial Times* noted recently, the Industrial and Commercial Bank of China (ICBC) has become the largest "world bank" in terms of market capitalization; it was "expected to report the biggest profit of any bank in the world" for the first half of 2008 (Anderlini 2008: 15). To this we may add the emergence of "sovereign wealth funds" in the world economy as "alternative" pools of foreign exchange reserves held by states in West Asia, Eurasia, and East Asia. China's large state-managed investment funds represent the largest concentration of money capital available for far-reaching global investments—as was evident in the aftermath of the U.S.-generated subprime mortgage crisis (2007–2008) that led to the bankruptcy of different global investment banks (in some of which the PRC has acquired important shareholder stakes).

The Future of East Asian Regionalism

Each of the three overlapping phases of East Asian regionalism appears to have widened and deepened the structured coherence and prosperity of the region. This enhanced regional coherence and prosperity, led by the PRC since the 1990s, appears to be strengthening the foundations of what Arrighi and his collaborators (Arrighi et al. 2003: 263–264; see also Arrighi 2007: 329–332) see as a distinctive market-based development drawing upon late Imperial China's strong traditions of leading the region along a *noncapitalist* market economy–based developmental path. On the other hand, Arrighi et al. also point out a major contradiction of the East Asian regional resurgence. Although the rise of East Asia emerged out of a process of "hybridization" of the East Asian developmental path under U.S. hegemony—the outcome of political and economic interaction that combined features of the Western and East Asian systems—that reduced the *inter*regional gap in incomes *between* East Asia on the one hand and Europe and North America on the other, the same hybrid developmental path also widened *intra*regional income gaps between different countries in the region. As such, the regional renaissance has been "an extremely uneven process that has magnified inequalities among and within the region's political jurisdictions and brought palpable benefits to no more (and probably less) than one-fifth of the region's population, while sharply raising expectations of the benefits of prosperity for all." The hybrid China-led East Asian developmental path thus diverges significantly from "the pattern of more even development characteristic of the historic East Asian system during the era of Chinese preponderance in favor of the Western pattern of uneven development" (Arrighi et al. 2003: 319).

From a somewhat different perspective, Katzenstein and Shiraishi (2006) and their collaborators trace the social foundations of the hybrid market-centered regionalization in East Asia to the emergence and growth of middle classes in the region. Shiraishi (2006: 237) argues that although East Asian capital inflows have affected different areas in the region in different ways, "everywhere it has given rise to new urban middle classes" whose regional significance "is without doubt because they constitute the expanding regional consumer market." As a social class the expansion and reproduction of these middle classes is contingent on the economic growth performance of their respective countries, on a politics that transforms "political issues into problems of output" and seeks "to neutralize class conflict in favor of a consensus on economic growth" (Shiraishi 2006: 241–242). If "the processes of Japanization and Americanization have fused to create regionalization that goes beyond any national model" in East Asia, then the rise of China "*and* the social, economic, and political reassertion of the Chinese populations living in Southeast Asia" only reinforces the general trend toward "hybrid regionalism." The growing importance of China and that of the Overseas Chinese makes the "Sinicization" of the region a market-driven phenomenon—as much as the "Japanization" and "Americanization" of the region (Katzenstein 2006: 10–12). In this it is the middle classes who are the main engine of the hybridization process of regional formation. "Americanization and East Asian hybridization are twin processes that shape middle-class consumer cultures" (Shiraishi 2006: 245). Personal consumption expenditures in East Asia totaled $5 trillion in 2002, which is the same as the figure for the EU and close to the $7 trillion figure for the United States (Katzenstein 2006: 27; Shiraishi 2006: 269). With the opening of China's popular culture market to imports, an East Asian popular culture is also well under way complementing the Japanization that has rapidly altered urban life in the region (Katzenstein 2006: 13). Geoffrey McNicoll (2005: 71–72) points to this East Asian urban middle class that is "acculturated to Japanese cartoons, Hong Kong martial arts films, and Western computer technology—embodied in equipment increasingly of Chinese manufacture, with the latest, if pirated, software" but "recognizably akin to the middle class of Europe or America." Although the particular consumption basket is "distinctive," it does not "differentiate" Asian consumers from consumers elsewhere. Even though ethnic, linguistic, and religious divisions remain alive in the region, the cultural clashes work only on a small scale.

In particular, Takashi Shiraishi (2006: 242–243) identifies three overlapping "waves" of middle-class formation. The first wave of middle-class formation took place in postwar Japan (between 1955 and the early 1970s), before spreading in a second wave to the newly industrialized economies of South Korea, Taiwan, Hong Kong, and Singapore (1960s–1980s). The first two waves of middle classes emerged within the context of an East Asian regional system fashioned under U.S. hegemony and the spread of "Americanism" in the course of the Cold War project of containing communism. The standard consumption basket—which included cars, radios, refrigerators, washing machines, cosmetics, and other goods—that made American consumers part of the middle class also became the standard for the construction and self-representation of East Asian middle classes. By the 1970s, phenomenal economic growth in Japan had enabled the appropriation of the American way of life. The third wave of East Asian integration and expansion led to the emergence of middle classes in major urban centers of Southeast Asia during the last years of the Cold War (Thailand, Malaysia, and to a lesser extent in Indonesia and the Philippines), and a fourth wave (since the late 1990s) of middle-class formation is taking place in urban centers of China's coastal provinces. "All of these factors," Katzenstein (2006: 27) claims, "are laying the social foundations for a market-centered regionalization in East Asia." To this we may add that the rise of the Asian middle class is also symbolized by a "supermarket revolution" in China since 2000 (and in India as well since 2006), where top global retailers operate in its prosperous urban markets (McMichael 2008: 287).

What, however, is the size and extent of this middle-class formation in the region? In Taiwan the technology-intensive growth of small and medium-sized industries expanded the middle classes from 12 percent in 1963 to 40 percent in 1983. In South Korea extensive urbanization (nearly 70 percent of the population became urbanized in the 1980s, and 82 percent of the population were urban by 1990) and industrialized economic growth expanded the size of the middle class from 15 percent in 1960 to 26 percent in 1980 to 32 percent in 1985. In the late 1980s powerful democratization movements in the country eroded the power of the U.S.-supported dictatorships, and in the 1990s South Korea became a mass consumer society. But the gap between rich and poor in South Korea, despite recovery from the 1997 financial crisis, "climbed to the third-highest in the OECD" (Armstrong 2008: 127). In both South Korea and Taiwan the rise of the middle classes is associated with growing democratization as well—but whereas in South Korea democratization came with grassroots movements, in Taiwan the initiative came from above, from the Guomindang party-state in the mid-1980s.

Across most of Southeast Asia the growth of middle classes has in fact been much less sizable or impressive. In Thailand an educational expansion (1975–1980) disproportionately benefited the Sino-Thai Bangkok middle classes (who were also the main agents of the "successful middle-class revolt" in 1992), and the economic boom of 1987–1995 produced middle-class jobs in manufacturing, finance and insurance, real estate development, and the hotel and entertainment industries. Insofar as the 1997 Asian financial crisis arrested economic growth in Thailand, the aftermath of the crisis does not appear to be associated with a middle class growing outside of the Bangkok metropolitan area. In Malaysia a developmental state governed by the business-oriented United Malay National Organization (UMNO) Party fostered the emergence of a predominantly ethnic Malay middle class. In Indonesia under General Suharto's New Order, fewer than 10 percent of the Indonesian population (professionals and technicians, executives and managers, and white-collar workers) comprise the Indonesian middle classes, whereas the poor expanded from 22.5 million in 1996 (11 percent of the population) to 48 million in 1999 (24 percent of the population). In the Philippines the middle classes comprise not more than 10–11 percent of the population (Shiraishi 2006: 245–267). Although a numerically large number of people in China, Indonesia, and the Philippines belong to the middle class, the per capita income levels in these three nations are still around 10–12 percent of the average per capita income level in the United States (McNicoll 2005: 71).

As Dieter Ernst points out, the middle- and higher-income classes in the East Asian regional market comprise some 141 million consumers who represent only 10 percent of the total East Asian population. These high-end markets are dominated by the city-states of Hong Kong and Singapore and the semisovereign states of South Korea and Taiwan. Somewhat paradoxically, the 41 million high-end consumers in the PRC account for nearly 30 percent of East Asia's higher-income market (Ernst 2004: 9). More generally, the picture of rising and prosperous Asian middle classes appears more characteristic of the "diamond-shaped" social structures typical of Japan, Hong Kong, Taiwan, and South Korea. The social structure of the PRC by contrast appears as a "pyramid" with small percentages of high-income groups, small numbers in the intermediate income groups, and very large numbers in the lower social strata. The affluent strata comprise 2.2 percent of the population (around 3 million) in the younger and middle generations (between thirty and forty-five years old) living mostly in the southern cities of Shenzhen and Guangzhou, Beijing, and the coastal cities of Shanghai and Tianjin, as well as in the richer suburbs of most cities. In terms of assets, income, occupation, and education, they include high- and middle-ranking officials of government and party and managers of successful state-owned enterprises; owners and managers of private enterprises; and new high-income white-collar strata who benefited from expanding educational opportunities in top universities either in China or abroad. The income level defining the newly affluent is around yuan (Y) 2,000 (U.S.$250) per capita per month plus bonuses, profits, and other kinds of incomes. According to a 2002 study by the Chinese Academy of Social Sciences (CASS), some 15 percent of Chinese belonged to the middle class (compared to 60 percent in the United States) and CASS's forecast is that the country's middle class would not exceed 100 million in the future (cited in Croll 2006: 101). There is also a large and growing gap between the very rich and the middle classes. As against these two strata, most of China's urban population of 500 million is located at or near the base of the urban wealth pyramid. Compared to the average annual urban income levels of Y8,000 per year, very few urban Chinese have experienced upward mobility into elite income levels of Y2,000 per month. Although average urban per capita income has grown at the steady rate of 14 percent per year (from Y5,425 in 1998 to Y6,280 in 2000, to Y7,703 in 2002 to Y9,422 in

2004), official estimates for the urban Gini coefficient show urban inequality rising from 0.16 in 1978 to 0.28 in the early 1980s to 0.38 in 1995, 0.46 in the late 1990s and 0.50 in subsequent years. With the urban poverty line set at between Y1,700 and Y4,200 per year (or Y150–Y200 per month), there were 13 million urban poor in the mid-1990s and 23 million urban poor (excluding migrants) in 2004 (Croll 2006: 102–106, 112–114). To this we should add the huge spatial and interprovincial income disparities in the PRC. Most if not all of the leading high-end growth markets in the PRC are concentrated in Beijing, the Yangzi Delta around Shanghai, and the southern coastal provinces, places which "even launch markets for digital consumer and mobile communication devices." In the rest of China, however, "persistent poverty keeps strangulating effective demand" (Ernst 2004: 40n10).

Thus a first consequence of rising material inequalities is the constraint they exert on the growth of domestic and regional markets. Even though growth and distribution in the PRC have been relatively higher and more egalitarian than in India—the average Chinese citizen earns almost twice as much a year as the average Indian citizen (McMichael 2008: 285)—China remains one of the more unequal countries in the world. This reproduces the dependence of the Chinese and East Asian expansion on the willingness and capacity of the United States and the EU to absorb ever increasing labor-intensive East Asian labor exports. "This willingness and capacity cannot be taken for granted in view of the growing indebtedness of the United States and the near economic stagnation of the EU" (Arrighi et al. 2003: 319). "Even though China controls 55% of the world market for laptop computers and produces 30% of all flat-screen televisions and 20% of microprocessors, it essentially assembles components designed and made elsewhere, or uses copied designs. The other 40% of manufactured products is constrained by the size of China's home market, given the historic low wage structure" (McMichael 2008: 286).

A second consequence of the skewed distribution of the benefits of economic growth is the emergence of sustained, widespread, and explosive social conflicts in the PRC. The documentation for this is extensive (Perry and Selden 2004; Lee 2007). Migrant workers (mostly women) who have been central to the PRC's coastal development strategy for upward mobility in the world-system are among the most exploited workers in the world. Millions of urban workers laid off by the extensive post-1997 restructuring of state-owned enterprises are the other great losers in China's emergence as the workshop of the world. These two social groups—superexploited migrant workers and laid-off urban workers—confront increasingly common predicaments of destitution and degradation of social status. If they have not yet combined to confront the inequities produced by the economic growth process, we may not rule out the possibility of such combinations emerging in the future. Neither may we rule out the other possibility that Perry and Selden (2004: 19) point out. The long history of popular social unrest in China suggests that "it could ... be managed by adept state leaders in such a way as to under*pin* rather than under*mine*, their rule." Whether or not, and how, the Chinese Communist Party rises to meet this challenge in the new millennium may well determine whether or not the future of the PRC, and with it the future of the world-system, moves in a socialist direction.

References

Anderlini, Jamil. 2008. "ICBC Eyes Biggest Profit in the World." *Financial Times* (August 21).
Armstrong, Charles. 2008. "Contesting the Peninsula." *New Left Review* 51 (May-June): 115–135.
Arrighi, Giovanni. 1994. *The Long Twentieth Century*. London: Verso.
———. 2007. *Adam Smith in Beijing: Lineages of the Twenty-first Century*. London: Verso.
Arrighi, Giovanni, Po-keung Hui, Ho-fung Hung, and Mark Selden. 2003. "Historical Capitalism, East and West." In Giovanni Arrighi, Takeshi Hamashita, and Mark Selden, eds., *The Resurgence of East Asia: 500, 150, and 50 Year Perspectives*. London: Routledge, 259–333.
Arrighi, Giovanni, Satoshi Ikeda, and Alex Irwan. 1993. "The Rise of East Asia: One Miracle or Many?" In Ravi Palat, ed., *Pacific-Asia and the Future of the World-System*. Westport, CT: Greenwood.
Brenner, Robert. 2002. *The Boom and the Bubble: The US in the World Economy*. New York: Verso.
Burton, John. 2008. "Singapore and Malaysia Struggle as US Stalls." *Financial Times* (August 12).
Croll, Elisabeth. 2006. *China's New Consumers: Social Development and Domestic Demand*. London: Routledge.
Cumings, Bruce. 1984. "The Origins and Development of the Northeast Asian Political Economy: Industrial Sectors, Product Cycles, and Political Consequences." *International Organization* 38(1): 1–40.
Ernst, Dieter. 2004. "Searching for a New Role in East Asian Regionalization: Japanese Production Networks in the Electronics Industry." East-West Center Working Papers, Economic Series: No.68, Honolulu, Hawaii, 1–43.
Ferguson, James. 2006. *Global Shadows: Africa in the Neoliberal World Order*. Durham, NC: Duke University Press.
Giles, Chris. 2008. "Bleak Outlook Sends Pound Lower Against Dollar." *Financial Times*(August 14).
Hamilton, Gary. 1999. "Asian Business Networks in Transition: or, What Alan Greenspan Does Not Know About the Asian Business Crisis." In T. J. Pempel, ed., *The Politics of the Asian Economic Crisis*. Ithaca, NY: Cornell University Press, 45–61.
Hamilton, Gary, and Wei-An Chang. 2003. "The Importance of Commerce in the Organization of China's Late Imperial Economy." In Giovanni Arrighi, Takeshi Hamashita, and Mark Selden, eds., *The Resurgence of East Asia: 500, 150, and 50

Year Perspectives. London: Routledge, 173–213.
Hamilton-Hart, Natasha. 2006. "Creating a Regional Arena: Financial Sector Reconstruction, Globalization, and Region-Making." In Peter Katzenstein and Takashi Shiraishi, eds., *Beyond Japan: The Dynamics of East Asian Regionalism*. Ithaca, NY: Cornell University Press, 108–129.
Harvey, David. 2005. *A Brief History of Neoliberalism*. Oxford: Oxford University Press.
Ikeda, Satoshi. 2004. "Japan and the Changing Regime of Accumulation: A World-System Study of Japan's Trajectory from Miracle to Debacle." *Journal of World-Systems Research* 10, no. 2 (Summer): 363–394.
Katzenstein, Peter. 2003. "Japan, Technology, and Asian Regionalism in Comparative Perspective." In Giovanni Arrighi, Takeshi Hamashita, and Mark Selden, eds., *The Resurgence of East Asia: 500, 150, and 50 Year Perspectives*. London: Routledge, 214–258.
———. 2006. "East Asia—Beyond Japan." In Peter Katzenstein and Takashi Shiraishi, eds. 1997. *Network Power: Japan and Asia*. Ithaca, NY: Cornell University Press, 1–33.
Katzenstein, Peter, and Takashi Shiraishi, eds. 1997. *Network Power: Japan and Asia*. Ithaca, NY: Cornell University Press.
———. 2006. *Beyond Japan: The Dynamics of East Asian Regionalism*. Ithaca, NY: Cornell University Press.
Lee, Ching Kwan. 2007. *Against the Law*. Berkeley, CA: University of California Press.
Macintyre, Andrew, and Barry Naughton. 2005. "The Decline of a Japan-Led Model of the East Asian Economy," in T. J. Pempel ed., *Remapping East Asia: The Construction of a Region*. Ithaca: Cornell University Press: 77–100.
Karl Marx (1976) *Capital* Vol.1, Penguin Books, London.
McMichael, Philip. 2008. *Development and Social Change: A Global Perspective*. Thousand Oaks, CA: Pine Forge Press.
McNicoll, Geoffrey. 2005. "Demographic Future of East Asian Regional Integration." In T. J. Pempel, ed., *Remapping East Asia: The Construction of a Region*. Ithaca, NY: Cornell University Press, 54–74.
Nakamoto, Michiyo. 2008. "China Ousts US as Biggest Japanese Market." In *Financial Times* (August 22).
Naughton, Barry. 1997. "The Emergence of the China Circle." In Barry Naughton, ed., *The China Circle: Economics and Technology in the PRC, Taiwan, and Hong Kong*. Washington, DC: Brookings Institution Press, 3–37.
Norris, Floyd. 2006. "Accessory for a U.S. Border Fence: A Welcome Mat for Foreign Loans." *New York Times* (November 4).
Ong, Aihwa. 1997. "Chinese Modernities: Narratives of Nation and of Capitalism." In Aihwa Ong and Donald Nonini, eds., *Ungrounded Empires: The Cultural Politics of Chinese Transnationalism*. New York: Routledge, 171–202.
Pempel, T. J. 1999a. "Introduction." In T. J. Pempel, ed., *The Politics of the Asian Economic Crisis*. Ithaca, NY: Cornell University Press, 1–14.
Pempel, T. J. 1999b. "Regional Ups, Regional Downs." In T. J. Pempel, ed., *The Politics of the Asian Economic Crisis*. Ithaca, NY: Cornell University Press, 62–78.
———. 2005. "Introduction: Emerging Webs of Regional Connectedness." In T. J. Pempel, ed., *Remapping East Asia: The Construction of a Region*. Ithaca, NY: Cornell University Press, 1–28.

———. 2006. "A Decade of Political Torpor: When Political Logic Trumps Economic Rationality." In Peter Katzenstein and Takashi Shiraishi, eds., *Beyond Japan: The Dynamics of East Asian Regionalism*. Ithaca, NY: Cornell University Press, 37–62.

Perry, Elizabeth, and Mark Selden, eds. 2004. *Chinese Society: Conflict, Change, and Resistance*. New York: Routledge.

Rozman, Gilbert. 2004. *Northeast Asia's Stunted Regionalism: Bilateral Distrust in the Shadow of Globalization*. Cambridge: Cambridge University Press.

Selden, Mark. 1997. "China, Japan, and the Regional Political Economy of East Asia, 1945–1995." In Peter Katzenstein and Takashi Shiraishi, eds., *Network Power: Japan and Asia*. Ithaca, NY: Cornell University Press, 306–340.

Shiraishi, Takashi. 2006. "The Third Wave: Southeast Asia and Middle-Class Formation in the Making of a Region." In Peter J. Katzenstein and Takashi Shiraishi, eds., *Beyond Japan: The Dynamics of East Asian Regionalism*. Ithaca, NY: Cornell University Press, 237–271.

Siebert, Horst. 2007. "Asia's Economic and Technological Outlook." In Malte C. Boecker, ed., *Asia Changing The World:* Hamburg: Verlag Bertelsmann Stiftung, 32–50.

Solingen, Etel. 2005. "East Asian Regional Institutions: Characteristics, Sources, Distinctiveness." In T. J. Pempel, ed., *Remapping East Asia: The Construction of a Region*. Ithaca, NY: Cornell University Press, 31–53.

Tachiki, Dennis. 2005. "Between Foreign Direct Investment and Regionalism: The Role of Japanese Production Networks." In T. J. Pempel, ed., *Remapping East Asia: The Construction of a Region*. Ithaca, NY: Cornell University Press, 149–169.

Therborn, Goran, and Habibul Haque. 2006. "Asia and Europe in the Contemporary World." In Goran Therborn and Habibul Haque, eds., *Asia and Europe in Globalization: Continents, Regions, and Nations*. Leiden: Brill, 1–10

Wallerstein, Immanuel. 1982. "Crisis as Transition." In S. Amin, G. Arrighi, A. G. Frank, and I. Wallerstein, eds., *Dynamics of Global Crisis*. New York: Monthly Review Press, 11–54.

———. 2000. "The Three Instances of Hegemony in the History of the Capitalist World-Economy." In Immanuel Wallerstein, ed., *The Essential Wallerstein*. New York: The New Press, 253–263.

———. 1999. "The Rise of East Asia, or The World-System in the Twenty-First Century." In Immanuel Wallerstein, *The End of the World As We Know It: Social Science for the Twenty-First Century*. Minneapolis: University of Minnesota Press, 34–48.

2

THE POLITICS OF GEOPOLITICS
THE CASE OF NORTHEAST ASIA

Immanuel Wallerstein[1]

In 2007, there were two central foci of the world's attention. One was Iraq and the other China. Iraq symbolized for most people in most parts of the world a fiasco in which the world's strongest military power had demonstrated that it is unable to win a relatively small war. China, in contrast, was seen by many people as the incarnation of rising forces in the world-system.

This view that the media emphasized in 2007 was quite the opposite of how the media had described the world just a few years earlier, say in 1989. In 1989, the historic rival of the United States, the Soviet Union, was in the process of disintegration. Consequently, the media saw the United States as the lone superpower, unchallenged and unchallengeable in its hegemonic position. In 1989, China was in great internal turmoil made clear by the Tiananmen Square protests and their suppression. China was viewed as politically shaky, en route perhaps to falling apart.

How fast views change! But why do they change so fast? The media, the politicians, and alas the social scientists as well have a tendency to read the headlines day by day and strive to explain each small bump in every curve as something new and fundamentally different. We get thereby a much distorted view of what is happening and furthermore a constantly and rapidly changing view. Social science analysts need to be more sober than that.

Let us start with the observation that there is a significant difference between politics and geopolitics, and therefore between political and geopolitical explanations of world reality. Politics is about the existential present. It is the description of the interplay of multiple forces seeking to achieve and/or maximize their immediate interests. These political forces react regularly to every bump in every curve because each small change may alter in the short run the tactics of other players and therefore make possible constant small-scale realignments of political forces. Political skill is knowing how best to take advantage of these constant possible realignments.

Geopolitics is about something quite different. Geopolitics is about the structural constraints that govern, over a medium run, the interplay of the longer-term political and economic interests of the major players in the world-system. Geopolitical trends are not found in headlines. Indeed, they are largely hidden from the view of the political actors. The geopolitics of the world-system nonetheless shapes the short-run actions of political agents, quite often without their being aware of it. Geopolitics takes place in the structural and cyclical TimeSpaces about which Fernand Braudel was so eloquent, and not in the episodic short-run events we call politics.[2]

For example, in the spring of 2007, the U.S. Congress debated whether or not the appropriations bill for the military in Iraq should or should not include provisions about a date for U.S. withdrawal of troops. Politically, this was very important. It was expected to have a big impact on the 2008 elections, or so the actors seemed to think. But geopolitically, it was of no significance whatsoever. The United States had already been defeated in Iraq, and this defeat could be expected to have an enormous impact on the world-system for the subsequent twenty-five years at least. Whether or not the 2007 U.S. appropriations bill carried an Iraq withdrawal clause would not change that one way or the other.

An analysis of geopolitics is therefore an analysis of middle-run structures and trends. At any given moment, it is about a future that is uncertain. We can lay out the trends that we perceive in the present. We can project ahead what kinds of options this offers to various major forces. We can suggest the probable consequences for one set of players if another set of players moves in one direction rather than another. But we cannot assume that what anyone will do is inevitable and determined. There are too many aleatory factors, too many small decisions to be taken. And we can never be sure what the actors will actually do. What I mean by the politics of geopolitics is an analysis of the probability that actors will go down one path rather than another, and an appreciation of how much difference this will make for everyone else.

The single most important geopolitical change at the moment is the precipitate decline of the world-systemic power of the United States.[3] I shall not discuss here the causes of this, but rather the consequences. The world-system has moved from a situation of *creeping* multipolarity to one of *undisguised* multipolarity. The United States, far from being the "indispensable nation," as Madeleine Albright proclaimed a mere decade ago, has become a country from which other countries are willing to take distance, openly. They are even ready to ignore the United States. This means that other loci of power—political, economic, military—are beginning to consolidate themselves and assert themselves forcefully on the world scene.

Which are these other loci of power? There are many candidates for these positions. The list includes at the very least Western Europe, Russia, China, Japan, India, Iran, and Brazil/South America. I propose to discuss one probable locus of power over the coming twenty-five years, which I denominate as Northeast Asia—meaning the combination of China, Korea, and Japan. Politically and juridically, Northeast Asia is composed today of five entities—the People's Republic of China (PRC), Taiwan/the Republic of China, the Republic of Korea (ROK), the Democratic People's Republic of Korea (DPRK), and Japan.

If we are to imagine them as a singular locus of geopolitical power in the coming decades, the first question that is posed is whether or not there will be some sort of reunification of the two Chinese and the two Korean entities. For if there is not, it is hard to see how there could be some sort of structure that would link meaningfully China, Korea, and Japan, at least to the level that exists in the European Union.

Korea's de facto division into two states dates from 1945, and China's division from 1949. The origins of the divisions basically derive from Cold War conflicts and ideologies. Resistance to unification (or should one say reunification?) has been very deep, and the antagonisms between the divided entities substantial. There has been no serious attempt to overcome these divisions up to now. Yet, on the other hand, both Chinese and Korean nationalism is a very strong force, and the sense that one day these two countries will be reunified is a potent element in the mentalities of the populations and their political leaders. To be sure, this has to be qualified in the case of Taiwan, where a Taiwanese nationalist and separatist movement has strong support, but only of part of the population.

One has to ask therefore what are the geopolitical pressures for these reunifications? The answer is somewhat different in the two cases. The People's Republic of China has been quite clear, and as far as one can tell unbudgeable, in its basic position. Its position is that Taiwan is an integral part of China and must therefore be reintegrated within the legitimate authority of the central government. In the past, China made special provisions when it reincorporated Hong Kong and then Macao, and no doubt the PRC would be willing to consider similar kinds of provisions for Taiwan. But it insists on the abandonment of any pretension to independent sovereignty.

The reasons for China's very strong stand on this issue are not hard to see. It takes the same basic position with regard to any area that fell within the borders of China as of, say, the early nineteenth century. This includes not only

Taiwan, Hong Kong, and Macao but also Tibet, Xinjiang, and Inner Mongolia. Part of the reason is long historical experience. What we call China has, over the past several thousand years, gone through cyclical phases of relative unity under a central authority and a breakdown of this central authority.

This sort of breakdown was manifest as recently as the twentieth-century interwar period when the Kuomintang was in power in the center, but was faced with great difficulties in asserting effective authority in many parts of China. The coming to power of the Chinese Communist Party (CCP) involved, among other things, the reassertion of effective central authority. The CCP, however, sees this task as incomplete. It fears that, if it does not constantly pursue this objective with vigor, not only will Taiwan remain outside this central authority but there also could be a breakdown of central authority in general. And this brings us to the second reason. The CCP believes that any kind of internal breakdown of central authority within China would deal a devastating blow to China's ability to strengthen its power and its role in the world-system as a whole. It is probably correct in this assessment.

Seen from the perspective of those living in Taiwan, views are much divided. Politically, the Kuomintang forces that retreated to Taiwan in 1949, and who long controlled the regime politically, seem inclined in their latest version to work out some sort of arrangement with Beijing. But those one might call the Taiwanese nationalist forces are by and large very resistant to any arrangement of any kind and are frequently threatening to declare Taiwan an independent, non-Chinese state.

This division within Taiwan is partly ethnic, partly generational. Ethnically, the pro-Taiwan independence group is drawn from those whose ethnic links are to groups that have long been located in Taiwan and are largely only located there. The group that was historically Kuomintang is drawn from persons whose ethnic links are to groups on the mainland and who, in many cases, arrived in Taiwan only with the retreat of Chiang Kai-Shek in 1949.

The Kuomintang group was of course for a very long time extremely hostile to the Communist regime in power in Beijing. But times have changed. The United States–Soviet Union Cold War is no more. The regime in power in Beijing has modified its ideological line in significant ways and no longer seems so diametrically different in economic practices from those current in Taiwan. And there is a generational change. The group that actually came in 1949 has largely died out, and their children and grandchildren have been molded politically in later times.

The major pressures leading to a revision of Taiwanese views about reunification are economic. Taiwanese entrepreneurs have been massively investing in mainland China, and an increasing number see their own economic future tied to China's continuing economic transformation. For this group, any move toward Taiwanese independence would represent the double negative of hurting their economic prospects and diminishing the legitimacy of their continued political and social role in Taiwan. In addition, even those who are ethnic Taiwanese, if they are also active entrepreneurs or employed within such structures, may see the economic logic of closer rather than looser ties with the PRC.

Of course, the continuing fear of persons in Taiwan is that they will find the political implications of reunification not at all to their taste. The political history of Hong Kong since its reintegration in 1997 has left an ambivalent message for this group. So they are proceeding with much caution. But one must not underestimate the effect of time. As time goes by, there may be further liberalizations of the Beijing regime. And early discomforts with the impact of reintegration in Hong Kong may fade. And therefore the example to Taiwan may begin to be analyzed differently in Taiwan. Above all, the growing world strength of China is a source of pride whose impact on persons in Taiwan may be to wish to be part of it, especially as the role and importance of the United States in the region continues to recede. Overall, it seems that the geopolitical pressures toward reunification are significantly greater than those against it.

The case of the two Koreas is rather different. They were divided promptly after World War II at the 38th Parallel, a line drawn by the Soviet and U.S. military forces as the limits of their occupation powers. In 1950, a war broke out, one that involved the active participation of the United States (and other Western powers) on one side and of the People's Republic of China on the other. This war ended with an armistice in 1953, at the same line of demarcation as where it began. During the next thirty years, North and South Korea displayed tense and seemingly unremitting hostility to each other. Reunification seemed out of the question.

But once again, geopolitical realities changed. The Cold War came to a close. Nixon's visit to China in 1972 launched a political warm-up process between the two countries, which could not fail to have an impact on Korea. The economy of the DPRK took a severe downward turn. And the dictatorial regimes that South Korea had known almost continuously were brought to an end. In 1998, President Kim Dae Jung announced a so-called sunshine policy, which called for active cooperation with the DPRK without any attempt by South Korea to "absorb" North Korea. This was not a policy that pleased the United States, but South Korea pursued it nonetheless. How successful it has been thus far in modifying North Korean policies remains a matter of great controversy.

One consideration that has weighed heavily on attitudes in South Korea has been the experience of Germany when it achieved its reunification in 1990. Basically, in the German case, there was no merger of the two countries. Rather, the multiple states, so-called *Länder*, that made up the former German Democratic Republic were simply absorbed as individual states within the German Federal Republic. This was called "unity" (*Einheit*) and not "reunification" (*Wiedervereinigung*). This process, although politically advantageous to West Germany, turned out to be enormously expensive. The result has been a unified country that has remained persistently divided, even polarized, economically.

South Korean politicians observed this and drew the conclusion that, even were they able to follow the German path (simple absorption of North Korea), this might be a very unwise choice. The economic bill might be much higher than that paid by West Germany, and the polarizing results even more serious. They decided to pursue a slower, more gradual route to further unification rather than hoping for a sudden transformation, as happened in the German case. And of course this fit the desires of the North Korean regime, which has seemed to be fixated on remaining in power in the form in which they had been exercising it.

Here again, however, time may make a difference. It is impossible to predict whether, within North Korea, there will be any gradual political or economic transformation comparable to either the Soviet or the Chinese experience. But it surely cannot be ruled out, again with the change of generations. And here the outside pressures, particularly from China, may exercise some influence on what happens within North Korea. As for South Korea, their immediate economic interests lead them to want closer ties, ultimately reunification, with North Korea. But perhaps even more, South Korea's ability to stand tall in its relations with both China and Japan would be enormously strengthened by a successful reunification, augmenting its population size and its economic potential.

So, let us say that by 2025, both China and Korea were reunified. Then what? At that point, the big question at the forefront will be: to what degree, and under which terms, can there be greater geopolitical cohesion in Northeast Asia? It depends, of course, primarily on the middle-run interests of the three countries. And these middle-run interests are different.

Japan has, in a sense, the most to gain and the most to lose. And somewhat curiously, Japan seems to be politically the least flexible of the three countries. There are some reasons for this, which are reasonably obvious. Japan lost World War II. The political result was the military neutering of Japan and its continuing subordination to the United States, which has played the role of both its protector and its neocolonial superordinate. But in addition, there has been its anguished shame about what it seems to regard as its geopolitical failure in the national project launched by the Meiji revolution.

Japan compensated for its discomfort with its geopolitical status by concentrating on economic achievement, which has been in fact quite remarkable. In the early post-1945 period, Japan still functioned as a semiperipheral power with a moderate standard of living. But suddenly its economic productive forces surged forward in a combination of much increased economic efficiencies, organizational innovations, and aggressive marketing. It was in fact much aided in surge by the United States, for reasons comparable to those that impelled the Marshall plan in western Europe. By the 1970s, Japan would come to be seen as a member of the so-called Triad (a term invented by a Japanese economist), which meant that it was regarded as the economic peer of Western Europe and the United States. And by the 1980s, Japan was being touted by many U.S. analysts as an unbeatable economic colossus. Even when the overstated economic bubble seemed to suffer a severe setback in the 1990s, Japan never ceased to be an economic powerhouse with a very high standard of living.

And in Japan as elsewhere, the world moved on. The Cold War had ended. Relations between the United States and China had markedly improved. And the generations that came to power in Japan no longer wished to live in the shadow of Japanese defeat in 1945. Call it nationalism or simply pride, Japan wanted desperately to be accepted as a "normal" nation. This meant that it wanted to play a geopolitical role appropriate for a major state, aspiring, for example, to obtain a permanent seat on the UN Security Council. And, most of all, Japan (or at least its more conservative elements, who have consistently controlled the government) wished to end the mandatory nonmilitary status that had been imposed on it by the U.S.-drafted postwar constitution. On May 3, 2007, Prime Minister Shinzo Abe, on the occasion of the sixtieth anniversary of the constitution, called for its revision to permit Japan to play a larger role in global security.

Japan's relationship to the United States became ambiguous or perhaps one should call it contradictory. On the one hand, the conservative forces fully sympathized with U.S. objectives and policies in the world-system. But on the other hand, the United States was an economic rival, and a constraint both on Japan's achieving its full military status and on its pursuit of its own political objectives in the world-system, particularly regionally in Asia. There was also the lingering irritant of U.S. use of Okinawa as a major military base.

In the major effort of the United States to contain and reverse the acquisition by the DPRK of nuclear weapons, Japan was part of the six-power consortium created to confront the DPRK. And Japan was the only one of the other five to support more or less consistently the U.S. positions within this consortium—indeed to support a stronger position vis-à-vis the DPRK than even the United States. Nonetheless, one cannot help wondering whether Japan has not been privately savoring the possibility that North Korea's defiance of the United States, if— as seems likely—it continues unabated, would give Japan the excuse it needs to become itself a nuclear power. Pulling away from the United States would be much easier if and when Japan pulled closer politically to China and Korea.

However, Japan has another dilemma that interferes with closer political relations with China and Korea. Since Japan regards its defeat in World War II as a national humiliation, it has been extremely unwilling to accept responsibility for behavior that other countries—and most particularly China and Korea—consider reprehensible, to put it mildly.

One striking example is the continuing furor over the fact that Japan forced women of various nationalities to serve in brothels for the Japanese army. Japan has never been willing to accept moral responsibility for this policy. Indeed, in 2007, Prime Minister Shinzo Abe retreated even from the restrained apology of a former prime minister. Nor is this the only bone of contention. China and Korea were repeatedly and publicly upset with the annual visits of Prime Minister Junichiro Koizumi to the Yasukuni temple in Tokyo. The temple is for many conservative Japanese a symbol of Japanese nationalism. The same temple is for China and Korea a symbol of Japanese militarist aggression. Furthermore, there is an active movement of revisionism in Japan concerning widely accepted accounts of the Nanjing massacre of 1937 in China. A society to revise textbooks to exclude accounts of this massacre, the Society for History Textbook Reform, counts among its members Prime Minister Shinzo Abe (McNeill 2007).

So, in the immediate politics of recent years, the Japanese have constantly engaged in actions that have revived hostile reactions in China and Korea. But, seen from the Japanese point of view, these actions were part of Japan's resuming its role as a "normal" nation. Why did Japan insist on doing this? Here again, a comparison with Germany might be helpful. Germany has, in the past thirty to forty years, made many statements and taken many actions that involved assuming responsibility for the misdeeds of the Nazi era and trying to make some kind of compensatory atonement. This is exactly what the Japanese have refused to do.

Here again, a geopolitical assessment might help to explain this different reaction of the two defeated powers. In the case of Germany, the Cold War imposed the necessity on West Germany of coming to terms with its historic enemy, France, in order to establish a West European front against the Soviet Union. Part of the price Germany had to pay for the burying of the hatchet by France (and by other Western countries, and indeed by Israel as well) was for Germany to disavow its Nazi past and to seek atonement.

Japan had no France. China and North Korea were on the other side of the Cold War alignments. South Korea was at the time tightly controlled by the United States, and Japan had no need to create closer links, especially since South Korea was still very angry about the Japanese colonial period. In the 1960s and 1970s, there was thus no geopolitical need to imitate the German path. And by the 1990s, when the Cold War was over, Japan had arrived at the stage of nationalist reassertion. So had Germany, of course, but it had already admitted its responsibilities, so its nationalist reassertion could take the form of even closer links with France, as in its opposition to the U.S. invasion of Iraq in 2003.

Japanese nationalism is regarded as both an irritant and a potential danger by both China and Korea. Nonetheless, in the economic arena, Japan's relations with China and Korea are very important for its long-term economic well-being. Japan's economic ties with China have been increasing steadily. In the 1990s, "the Japanese economy [shifted] from the 'full-set' structure of the past to a structure based on divisions of labor within East Asia" (Mukoyama 2003: 9). As of 2002, Japan began to import more from China than from the United States. And Japanese investment in China has become oriented not merely to "reverse importing"—that is, as a production base for exporting to Japan—but also as a "production and sales base for local markets" (Mukoyama 2003: 45).

The trade has become complementary. It is still based on "divisions of labor between products at different levels of technology" (Mukoyama 2003: 27). Undoubtedly, over time, production in China may rely less on the low wage-level of its workers. But, even so, there will be a large place for China to profit from advanced technology developed in Japan. And it will still be true for a long time that "the exodus of production from Japan to China has occurred in areas in which Japan has lost its comparative advantage" (Mukoyama 2003: 46).

There is as well a geopolitical element in Japan's increasing economic links with China. It has to do with its slow, but real, delinking from the United States. Saori Katada (2003) traces the rise of East Asian "regionalism" to the impact of the so-called Asian financial crisis of 1997. Katada notes that Japan's immediate reaction to the crisis was to seek to reinforce regional financial cooperation. This effort was strongly opposed by the United States. Katada cites three bases for Japan's efforts: material interests, power politics, and ideological differences. It is the last that is the most striking. Katada speaks of Japan's opposition to the Washington Consensus, which had led to the explanations that were given in Western countries for the financial crisis. For Western analysts, the crisis was the fault of the economic structures of Asian countries. Japanese experts, on the contrary, argued that it was a liquidity crisis deriving from the flaws in international financial structures. Very different policy conclusions derive from the contrasting analyses.

The situation in Northeast Asia looks, of course, somewhat different from China's point of view. For one thing, China was historically the dominant force in this pair. It only lost that advantage in the nineteenth century, and most emphatically in the 1970s. China does not intend to allow this momentary shift in Japan's favor to mark a permanent realignment of the two. In the twenty-first century, China is already ahead militarily and intends to keep ahead. As of the first decades, it was still behind in terms of its economic structures but the gap was beginning to narrow. And China began, once again, to be taken more seriously on the world scene than Japan, whether its political stances were seen by others as something to applaud or something to fear.

Still, the Chinese leadership has been demonstrating a very sophisticated appreciation of geopolitics. And they know that including Japan in a Northeast Asia arrangement has more pluses than minuses for them. It would temper Japanese militarism, which many Japanese themselves still fear. It would markedly reduce the capacity of the United States to be a major player in the region. It would serve to reassure Western Europe, Australia, and possibly even India, since all of them might see Japan as a moderating political force on China.

China surely does not want to have Japan as a hostile power. Some concessions are possibly worth it. So while China has continued to protest vigorously Japan's unwillingness to atone for what the Chinese see as its manifest sins, it has not followed that China has allowed this to poison their relations. Rather, the Chinese have seemed to be trying to transform the political situation by further engagement rather than by distancing themselves politically.

It is, however, in the economic arena that China has most to gain from closer links with Japan. China is constantly increasing considerably its productive output and its profit levels on the world scene. But, as of 2007, it still had some ways to go. It still needs extensive foreign investment. It still needs to borrow or otherwise obtain much technology. Although its research capacities are ever better China is still behind Japan. And it still needs access to markets as well as access to raw materials. It especially needs to be able to market goods of higher technological input, and to do this amid continuing world economic turbulence.

The question for China is not whether or not it needs to continue to expand its world economic links, but with whom. It is all very well to say that it should spread its connections, and of course it has been doing that. But in terms of markets for its own production, the obvious large markets are the United States, Western Europe, and Japan. The U.S. economy is and will continue to be shaky, and Western Europe has had too few cultural ties to extensively modify its import patterns so as to increase the Chinese part. It seems obvious that Japan is the place to concentrate China's efforts. Whatever the current political analysis, a geopolitical analysis points to increased ties.

Of course, there remains the question of the long-standing and quite acute rivalry of China and Japan to preeminence in their mutual relationship. This is where Korea comes in. Korea, as a competitor in the world-economy, although it has been improving its position markedly, is still not quite up to the Japanese level. And Korea seems a small country when one compares it to China. Actually, Korea has a quite significant population size (which would of course be much increased after reunification). And, by global standards, Korea has become quite a strong player in the world-economy,

From a Korean point of view, what would Chinese-Japanese rapprochement look like? If Korea was outside the arrangement, it would look quite threatening. The Koreans have unsettled political grievances with Japan and fears of being regarded in China as a client state on the periphery of the Middle Kingdom. But, if Korea was inside, it would clearly benefit from the overall advantages a Northeast Asia consortium has to offer.

In terms of the politics of such a consortium, Korea could act as a mediator in the China-Japan rivalry. It would probably do this by insisting on a sort of equality among all three members, and this might work. In terms of the economics of such an arrangement, not only would Korean goods have easy access to a very large and flourishing market and be able to import what they needed on optimal terms, but also Korea could position itself to "function as a distribution hub for the rapidly expanding flows of goods between China and the world" (Mukoyama 2003, 21). It would, of course, also allow Korea to end its dependence on U.S. military guarantees and thereby permit it to pursue its own interests geopolitically much more freely.

Let us assume that over the next twenty years or so such a consortium in Northeast Asia becomes firmly established. What would its impact on the overall geopolitical scene be, and in particular who might be the losers in such an arrangement? We would have to begin with the two other members of the Triad—the United States and Western Europe.

The United States would have to make a fundamental geopolitical decision—to fight them or to join them. Given the overall decline of the U.S. position in all arenas, and given my presumption that a Northeast Asia consortium would rapidly emerge as the member of the Triad that would be strongest in the world market, the United States would find that it would have to join with somebody—with either the Northeast Asia consortium or with the European Union. The United States might find that the Northeast Asia group would welcome U.S. adhesion, provided it was as a very honored junior partner, whereas the Europeans would be much more reluctant to include the United States in their arrangements, despite existing rhetoric and long-standing historic links.

It is indeed precisely because of these historic links that Europe would demonstrate reluctance. Right up to World War II, Europe considered the United States as its geopolitical and cultural offshoot, and therefore its subordinate. The war and the unquestioned assumption of hegemony by the United States after 1945 transformed the relationship, and in a sense humiliated Europe, especially Western Europe. Quite aside from any other consideration, Europe can never culturally assert itself again unless it breaks its political ties with the United States. And geopolitically, this seems to me inevitable, despite the fact that so many of the current political elites seem nostalgic for what now seems to be the halcyon days of the Cold War. These elites will die out, and their children will not retain these memories.

The situation in Northeast Asia is exactly the opposite. Their memories are of Western, not merely U.S., domination, which was institutionalized in the nineteenth century and has lasted up to now. Their cultural needs are precisely to assert their centrality in the world-system. And nothing would serve this better than to have the United States as a very honored junior partner. So once China, Japan, and Korea overcome their own difficult relations and establish a common front, they will almost surely work to respond to the United States' need for linkage.

If there becomes clear linkage between Northeast Asia and the United States, Europe may be freed culturally, but it will be in trouble economically and militarily. This will force the European Union to come to terms with Russia in an effort to balance the new geopolitical mammoth of Northeast Asia plus the United States. The fierce opposition of the political elites in those parts of Eastern Europe that had been part of the USSR or had been Soviet satellites in the post-1945 era will crumble before the very strong insistence on the part of the rest of the European Union to strengthen its geopolitical power by linking with Russia. This will be especially reinforced by what will be by then the visible decline of United States geopolitical power.

If we turn our attention to other parts of the world-system, and especially to Asia, it seems clear that there could be different responses by Southeast Asia, by India, and by Southwest Asia. Southeast Asia would not have too much choice. Faced with a united Northeast Asia, Southeast Asia would probably not have the political, economic, or military energy to fight the role of being a sphere of interest of Northeast Asia. They might not like it, but geopolitics is not about utopian desires but about relative strengths.

India is a different case. Given its size, and its potential strengths, India would not be ready to play the role of a subordinate semiperipheral sphere of interest for Northeast Asia. Nonetheless, India would probably need some assistance to resist and to be able to pursue its own economic ascent. If the geopolitical lines were shaping up as Northeast Asia plus the United States versus the European Union plus Russia, India might well find more reason to join itself in some way to the Euro-Russian pole. And undoubtedly, its adhesion would be very welcomed, and therefore India might be able to command very good terms in the arrangements.

Finally, Southwest Asia is in a different position still. Politically and militarily, they remain on a world scale rather weak. They are increasingly unhappy with the United States politically. This is true not only of Iran but also of the Arab states as a whole. The Israeli thorn in their side may not cease to be one for some time. However, neither do they have fond memories of their relations with Europe and Russia.

Their major geopolitical card remains energy. And in the first decade of the twenty-first century, they were slowly but surely shifting in the direction of linkage with East Asia. In 2007, for the first time, Saudi oil exports to Asia were greater than their exports to Europe. There are two clear reasons, at least, for such a shift. The United States has become less reliable. Its military power is on the defensive, and the dollar's role as the sole world currency seems about to crumble entirely. On the other hand, Northeast Asia, indeed all of Asia, has been steadily expanding as a consumer of oil and gas. Given long-term demographic trends, not to speak of economic trends, this should become a stronger reality as the decades move on. Once again, we have a situation in which the shift may be slow for the moment, but the pace is increasing, and at one point the shift might become quite dramatic.

There is one last question we have to treat in this survey of the geopolitical future we face. Geopolitics is more long-term than politics. But systemic realities are still more long-term and powerful. We have to place this entire analysis within the framework of the structural crisis of the capitalist world-economy as a historical system. I have a long-standing position that the modern world-system has reached its moment of structural crisis. Consequently, we are in a period of transition from the existing capitalist world-economy to something else. The way this happens is via systemic chaos and structural bifurcation. There are and will be two alternative paths of replacing the existing system, modes of transformation that are in direct conflict one to the other.

I have given arguments as to why this is happening elsewhere (Wallerstein 1998), and I shall not repeat them here. I have called this the struggle between the spirit of Davos and the spirit of Porto Alegre. I have said that this may continue another twenty-five to fifty years before one fork or other of the bifurcation is definitively chosen and that it is intrinsically impossible to predict the outcome. The only thing that is sure is that the existing historical system has become unviable in its own terms, and therefore will disappear.

I shall simply assume this argument for the moment, and ask what impact this systemic struggle will have on the geopolitical analyses of the prospective future that I have been making. It means one thing above all. All the trends that I have been outlining will proceed. But none of them will have the normal end point that similar reshufflings of the world's geopolitical relations have had throughout the history of the capitalist world-economy.

The normal outcome one could expect from the patterns I have claimed to discern would be that by 2050 the East Asia consortium would assume the shape of an emerging new hegemonic center of the modern world-system. One might even anticipate that the fierce struggle between the East Asian consortium, to which the United States would be allied, and the European Union, to which Russia would be allied, might even result in another "thirty years' war" before East Asia would win out clearly.

But will this happen? I doubt it. This is not because this pattern of relocation of hegemonic centrality would not reassert itself but because this pattern of hegemonic shifts is dependent on a functioning capitalist world-economy. If we move into another kind of system, all bets are off. We do not know what this other system would look like. We do not know if geographic differentiation will continue to play in the future world-system the kind of role it plays in the present one. We do not know if the new system will be more egalitarian than the present one or even more polarized.

The conclusion I draw from this is that politically the struggle between the spirit of Davos and the spirit of Porto Alegre is far more important than the struggle among the Triad for supremacy as well as the struggle between the North and the South for allocations of surplus value. But analytically, I draw the conclusion that we should be far more prudent than most analysts have been about generalizing from relatively short-term shifts what it is that is most important to discern. Because this is a world in systemic crisis—that is, in chaos—the fluctuations we encounter are enormous. This is true in all the arenas of social action—economic, political, cultural, social, and military. We are living not only amid the long-term uncertainties of transition but the short-term uncertainties of a world that is far more chaotic than the one that we have known for the past 500 years.

This makes our daily lives very difficult. And while we are all required to navigate the dangers of daily life, if we intend to be intellectually and politically useful, we must keep our eye on the ball of systemic transition—something rather difficult to do. Let us hope that we do it well.

Notes

1. Keynote address at Thirty-First Annual Conference of the Political Economy of the World-System Section of the American Sociological Association, St. Lawrence University, May 11–12, 2007.

2. See my discussion of multiple TimeSpaces, amplifying the Braudelian distinctions (Wallerstein 2001).

3. I have spelled this out in many places. The most recent version is Wallerstein 2007.

References

Katada, Saori N. (2003). "Constructing Regional Interests in Japan and China." *The Japanese Economy* 31, nos. 3–4 (Fall 2003/Winter 2004): 126–150.

McNeill, David (2007). "Japan's History War." *Chronicle of Higher Education*, April 27.

Mukoyama, Hidehiko (2003). "How Globalization Will Change Japan-China Trading Patterns." *The Japanese Economy* 31, nos. 3–4 (Fall 2003/Winter 2004): 8–50.

Wallerstein, Immanuel (1998). *Utopistics: Or, Historical Choices of the Twenty-first Century.* New York: New Press.

——— (2001). "The Invention of TimeSpace Realities: Towards an Understanding of Our Historical Systems." In *Unthinking Social Science: The Limits of Nineteenth-Century Paradigms,* 2nd ed. Philadelphia: Temple University Press, 135–148.

——— (2007). "Precipitate Decline: The Advent of Multipolarity." *Harvard International Review* (Spring): 54–59.

3

ASIA, EURASIA, EURASIANISM

THE ROLE OF RUSSIA IN THE TRANSITION FROM U.S. HEGEMONY

Boris Stremlin

The last quarter century has witnessed the growth of interest in Asia as the most economically dynamic region of the capitalist world-economy. The shift of the center of gravity away from the "organic core" centered on the Atlantic has, for many analysts, elicited a related shift in the epistemological foundations of the modern world-system. It has been stipulated, for instance, that "[a] focus on 'Asia' has the potential to destabilize the categories and paradigms associated with world-systems perspectives" (FBC 2006:. 4).

This chapter, conversely, argues that the concept of "Asia," far from destabilizing the categories and paradigms associated with world-systems perspectives, has always been constitutive of the structures of knowledge of the modern world-system. Instead, it undertakes to examine the historical construction of the idea of "Eurasia," which emerged primarily in the Russian-Soviet sphere, and argues that this hybrid concept has represented a fundamental epistemological challenge to the existing system. Having established the historical construction of "Eurasia," the chapter then proceeds to examine the resurgence of Russian power in the Putin epoch in light of Eurasianist perspectives and inspects the role of Eurasianist ideology in challenging the unipolar global order in the first decade of the twenty-first century.

The Historical Construction of "Asia"

The name *Asia* seems to originate from Assuwa (or Arzawa)—a name that, in the diplomatic texts of the fourteenth century BCE referred to a kingdom or a confederacy located in western Anatolia (Bernal 1991: 201; Lewis and Wigen 1997: 214–215). Derived from the Akkadian word (*w)asu(m)*—"to go out"—the toponym referenced the direction of the setting sun (Narasimhan and Yefremov 2006: 1). The transmission of the place name to the Greeks involved a fundamental reorientation. Rendered as "Asia," the term is first encountered in the works of Herodotos, who, following sixth-century Ionian geographers, extended its designation in two profoundly new ways. First "Asia" now referred to the whole of Anatolia (hence "Asia Minor"). More important, in the sixth century, the kingdom of Lydia, which was situated in the region of the old confederacy of Assuwa, was incorporated into the Persian empire. Thus, "Asia" was also extended to the whole of the Persian-dominated East, which, along with Europe and Africa ("Lybia"), would henceforth be regarded as a continent (Bernal 1991: 201). The stipulation of distinct continents necessitated the extension of the very real division between the Balkan Peninsula and Anatolia formed by the Bosporus and the Dardanelles northward of the Black Sea, where the two continents were transected by the river Tanais (Don) (Lewis and Wigen 1997: 21–22; Bassin 1991: 2). Though Herodotos himself questioned the geographic utility of this division, it nevertheless conformed to his political agenda. Thus, what had been synonymous concepts in the Semitic worldview (*[w]asu[m]* and *erebu* West Semitic *sunset,* whence *Europe*), had, in Herodotos's *Histories,* turned into opposing cultural principles. Whereas Europe, composed of independent Greek *poleis,* embodied the principles of liberty, Asia, dominated by the Persian great king, was the domain of despotism. Henceforth, "Asia" would be projected as the anti-Europe, as Europe's Other (Said 1978; Lewis and Wigen 1997: 53–55; Wang 2007: 4–13).

The Romans and, later, the medieval Europeans, whose T-O maps continued to depict the main boundary between the two continents as running along a greatly exaggerated Don, subsequently adopted the Greek division between Europe and Asia. Whereas for patristic writers, the continental divide constituted a boundary between the patrimonies granted to the sons of Noah (Lewis and Wigen 1997: 23), by the fourteenth century CE "the geographic realm of Europe was increasingly identified with [the] newly circumscribed spiritual realm of [Western] Christendom" (Bassin 1991: 4). This division survived more or less intact until the eighteenth century, when the incorporation of Russia as a great power into the European interstate system necessitated a shift of the boundary between Europe and Asia eastward, to the Ural Mountains. After Peter the Great's victory over Sweden in the Great Northern War and his parallel recognition of the preeminence of European civilization, his court geographer, Vasilii Tatishchev (1686–1750), advanced the argument that

Russia, like European empires, consisted of a European metropole and an Asian colonial periphery, although unlike European empires, the metropole and the colonies were separated by a mountain range rather than by bodies of water. A similar demarcation of this boundary, proposed by Tatishchev's sometime collaborator Philip Johann von Strahlenberg (1676–1747), who served as an officer in the Swedish army and spent thirteen years as a prisoner of war in Siberia, gained general acceptance in European atlases after 1800. By the end of the nineteenth century, however, Tatishchev's more easterly variant ultimately triumphed (Bassin 1991: 5–8, 17).

Although the strictly geographic definition of Asia proposed by Tatishchev and von Strahlenberg has survived until the present day, its cultural and political outlines have undergone significant variation since the late nineteenth century. In the course of the 1800s, India and China displaced the Near East as the main objects of Orientalist research, as their economic significance to the colonial powers began to outdistance that of western Asia (Schwab 1984: 71). The eastward shift in Asia's center of gravity was further stimulated by the rise of Japan following the Meiji Restoration. The notion of Asia (*toyo*) introduced by Fukuzawa Yukichi (1835–1901), generally regarded as one of the principal founders of modern Japan, signaled the emergence of a Japanese empire that, like the Russian one, was modeled on European prototypes. Fukuzawa's *toyo* rested upon the double conceit of defining a region on the basis of cultural homogeneity (Confucianism) along with the reconfiguration of this region along European lines under the leadership of Japan. This "shedding of Asia" meant the "dissociation from China-centered imperial relations and construction of a European-style nation-state oriented toward 'freedom,' 'human rights,' 'national sovereignty,' 'civilization,' and 'independent spirit.'" (Wang 2007: 4). Fukuzawa's delineation of a distinct Asian region thus constituted its reconstruction as Europe's alter ego, as the "shedding of Asia" in a cultural sense went hand-in-hand with "joining Europe" and the invasion of Asia in order to establish a European-style colonial empire (Wang 2007: 13). By the 1930s, Kaname Akamatsu (1896–1974) reframed this empire, now branded as the Greater East Asia Co-Prosperity Sphere, in terms of his famous "flying geese" metaphor—a forcible attempt by the lead Japanese "goose," now hostile to the West, to impose its rule and its values on the rest of the Asian "gaggle" (Furuoka 2005: 1).

The association of Asia with the Far East continued to gain traction following the U.S. defeat of the Japanese empire in World War II, when Japan made a second attempt at East Asian integration by becoming the "lead goose" in a regional network of industrial production (Furuoka 2005: 1). In the context of U.S. efforts to promote the development of its satellites in maritime Asia during the Cold War, this region—including Japan, the Four Dragons (Taiwan, South Korea, Hong Kong, and Singapore), and subsequently the minidragon and Asian tiger economies of Malaysia, Thailand, Indonesia, Mainland China, and Vietnam—emerged to become the fastest-growing economy in history and, along with Europe and North America, became "one of the three great pillars of the modern industrial world" (Vogel 1991, 1–2). The success of the "East Asian model of growth" was regarded as "miraculous" and projected indefinitely into the twenty-first century, which, prior to the economic crisis of 1997–1998, was widely hailed as the "Pacific Century" (Palat 2004: xii, 1–2). As implied by the latter sobriquet, the leading power of the Asia-Pacific remained the United States, which, since Henry Luce had declared the Pacific a U.S. lake in 1953, had remade the region in its own image (Palat 2004: 8). U.S. Cold War area studies, which reconfigured the world into a series of regions on the basis of U.S. strategic interests, tended to metonymically identify "Asia" with the economically dynamic region in the eastern portion of the Asian continent (Lewis and Wigen 1997: 40).

World-systémic literature has, by and large (at least with respect to the modern period), confined its interest in Asia to these East Asian and U.S. predilections. For Wallerstein, as for Vogel, East Asia forms one leg of the triad of core regions in the world-economy that are now engaged in a three-cornered contest for hegemony that would likely take the form of a struggle between a territorialist alliance between the EU and Russia against a maritime alliance between the United States and East Asia in the medium-term future (Wallerstein 1991: 43–45). Giovanni Arrighi, for his part, has followed the argument set out by Takeshi Hamashita in the article "The Tribute-trade System and Modern Asia" to the effect of positing East Asian dynamism in the late twentieth century as a reconstitution of the Sino-centered tribute-trade system, which had survived despite its partial incorporation into the Euro-centered world-system after 1850 (see Hamashita 1987; Arrighi, Selden and Hamashita 2003). For Arrighi and his collaborators, the survival of the tribute-trade system was effected, in the first instance, by the Japanese displacement of China as the center of this system after 1850 and, second, by the survival of networks of Overseas Chinese family enterprises that have taken the lead role in investment in mainland China after 1979.

The inclusion of China within the East Asian region (recognized by scholarly consensus by 1975 at the latest [see Lewis and Wigen 1997: 168]), however, complicates the construction of East Asia as an integrated region in several important respects. The economic crisis that afflicted the region in 1997–1998 has resulted in a shift of the regional center of gravity from Japan to China. This reconfiguration buried the dreams of a Pacific century as inter-Asian trade increased at the expense of transpacific trade while China stepped into the vacuum left behind by disastrous IMF structural adjustment policies in the wake of the crisis and cemented its role as the main engine of East Asian economic growth (Palat 2004: 227–236). Yet, the reconfiguration of East Asia around Chinese, rather than Japanese, leadership not only lessens the U.S. role as the dominant power in the region but may also, in the longer run, contribute to the rise of alternate regional formations. Since the 1990s, the most dynamic growth rates have been exhibited not by the East Asian region, but by large, semiperipheral states collectively referred to as the BRIC countries (Brazil, Russia, India, and China) (Wilson and Purushothaman 2003). Even though these countries in no sense form a region, they are increasing political and economic coordination. Three of the BRICs (Russia, India, and China) are situated on the Eurasian supercontinent, belong to the Shanghai Cooperation Organization as full or associate members, and may be in the process of constructing a geopolitical axis that will form a counterweight to the U.S.-led unipolar world order (Stroupe 2006).

The construction of (East) Asia on the basis of the tribute-trade system as instantiated by maritime commercial networks may have been directed at rectifying traditional Eurocentric models that posited Asia as the anti-Europe or a European periphery, but, as pointed out by Wang Hui, this construction in fact recapitulates Eurocentrism (and U.S.-centrism) by fashioning Asia primarily in economistic, commercial, and maritime terms. For Wang, Hamashita's construction of Asia underemphasizes transcontinental transportation and communication networks, which were only subordinated to Japan-centered maritime networks in the age dominated by European expansionism (Wang 2007, 36–37). Instead, Wang proposes to replace Japanese-centric (and U.S.-centric) constructions of Asia in the image of Europe with more broadly political notions rooted in social-revolutionary constructions such as "Great Asianism" or "Pan-Asianism" that are associated with Sun Yat-sen. Unlike *toyo,* these constructions transcend the dichotomy between (European) agency and peripheral (Asian) passivity and open the way for locating political and terrestrial actors (e.g., partisans) and wide-ranging antisystemic alliances (such as those between the Russian and Chinese revolutionaries) that aim at the fundamental transformation of the modern world-system rather than the endless replication of its structures in diverse regions throughout the world (Wang 2007: 19–29, 38–40). Given the apparent resonance between Wang's proposal and the emergence of a Eurasian challenge to U.N. hegemony outlined above, I will now proceed to outline the construction of the idea of Eurasia in greater detail.

The Historical Construction of Eurasia

Given the rather flimsy basis for the separation of Europe and Asia at the Urals, geographers experienced persistent misgivings regarding Europe's status as a distinct (much less the archetypal [see Lewis and Wigen 1997: 36]) continent and worried that it was in reality nothing other than a peninsular formation on the western edge of Asia. By the 1880s, the existence of a geographic hybrid could no longer be denied, and the Viennese geologist Eduard Suess (1831–1914), one of the founders of the theory of plate tectonics and the originator of the concept *biosphere,* "coined the term 'Eurasia' to refer to the combined European-Asiatic landmass" (Bassin 1991: 10). This denial of a hard natural-scientific basis for the notion of distinct European and Asian continents left them intact (as we have seen) as cultural conventions, but as such, they remained vulnerable to attack on both scientific and cultural grounds.

Not surprisingly, the epicenter of such attacks was located in Russia, which was most directly affected by its geographic division into European and Asian sections and which, since the Napoleonic Wars, had begun to experience increasing difficulties in its attempts to become a core power within the European interstate system. Among the Russian elites, these tensions elicited the formation of the Slavophile movement, whose spokespersons took aim at Peter the Great and all his followers who insisted that Russia's only path to progress lay in its Westernization. The Slavophiles' most eloquent spokesman, the botanist and biogeographer Nikolai Danilevskii (1822–1885), not only denied that the Urals constituted a significant geographic boundary but also insisted that the topography of the Russian empire and outlying regions constituted a cohesive "natural geographic region." For this reason, he stipulated, Russia, along with its Slavic cousins in East-Central Europe, constituted a distinct "historico-cultural type" (or "civilization"), with its own laws of motion and its own historical destiny. He further added that it made little sense for this civilization, on the verge of transitioning from the stage of a universal state into a mature interstate system, to try to merge with a foreign Western civilization that had already entered the stage of decrepitude (Danilevskii 1965 [1869]: 21–22, 87–95).

The Slavophiles' rejection of the Europe/Asia dichotomy and their insistence on the unique character of Russian (or Russo-Slavic) civilization proved to be only the opening salvo of the assault on Westernizing paradigms. This initial attack still suffered from profound inconsistencies, because Pan-Slavism in effect replicated the Asia/Europe dichotomy by including Russia in a world much of which lay to Russia's west, and thereby implicitly counterpoising it to the Orient (Bassin 1991: 12–13). In the wake of World War I and the Russian Revolution, however, the Russian opposition to Europe and the West became radicalized. Within Russia itself, the Bolshevik Party, which claimed legitimacy as representatives of the Russian masses and as true adherents to Marxist ideology, captured state power. Despite the Bolsheviks' explicit commitment to national self-determination and their emphasis on economic development and despite the European origin of Marxism, their accession signified a fundamental break with Westernization. For Lenin, the *capitalist* development of Russia (and Asia) was possible only under the conditions of a peasant revolution led by a Marxist vanguard (see Wang 2007: 14–19), and the pursuit of national self-determination could only be realized by the reconstitution of the Russian empire as the USSR (see Martin 2001; Hirsch 2005), which, furthermore, would ensure the efficaciousness of the international Marxist movement by assuming the leading position in anticolonialist struggles. Although during the seventy-four-year history of the Soviet Union, its performance along all these dimensions was decidedly mixed, in the brief period between 1949 (the victory of the Chinese Revolution) and 1960 (the beginning of the Sino-Soviet split), the bloc of Council for Mutual Economic Assistance (COMECON) countries can fairly be characterized as constituting a distinct, Eastern (indeed, Eurasian) bloc, rivaling the opposing U.S.-led bloc of the West.

It was among the anti-Bolshevik Russian diaspora, however, that a distinct Eurasianist movement emerged. Led by the geographer Petr Savitskii (1895–1968) and the linguist Prince Nikolai Trubetskoi (1890–1938; spelling is according to the currently accepted Library of Congress transliteration), the Eurasianists formulated a geopolitical doctrine that built on the Slavophile notion of Russia as a distinct "geographical world" and a distinct, non-Western civilization. Their position was more radically and consistently anti-Western, however, than that of Slavophiles such as Danilevskii (Bassin 1991: 14–16; Vinkovetsky 2007: 5), because they insisted that the primary geographic, ethnic, cultural, and political bonds linked Russia not with the Slavic peoples of east-central Europe but with the nomadic (and largely Turkic- and Mongolian-speaking) peoples of Central Asia and Siberia. Not only the physical-geographic unity of the Eurasian plain, stretching from Hungary to the Pacific but also the ethnic intermixing, the traditionally southern and eastern orientation of Russian trade routes, a mystical bent in religious observance, and above all, an imperial polity built upon the foundations of nomadic steppe confederacies connected Russia organically to the Khazars, Pechenegs, Mongols, and Qipchaks (Trubetzkoy 1991a [1925]: 165).

The geographic identity of Eurasia in this construction differed from that of Suess's geophysical definition of Eurasia as Europe plus Asia. Rather, it corresponded more or less with the perimeters of the Russian empire (and after that, the USSR) or to the region that Eursianists' contemporaries, the founders of geopolitics (Halford Mackinder [1861–1947], Karl Haushofer [1869–1946]) referred to as the "heartland" (Dugin 1997: 445; von Hagen 2004: 9). "Eurasia" in this sense constituted the Russian "trunk" of the Eurasian supercontinent, and both "Europe" and "Asia" formed its maritime peripheries (Savitskii 1997a [1993]: 297–298).

This construction of "Russia-Eurasia" as a "continent" that, rather than being prone to political Balkanization and racial hierarchies that characterize both Europe and Asia, historically promotes the unification of its geographically mobile and politically mobilized populations as "brotherly peoples" living under the aegis of a single state (Savitskii 1997a [1993]: 301–302) set the Eurasianists apart from others in the White Russian émigré diaspora, and it evinced their rather more nuanced attitude toward the Bolshevik regime that had sent them into exile. Although they condemned the Bolsheviks' atheism and what they regarded as the abstract and doctrinaire ideology, they nevertheless believed that the Soviet regime had been forced by the logic of history and by the Russian people to become the saviors of Russian statehood and the objective promoters of Eurasianist ideology and geopolitics (Savitskii 1997b [1926]: 13–16). Moreover, the Eurasianists supported the Soviet reconstitution of the empire on supraethnic principles that they understood as Pan-Eurasian (Trubetskoy 1991b [1927]: 239). Anticipating the 1922 Treaty of Rapallo between Weimar Germany and the Soviet Union, they also posited the possibility of a partnership between these two territorialist powers in order to counterbalance the oceanic power of Great Britain (Savitskii 1997c [1919]: 393–397). Last, in their decisive rejection of the market-oriented "capitalist road" of development (associated with sea powers) and in their transdisciplinary "geosophic" scholarship, the Eurasianists both resembled and looked up to Lenin and the Bolshevik vanguard (Dugin 1997; Savitskii 1997b [1926]: 16).

Isolation within the Russian émigré community, personality clashes and sectarianism among the Eurasianists themselves, as well as the consolidation of the Stalinist wing of the Bolshevik Party in power and the approach of World War II, doomed the first incarnation of the Eurasianist movement. The Eurasianist torch was subsequently taken up by the Soviet Turkologist Lev Gumilev (1912–1992), however, who in the postwar period had established a correspondence with several leading Eurasianists. Although prohibited from publishing an account of his heterodox views until the onset of *perestroika,* by the late 1980s Gumilev resurrected Eurasianism as a living movement and became, arguably, the most prominent public intellectual in the country.

Owing to the impossibility of addressing sensitive issues with bearing on contemporary politics and to his own historical and scientific interests, Gumilev's development of Eurasianist geopolitics was negligible. His major contributions to Eurasianism were twofold. First, he utilized the idea of the biosphere developed by Suess and Russian ecologist Vladimir Vernadsky (1863–1945)—the father of Eurasianist historian George Vernadsky (1887–1973)—to work out a unique notion of ethnogenesis that was implicated in the environment of a particular terrain and in the process of solar irradiation. Thereby, Gumilev emphasized the transdisciplinary character of Eurasianism, and in stressing the self-organizing nature of ethnogenesis, he insisted that Eurasianists were the pioneers of systems science (Gumilev 2003: 24–25; Gumilev 1997: 385–387). Second, as a Turkologist, Gumilev placed much more emphasis on the early history of pastoral nomadism and on the role of Turkic and Mongolian peoples in the cycles of ethnogenesis in Eurasia than had Savitskii and Trubetskoi (Gumilev 2003: 24). For Gumilev, the Russian ethnos was merely the leading group of a Eurasian *superethnos,* defined as a "group of ethnoi simultaneously originating in a certain region, and mutually interlinked by mutual economic, ideological and political relationships" (Gumilev 1992; Gumilev 1997: 141). As such, Gumilev provided the basis for a shared post-Soviet identity that was not premised on the postcolonial linkages between Russia and the newly independent states of Central Asia as well as the autonomous republics located in the south and east of the Russian Federation. Local elites in Kalmykia, Buryatia, Tuva, Sakha, Altai, and Kazakhstan saw Eurasianism as establishing their role as equal partners of Russia, and it provided them with a sense of importance on the global stage. Moreover, Gumilev's conception of ethnogenesis inspired a new and specifically post-Soviet form of spiritual ecologism, which leaders who claimed allegiance to Eurasianism counterpoised to the predatory and extractive capitalist consumerism that was spreading throughout the world in the form of U.S.-led globalization (Humphrey 2002: 263; Nazarbaev 2005).

Gumilev's prominence during the late 1980s and early 1990s thrust the concept of "Eurasia" into the limelight and created a veritable cottage industry of all things "Eurasian" within the bounds of the newly formed Commonwealth of Independent States. Aside from the Gumilev Foundation, a new Lev Gumilev Eurasian National University (founded by Kazakhstan's President Nursultan Nazarbaev as the country's flagship educational institution in 1996), a slew of Eurasianist journals, and a Eurasianist political party have all come into being. This explosion of Eurasianism can be attributed to the rather sudden demise of Marxist-Leninist ideology, which had served as an integrating force within the USSR for seventy-four years, creating a void that Eurasianism seemed well suited to fill. Owing to the political realities of Soviet disintegration and the cultural conditions ushered in by "globalization" and transnationalism (as well as the holistic and systemic predilections of Gumilev himself), contemporary Eurasianism, unlike Marxism-Leninism, more closely resembles a network of loosely related franchises rather than a centralized and hierarchical bureaucracy. As such, regional governors often promote their own variant of Eurasianism to legitimize their authority (which is in practice compromised by their economic dependence on Moscow) and to create the impression that the peoples over whom they govern are the direct heirs of Genghis Khan and other Eurasian empire builders (Humphrey 2002: 259). The official Eurasianism of Nazarbaev's Kazakhstan purportedly similarly upholds the nomadic traditions of the Kazaks (partly to forestall the emergence of a strong Islamist movement in the country) even as it calls upon Russia to assume the leadership position in a Eurasian Union (see Nazarbaev 2005; Amrekulov 2004; Vinkovetsky 2007: 7–15). The precise outlines of Eurasia thereby acquire a multidimensional character. Nazarbaev's vision of Eurasia, for instance, differs somewhat from that of the classic and contemporary Russian Eurasianists in that it extends the region to Iran and Pakistan, thus placing Kazakhstan, and specifically, its new capital at Astana, in Eurasia's geographic center (Nazarbaev 1997, 236–237). Russian president Vladimir Putin's 2000 proclamation of Eurasianism as the ideology of the new Russia on a visit to Kazakhstan's Gumilev University "shows he is fully aware of the currency of the notion in the Asian regions" (Humphrey 2002: 263, 272).

Eurasianism has also made an impact beyond the former Soviet sphere. In the West, it has emerged as an "antiparadigm" confronting traditional epistemological nationalism and traditional dichotomies between Europe and Asia. It allows scholars to dissolve the "monolithic and static cultural determinism of the Russia/Orient paradigm" and stimulates the "decentering of historical narratives from the powerful perspectives of the former capitals," thus opening the possibility of reconstructing a more total, and yet more multicultural, perspective on the regions that composed the Russian empire and the Soviet Union (von Hagen 2004: 8, 2). Perhaps most significant of all, the U.S. State Department—still the chief source of funding research abroad (and thus, of establishing epistemological categories in the social sciences)—"was among the first institutions to replace all the designations of 'former' (as in former Soviet Union) and 'newly' (as in newly independent states) with Eurasia" (von Hagen 2004: 19). Among Chinese scholars, too, as we have seen, Wang Hui has proposed a more Eurasinist context for the study of East Asian regionalism.

The transformation of Eurasianism from a minority movement among the émigré diaspora or the dissident underground into one of the principal integrating ideologies in the post-Soviet space has enabled it to shift from a primarily historical orientation and to emerge as the most coherent geopolitical school of thought in Russia. The main representative of this school today is Aleksandr Dugin (1962–)—a philosopher and the founder and chief ideologue of the International Eurasian Movement. According to Dugin, each phase of retreat from Russia's Eurasianist mission has been followed by a new period of expansionism, which has been accompanied by the expanding consciousness of Russia's Eurasianist destiny (Dugin 2004: 59). Thus, the temporary retreat into Western-style liberal democracy and a turning away from imperial ambitions during the late 1980s and early 1990s has opened the way for the implantation of Eurasianism in the post-Soviet territories that was impossible during the Soviet period, although this neo-Eurasianism builds on, and does not reject, the Soviet experience (Dugin 2004: 43).

Dugin's Eurasianism stresses Russian hegemonism perhaps to a greater degree than did Gumilev's (the latter was even accused by one of his opponents of "Russophobia" [Gumilev 2003, 26]). Dugin argues that the character of the Russian polity is unthinkable as anything other than an empire, given the absence of any historical experience of Russia as a European style nation-state. Following the Slavophiles and the classical Eurasianists (and, it must be added, most mainstream Soviet Marxists), he contends that Russian expansionism has generally been of the peaceful variety, incorporating peoples who voluntarily subjugated or allied themselves to the Russian state in view of their common Eurasian destiny. In rejecting the nation-state model, however, Dugin also rejects narrow nationalism, including the forcible Russification or Christianization of other ethnic groups that compose the imperial whole. Like most Eurasianists today, Dugin is in favor of a federal imperial structure and of the preservation of all traditional Eurasian religions (Orthodoxy, Islam, Buddhism, Judaism, Taoism, Hinduism, etc.) (Dugin 2004: 342–368, 168–169), which he counterpoises to the profit-driven, expansionist, thallasocratic, cosmopolitan, and culturally relativist ethic of the contemporary West (Dugin 2004: 90–125).

This federated imperialism and religious ecumenicism is contextualized in a Eurasian framework that transcends the more limited notion of "Russia-Eurasia" that was propounded by the Eurasianists of the early twentieth century. For Dugin, Russia's geopolitical role consists of assuming the leadership of a new, Eurasianist continental bloc—to restore the balance between land and sea powers that had been undermined by the collapse of the Soviet Union (Dugin 2004: 369) and to reconstruct bipolarism (Dugin 2004: 427–432), possibly en route to the creation of a new global Eurasianist empire (Dugin 2004, 404). In his conception, Russia must resist attempts by the United States and its allies to create regional powers, to promote the nationalism of small states, to situate *cordons sanitaire*, and to provoke "clashes of civilizations" on the Eurasian continent. It should also strive to combat liberal economics by establishing a continental autarky and by returning to nonmaterialistic and religious values (Dugin 2004: 366–367, 373). More broadly, Dugin and other Eurasianists call on Russia to support the countries that have been victimized by neoliberal globalization and to assume the mantle of leadership in an alternative global project (Dugin 2002: 217; Panarin 2002, 117).

In his calls to combat U.S. unipolarism and to establish the supremacy of the Eurasianist "heartland," Dugin follows in the footsteps of Karl Haushofer, who in the 1930s proposed the formation of a Berlin-Moscow-Tokyo axis as the most effective way to checkmate Atlanticist seapower (Dugin 2004: 373–404). Dugin's reasoning centers on the complementarity of, on the one hand, Germany and Japan as economic giants that were politically emasculated by the United States at the end of World War II, and, on the other hand, an economically impoverished but politically sovereign and militarily formidable Russia. Russia's role in this alliance would reside in helping Germany and Japan escape U.S. domination by restoring their full sovereignty and promoting the creation of a German-dominated Central European union and a Japanese-dominated East Asian coprosperity sphere. In contrast to their prototypes in the 1930s, however, neither of the lateral powers would pursue ethnic hegemony in its respective sphere. Russia would furthermore take the lead on the establishment of united Eurasian armed force and provision the new German (or, possibly, Franco-German) empire with "ideological, political and spiritual energy" (Dugin 2004: 377–378). Germany and Japan would in turn help in the economic development of Russia, given the extra incentives provided by the return of Kaliningrad (to Germany) and the Kurile Islands (to Japan) (Dugin 2004: 383, 394). This axis would be supplemented in the south by a Moscow-Tehran axis, which would give Russia an outlet to the sea and contain Russia's Muslim periphery while allowing Iran to escape isolation by the Atlanticist powers and to outcompete rival projects aiming to establish an Islamic Caliphate (Dugin 2004: 395–401). Dugin also views India as Russia's natural ally but considers

India's importance to Russia secondary in comparison with Germany, Japan, and Iran (Dugin 2004: 384–385).

Notably, Dugin asserts that China always tends to ally with maritime powers and disdains its contemporary liberalism (established by totalitarian methods) as devoid of any geopolitical conception that can serve as a basis for independence (Dugin 2004: 385–388). For Dugin, China, Britain, Turkey, and Saudi Arabia constitute the Eurasianist's "scapegoats" and Trojan horses of the United States on the continent (Dugin 2004: 374–403). Other Russian geostrategic thinkers sometimes admit China into a Russian alliance—Panarin (2002: 306) as a component of a vertical Eurasianist alliance anchored by Russia and India; Deviatov (2002: 271–272) as Russia's temporary senior partner—reluctantly; Khachatrian (2005: 151–183) as part of a broad alliance including Germany, Greece, Egypt, Iran, India, Korea, and China—enthusiastically; and Anatolii Utkin (2003: 558) as part of Yevgenii Primakov's Russia-China-India triad—more soberly.

Eurasianism in Contemporary Russian Geostrategy

Does the Eurasianist paradigm have any relevance in the contemporary global situation, and does it offer a realistic assessment of Russia's power potential? The critics, both among Western writers and Russian liberals, have not been kind. Dmitrii Trenin (2002) and Matthew Schmidt (2005) argue that Eurasianism effectively came to an end with the fall of the Soviet Union and that contemporary Eurasianist ideology constitutes a dead end—nothing other than a rehashing of old Slavophile pieties. Russia, they contend, is a weak country, whose only option is to realign itself with the Euro-Atlantic community. Furthermore, they insist, the Russian elite is decisively pragmatic and capitalistic and its cultural and economic interests lie in the West: "If things went sour at home, they would probably leave Moscow for London or Zurich, not Shanghai or Mumbai" (Trenin 2007: 96). Another perceived impediment to the establishment of Eurasianism as a coherent foreign policy doctrine is its obsession with the occult, pseudoscience, and mysticism and with radical nationalist parties such as Rodina and the Liberal Democrats (Schmidt 2005: 5–6). Even more sympathetic critics characterize Eurasianism as lacking a real ideology and economic content (Humphrey 2002: 271–272) or as perhaps suitable, shorn of its mystical connotations, for promoting economic globalization in its part of the world (Lavelle 2005).

Let us examine these objections one by one. The characterization of Russia as a fundamentally European country with no alternative but to join Western institutional structures is no less than a classification of "Russia-Eurasia" as a unique civilization, a cultural-reductionist argument. The data available to us, however, are ambiguous and may weigh more heavily on the Eurasianist side.

The idea of an economistic Russian elite, whose hearts and bank accounts lie in the West, is an anachronistic one, resembling more the reality of the 1990s than the conditions of today. According to the "Voices of Russia" poll jointly conducted by the Levada Center in Moscow and the EU Russia Center in Brussels, 75 percent of Russians consider Russia as a Eurasian state with its own path of development, and 45 percent think of the European Union as a potential threat to Russia (and this figure has risen steadily since the late 1990s) (EU Russia Center 2007). Today, the elite can ill afford to ignore such sentiments, and according to one analyst, "Eurasianism is fast becoming the ideology of the Russian ruling class" (Esobar 2003).

Economically, Russian dependence on the West is becoming more difficult to demonstrate. It is true that presently, slightly more than half (52.9 percent) of the foreign trade of the Russian Federation is with the European Union (RIAN 2005). Trade with other Eurasian partners has been increasingly steadily since the late 1990s, however. Of particular note is the 13.2 percent year-on-year increase in trade with the former Soviet Commonwealth of Independent States (CIS) countries (15.4 percent of total) (RIAN 2005), many of which are highly dependent on the remittances sent by their nationals working in Russia (Hill 2004: 3). Of at least equal importance has been an expansion of trade with China. In 2006, China became Russia's largest single trade partner, and Russia became China's eighth largest (Gvosdev 2007; Voskressenski 2007: 5). The growth of Sino-Russian trade (projected to reach $60 billion by 2010) has been matched by the expansion of Chinese trade with other countries belonging to the Shanghai Cooperation Organization (SCO), which has tripled (to $45 billion) since the late 1990s (Gvosdev 2007). This growth of inter-SCO trade reflects its strategic importance. Though still negligible in overall volume compared to transpacific trade between the United States and China (just over 20 percent), this trade provides China with strategically vital energy resources and contributes to the revitalization of China's "red rust belt" in the north of the country, making it less dependent on maritime trade and affording greater security to Russia's underpopulated Far Eastern territories (Gvosdev 2007). At the same time, the European Union depends on Russia for roughly 20 percent of its energy supply (Hill 2004: 27–28), and its stated goal of diversifying its supplies is undercut by the proposed formation of "a gas OPEC" cartel that would include, at a minimum, Russia, Iran, and Algeria (Stroupe 2007). Thus, EU dependence on Russia may equal or surpass any Russian dependence on the EU, or the West, broadly speaking.

Second, the arguments asserting Russia's fundamental weakness (which is responsible for its dependence on the West) have become untenable. More than a decade ago, Zbigniew Brzezinski (1997) was already voicing concern over the prospect of a resurgent Russia constituting the lynchpin of an anti-U.S. Eurasian alliance. Today, Russia "has transformed itself from a defunct military (although still nuclear) superpower into a new energy superpower," which is increasingly able to recycle profits into domestic consumption, to convert it into soft power (Hill 2004: 1–3). The rebound in Russia's energy sector has allowed its economy to grow at an average rate of 6.7 percent since 2000—the fastest rate in the world excluding the newly industrializing countries in Asia and its fellow BRICs (American Chamber of Commerce 2007: 5). Its economy is projected to surpass those of Germany, France, and Italy by 2030 and to become the sixth largest in the world by 2050 (Wilson and Purushothaman 2003: 3–4). Since 1998, when Russia defaulted on its loans, it has emerged as a creditor state, having accumulated $300 billion in foreign currency reserves—the third largest stock of such reserves in the world (after China and Japan). Russia has also become the largest producer of oil in the world at around 11 million barrels per day (though its reserves are still dwarfed by those of Saudi Arabia), and its state-run natural gas monopoly Gazprom alone holds 25 percent of the world's natural gas reserves (Whitney 2007; Hill 2004: 32). At the same time, Russia has recaptured its leading position in the global arms market (ABC 2006) and is using its traditional comparative advantage in strategic industries to gain leadership in such high-tech sectors as "nuclear energy, shipbuilding, aircraft, satellites and delivery systems, and computer software" (Korduban 2007).

The last few years of Putin's rule have also produced notable diplomatic successes. Russia has, at least for the time being, put an end to the Chechen insurgency, and it has raised its credibility in the Muslim world by inserting itself as a serious mediator in the Arab-Israeli conflict and in the conflict over the Iranian nuclear program. Russian perseverance has also stemmed the tide of the U.S.-sponsored "color revolutions," as these have thus far led not to economic prosperity and democratization but rather to increased instability in Georgia, Kyrgyzstan, and Ukraine. Fear of color revolutions has drawn Uzbekistan back into the Russian orbit, and Russia seems on the verge of establishing a working relationship with the republic of Moldova. And, of course, the Russian veto continues to offer a major stumbling bloc to U.S. initiatives in Kosovo and in the Gulf. Russia has also engaged in the construction of multiple pipeline networks throughout the Eurasian continent to strengthen its strategic position. Japan and China have extended offers for two variants of a transsiberian pipeline, leaving the choice of the more preferable route to the Kremlin. Russia has also struck a deal with Germany to build the Nord Stream Baltic Sea pipeline in circumvention of Poland, seemingly in conformity with a strategy recommended by Dugin to decide all issues with Germany prior to consulting with Germany's EU partners (see Dugin 2004: 382). In addition, the Kremlin has prevailed upon Kazakhstan to refuse to avoid using pipelines favored by the United States and its allies, thus keeping Kazakhstan within the Russian orbit (Socor 2007). Above all, the construction of the SCO has provided strategic depth and security to both Russia and China, allowing them to concentrate on other problems and preventing their encirclement by the United States and its allies (Voskressenski 2007: 28–35).

The most dramatic development is that Russian partnerships with other energy producers and consumers have destabilized the global free market in energy, which has constituted one of the lynchpins of the U.S.-dominated neoliberal world order since the 1970s. By shifting to long-term bilateral contracts between energy producers and consumers, Russia has undermined the highly liquid global energy market structured on short-term contracts that privileged the high-energy consuming states of the core by allowing them to circumvent potential embargoes and that played to their strengths as centers of finance capital (Stroupe 2007). As a result, Russia has laid the foundations for a new "global complex of ties and alliances [that] excludes completely the United States [and] progressively binds its participants ever closer together in mutual energy-based economic, political and diplomatic interdependence and helps to deepen the cohesiveness across the global grouping" (Stroupe 2006). An additional strength of this system is its institutional flexibility, since, unlike the Western grouping around North Atlantic Treaty Organization (NATO), it is not dependent on the establishment of formal multilateral alliances. Instead, it subsists on mid-level utilitarian organizational and institutional structures (such as the Shanghai Cooperation Organization, the Collective Security Treaty Organization, the Asia-Pacific Economic Cooperation forum, the Non-Aligned Movement, etc), which at present appear to lack only the conventional grand-level organizational structure (Stroupe 2006). This allows participants in the network significant freedom of action while binding them together in a relationship of mutual interdependence.

Third, the contention that the Russian leadership is too pragmatic to engage any sort of ideologically charged confrontation with the United States of the sort envisioned by Eurasianists is also belied by the slide toward a new "Cold War" in the last few years (Cohen 2007). It is true that despite his invocation of Eurasianism as the national ideology, Putin's partnership with China in the SCO and his sometime accommodation of the United States and the EU over the Iranian nuclear program are pragmatic policies that do not fully conform with Eurasianist prognoses. Nevertheless, Putin's 2007 speeches at the Munich Conference on Security Policy and at the St. Petersburg Economic Forum constituted clear challenges to the U.S.-led global order, challenging NATO expansion, dollar hegemony, and the institutions of global governance such as the World Trade Organization (WTO) and the IMF and depicting himself as "leading a global insurgency against the empire" (Whitney 2007). His declarations have been partly in response to those of Western elites, which, even as Russian Westernizers recognize, have adopted the Soviet habit of ideological hectoring (Trenin 2007: 96–97). He also seems partly to have been impressed by the actions of the antiglobalization protesters at the G-8 summit at Heiligendamm and has now taken up their critique of neoliberalism (Kagarlitsky 2007). If Russia emerges as a champion of the global South and joins forces with the antiglobalization movement, its rivalry with the United States will assume the global and ideological proportions of the confrontation between the United

States and the Soviet Union, which drew on the strength of the international communist movement (cf. Cohen 2007). Though the configuration of such an alliance will differ from specific Eurasianist prescriptions, it would conform to Dugin's and Panarin's vision of Eurasianism as a global alternative.

Is some variant of Eurasianism likely to emerge as a new unifying ideology for Russia and its allies in this struggle? Eurasianism's critics allege that it is a dead end, merely the latest recapitulation of Slavophilism, but this argument ignores the fact that there has been a progression toward more radically non-Western positions in Russia's homegrown ideologies, rather than a simple alternation between Westernist and autochthonous phases (Bassin 1991: 14–16). Eurasianism's champions do proclaim it as a Russian form of "neoconservatism" (Dugin 2004: 366–367; Panarin 2002: 249), but, as we have seen, Eurasianism is not a centralized doctrine but a flexible ideology that can be adapted to a multiplicity of local conditions, and its occasionally "New Age" character may actually make it suitable for making common cause with other opponents of neoliberal globalization. At the same time, Eurasianist ideologues, no less than Putin or Nazarbaev, are pragmatists. Much of Dugin's success as a public figure stems from his media savvy (he appears on Russian television almost daily) and his political connections (the most important one is to Putin's main "spinmeister," Gleb Pavlovsky) ("Alexander Gelevich Dugin" 2007). Meanwhile, it is Russian liberals that have recently made common cause with Dugin's erstwhile partners in the National Bolshevik Party—a right-radical grouping that is indeed without any future.

In sum, it is clear that Eurasia has become the "grand chessboard" on which the future of the world-system is being decided; that a resurgent Russia has become the first major country to openly challenge the unipolar world order; and that the retreat of neoliberalism has created an ideological vacuum, which Eurasian ideologies with universalist pretensions will increasingly rush to fill. At this point, Russia continues to encounter structural difficulties—it is still dependent on outside investment and technology, it is overreliant on its energy sector, it is still unpopular with many of its neighbors, and it is still experiencing demographic decline. But Russia is growing, is strategically central, and retains the ability to challenge the United States. Moreover, Russia, as the Eurasianists contend, can attain its goals by pursuing regional consolidation and building new institutions, whereas the U.S. goals in Eurasia require the exploitation of existing divisions and the sowing of conflict. In this period of transition, Eurasianism remains a project with a future.

References

ABC [ABC News Online] (2006). "US Drives World Military Spending to Record High." *ABC News Online,* June 12. URL: http://www.abc.net.au/news/news-items/200606/s1661277.htm. Accessed July 15, 2007.

"Alexander Gelevich Dugin" (2007). Answers.com. URL: http://www.answers.com/topic/alexander-gelevich-dugin. Accessed May 9, 2007.

American Chamber of Commerce (2007). "The Economy and Investment Climate in Russia." URL: http://www.amcham.ru/publications/investment_reports/ir2006. Accessed May 10, 2007.

Amrekulov, Nurlan (2004). *Armanzher: Mechta Chelovechestva* [Armanzher: The Dream of Humankind]. Almaty: Galym.

Arrighi, Giovanni, Mark Selden, and Takeshi Hamashita, eds. (2003). *The Resurgence of East Asia: 500, 150, and 50 Year Perspectives.* London: Routledge

Bassin, Mark (1991). "Russia Between Europe and Asia: The Ideological Construction of Geographical Space." *Slavic Review* 50, no. 1 (Spring): pp. 1–17.

Bernal, Martin (1991). *Black Athena: The Afroasiatic Roots of Classical Civilization.* Volume II: *The Archaeological and Documentary Evidence.* New Brunswick, NJ: Rutgers University.

Brzezinski, Zbigniew (1997). *The Grand Chessboard: American Primacy and Its Geostrategic Imperatives.* New York: Basic.

Cohen, Stephen F. (2007). "The New American Cold War." *The Nation,* June 8. URL: http://www.thenation.com/doc/20060710/cohen. Accessed June 19, 2007.

Danilevskii, Nikolai (1965 [1869]). *Rossiia i Evropa* [Russia and Europe]. New York: Johnson Reprint.

Deviatov, Andrei (2002). *Krasnyi Drakon: Kitai i Rossiia v Dvadtsat' Pervom Veke* [Red Dragon: China and Russia in the 21st Century]. Moscow: Algoritm

Dugin, Aleksandr (1997). "Posleslovie: Evraziiskii Triumf" [Afterword: The Eurasianist Triumph], in Petr Savitskii, *Kontinent Evrazia* [The Continent Eurasia], ed. Aleksandr Dugin, pp. 433–453. Moscow: Agraf.

——— (2004). *Proekt "Yevrazia"* [Project "Eurasia"]. Moscow: Yauza.

Escobar, Pepe (2003). "Russia's 'Liberal Empire.'" Asia Times Online, December 18. URL: http://www.atimes.com/atimes/Central_Asia/EL18Ag01.html. Accessed May 9, 2007.

EU Russia Centre (2007). "Voices from Russia: Society, Democracy, Europe." URL: http://www.eu-russiacentre.org/assets/files/EU-RC. Accessed April 5, 2007.

FBC [Fernand Braudel Center] (2006). "Newsletter No. 30, Activities, 2005–06," November. URL: http://www.binghamton.edu/fbc/newsletter30.pdf. Accessed July 13, 2007.

Furuoka, Fumitaka (2005). "Japan and the 'Flying Geese' Pattern of East Asian Integration." *eastasia.at* 4, no. 1 (October): pp. 1–7. URL: http://www.eastasia.at/vol4_1/article01.htm. Accessed May 5, 2007.

Gumilev, Lev. N. (1992). *Ot Rusi k Rossii: Ocherki Etnicheskoi Istorii* [From Rus' to Russia: Foundations of Ethnological History]. Moscow: EKO.

———. (1997). *Etnogenez i biosfera zemli* [Ethnogenesis and the Biosphere of the Earth]. Moscow: Di Dik.

———. (2003). *Ritmy Evrazii: Epokhi i Tsivilizatsii* [The Rhythms of Eurasia: Epochs and Civilizations], ed. V. A. Michurin, pp. 23–30. St. Petersburg: Kristall.

Gvosdev, Nikolas (2007). "China, Russia Shaking Economic Status Quo." *AsiaTimes online,* July 3. URL: http://www.atimes.com/atimes/China_Business/IG03Cb02.html. Accessed July 3, 2007.

Hamashita, Takeshi (1987). "The Tribute-trade System and Modern Asia." *The Memoirs of the Toyo Bunko* 46, 7–25.

Hill, Fiona (2004). "Energy Empire: Oil, Gas, and Russia's Revival." London: The Foreign Policy Centre.

Hirsch, Francine (2005). *Empire of Nations: Ethnographic Knowledge and the Making of the Soviet Union.* Ithaca, NY: Cornell University.

Humphrey, Caroline (2002). "'Eurasia,' Ideology, and the Political Imagination in Provincial Russia," in C. M. Hahn, ed., *Postsocialism: Ideals, Ideologies, and Practices in Eurasia,* pp. 258–276. London: Routledge

Kagarlitsky, Boris (2007). "A Liberal Interpretation of Normal." *Moscow Times,* June 21. URL: http://www.tni.org/detail_page.phtml?act_id=17015&username=guest@tni.org&password=9999&publish=Y. Accessed June 24, 2007.

Khachatrian, Vladimir (2005). *Proekt Orion* [Project Orion]. Moscow: TAKhO SV.

Korduban, Pavel (2007). "Putin Harvests Political Dividends from Russian Economic Dynamism." *Eurasia Daily Monitor,* June 18. URL: http://www.jamestown.org/edm/article.php?article_id=2372236. Accessed July 15, 2007.

Lavelle, Peter, ed. (2005). "RP's Weekly Russia Experts' Panel: Defining the 'Post Soviet Space.'" URL: http://www.untimely-thoughts.com/index.html?cat=3&type=3&art=1974. Accessed December 14, 2006.

Lewis, Martin W., and Kären E. Wigen (1997). *The Myth of Continents: A Critique of Metageography.* Berkeley: University of California.

Martin, Terry (2001). *The Affirmative Action Empire: Nations and Nationalism in the Soviet Union, 1923–1939.* Ithaca, NY: Cornell University.

Narasimhan, Chakravarthi V., and Yuri K. Yefremov, eds. (2006). "Asia." *Encylopaedia Britannica Online,* pp. 1–123. URL: http://www.britannica.com/eb/article-9110518/Asia. Accessed May 5, 2007.

Nazarbaev, Nursultan (1997). *Evraziiskii Soiuz: idei, prakika, perspektivy, 1994–1997* [Eurasian Union: Ideas, Praxis, Perspectives, 1994–1997]. Moscow: Fond sodeistvia razvitiiu sotsial'nykh i politicheskikh nauk.

——— (2005). *V Serdtse Evrazii* [In the Heart of Eurasia]. Almaty: Atamura.

Palat, Ravi Arvind (2004). *Capitalist Restructuring and the Pacific Rim.* London: Routledge Curzon.

Panarin, Aleksandr (2002). *Global'noe Politicheskoe Prognozirovanie* [Global Political Forecasting]. Moscow: Algoritm.

RIAN [Russian News and Information Agency] (2005). "Russian Foreign Trade Grows 34.2 percent in First Half of 2005—Customs Service." August 9. URL: http://en.rian.ru/business/20050809/41121038.html. Accessed July 15, 2007.

Said, Edward (1978). *Orientalism.* New York: Vintage.

Savitskii, Petr (1997a [1933]). "Geograficheskie i Geopoliticheskie Osnovy Evraziistva" [The Geographic and Geopolitical Foundations of Eurasianism], in Petr Savitskii, *Kontinent Evrazia* [The Continent Eurasia], ed. Aleksandr Dugin, pp. 295–303. Moscow: Agraf.

Savitskii, Petr (1997b [1926]). "Evraziistvo" [Eurasianism], in Petr Savitskii, *Kontinent Evrazia* [The Continent Eurasia], ed. Aleksandr Dugin, pp. 13–80. Moscow: Agraf.

Savitskii, Petr (1997c [1919]). "Ocherki Mezhdunarodnykh Otnoshenii" [An Essay on International Relations] in Petr Savitskii, *Kontinent Evrazia* [The Continent Eurasia], ed. Aleksandr Dugin, pp. 382–297. Moscow: Agraf.

Schmidt, Matthew (2005). "Is Putin Pursuing a Policy of Eurasianism?" *Demokrati-*

zatsiya (Winter): pp. 1–14. URL: http://findarticles.com/p/articles/ mi_qa3996/ is_200501/ai_n13640828/pg_11–30k

Schwab, Raymond (1984). *The Oriental Renaissance: Europe's Rediscovery of India and the East 1680–1880.* Trans. Gene Patterson-Black and Victor Reinking. New York: Columbia University.

Shlapentokh, Vladimir (2006). "China in the Russian Mind Today: Ambivalence and Defeatism." URL: http://www.msu.edu/~shlapent/china.htm. Accessed April 20, 2007.

Socor, Vladimir (2007). "Moscow Pressuring Kazakhstan to Frustrate Westbound Energy Transport Projects." *Eurasia Daily Monitor* vol. 4, no. 67. URL: http://jamestown. org/edm/article.php?article_id=2372078. Accessed April 7, 2007.

Stroupe, Joseph (2006). "The Rising Pole of the East." *AsiaTimes* online, December 19. URL: http://www.atimes.com/atimes/China/HL19Ad01.html. Accessed December 19, 2006.

——— (2007). "All Power to Russia." *AsiaTimes* online, April 27. URL: http://www. atimes.com/atimes/Central_Asia/ID27Ag01.html. Accessed April 27, 2007.

Trenin, Dmitrii (2002). *The End of Eurasia: Russia on the Border Between Geopolitics and Globalization.* Washington, DC: Carnegie Endowment for International Peace.

——— (2007). "Russia Redefines Itself and Its Relations with the West." *The Washington Quarterly* (Spring): pp. 95–105.

Trubetzkoy, Nikolai Sergeevich (1991a [1925]). "The Legacy of Genghis Khan: A Perspective on Russian History not from the West but from the East," in Nikolai Sergeevich Trubetzkoy, *The Legacy of Genghis Khan and Other Essays on Russia's Identity,* ed. Anatoly Liberman, trans. Kenneth Brostrom and Anatoly Liberman, pp. 161–231. Ann Arbor: Michigan Slavic Publications.

——— (1991b [1927]). "Pan-Eurasian Nationalism," in Nikolai Sergeevich Trubetzkoy, *The Legacy of Genghis Khan and Other Essays on Russia's Identity,* ed. Anatoly Liberman, trans. Kenneth Brostrom and Anatoly Liberman, pp. 233–244. Ann Arbor: Michigan Slavic Publications.

Utkin, Anatolii (2003). *Vyzov Zapada i Otvet Rossii* [The Challenge of the West and the Response of Russia]. Moscow: Algoritm.

Vinkovetsky, Ilya (2007). "Eurasia and Its Uses: The History of an Idea and the Mental Geography of Post-Soviet Space." Unpublished paper for SOYUZ symposium, pp. 1–16. URL: www.princeton.edu/~restudy/soyuz_papers/Vinkovetsky.pdf. Accessed May 5, 2007.

Vogel, Ezra (1991). *The Four Little Dragons: The Spread of Industrialization in East Asia.* Cambridge, MA: Harvard University.

Von Hagen, Mark (2004). Empires, Borderlands, and Diasporas: Eurasia as Anti-Paradigm for the Post-Soviet Era." *The American Historical Review* 109, no. 2 (April):pp. 1–28. URL: http://www.historycooperative.org/journals/ahr/109.2/ hagen.html. Accessed May 5, 2005.

Voskressenski, Alexei (2007). "The Rise of China and Russo-Chinese Relations in the New Global Politics of Eastern Asia." URL: src-h.slav.hokudai.ac.jp/coe21/ publish/ no16_2_ses/01_voskressenski.pdf. Accessed July 22, 2007.

Wallerstein, Immanuel (1991). *Geopolitics and Geoculture: Essays on the Changing World-system.* Cambridge: Cambridge University.

Wang, Hui (2007). "The Politics of Imagining Asia: Empires, Nations, Regional and

Global Orders." Trans. Matthew A. Hale. *Japan Focus,* April 16, pp. 1–53. URL: http://japanfocus.org/products/details/2407. Accessed April 16, 2007.

Whitney, Mike (2007). "Putin's War-Whoop: The Impending Clash with Russia." Global Research.ca, June 22. URL: http://www.globalresearch.ca/index.php?context=va&aid=6125. Accessed June 22, 2007.

Wilson, Dominic, and Roopa Purushothaman (2003). "Dreaming with BRICs: The Path to 2050." Goldman Sachs Global Economics Paper no. 99, pp. 1–24. URL: www2.goldmansachs.com/insight/research/reports/99.pdf. Accessed May 5, 2007.

4

CHINA IN THREE GEOGRAPHICAL CONTEXTS

Steven Sherman

Introduction

A popular notion recently (at least until the U.S. invasion of Iraq unintentionally focused interest in the continuing salience of geopolitics and the long historical trajectory of Sunni and Shia Islam) was that something fundamental had changed since 1989, resulting in a "flat world" or a placeless "empire" that rendered older national histories irrelevant (Friedman 2005; Hardt and Negri 2000). Although his work is typically far more historically grounded than these authors, Immanuel Wallerstein strangely converges with them when describing the demise of the modern world-system and its replacement by something else (see, e.g., Chapter 2). Although he has explored at length shifting geopolitical dynamics that repudiate the notion of a flat world unified only by capital (or by a networked "multitude" that is 'everywhere'), Wallerstein argues that we are at the beginning of a systemic crisis and a bifurcated transition to a new form of global organization. Because this transition is chaotic and unpredictable, it cannot be extrapolated from geopolitical trends. Because the transition hinges on the exhaustion of capitalism, shifts in power from one center of accumulation to another center are of limited significance. He thus denigrates the story of geopolitical shifts he has patiently described and arrives at a point similar to that of Hardt and Negri: a global contest between the vision of the

Davos-based World Economic Forum ("Empire," for Hardt and Negri) and the Porto Alegre–based World Social Forum ("multitude").

Yet a look back at the emergence of the modern world-system does not bear out these claims of total discontinuity. It certainly would not have been easy in 1400 to ascertain that Northwestern Asia would be the center of the new system. That said, many of the components of the geoculture that would only cohere around 1800 were already present—republicanism, the territorial state, the belief that the universe was organized around a few simple rules that could be rationally ascertained, interstate diplomacy, universities, and a crusading narrative of Christianity's universalizing thrust (see Stark 2005). To create the modern geoculture, these had to be brought together in new ways, secularized, and universalized. And even though European states and commercial enterprises drove the construction of the new system, it now seems less than obvious that many of the losers in this process (including empires, religions, indigenous peoples) simply folded their tents and gave up as the "modern" shed the "traditional."

In this spirit, I want to reflect in this chapter on some aspects of the long-term significance of the shift of economic power toward East Asia (in particular China). The historical geographies and narratives described below will not simply disappear as the modern world-system mutates into something else; instead they will combine with the spirit of Davos or Porto Alegre (or both) in new and complex ways.

I will frame an understanding of China's place in the world through three geographies. By *geography*, I mean particular ways to historically, socially construct space. The three spaces are the East/West divide, the North/South divide, and the division between those peripheral/semiperipheral areas of the modern world-system that were incorporated through direct, lengthy, colonial rule and those that were not. These spaces intersect with two historical themes currently out of fashion. One is the history of socialism (necessarily a part of the description of the global South and uncolonized spaces of empire); the other is the history of civilizations (which will be raised in discussing uncolonized empires and the East/West divide). The narrative of socialism is often seen as concluded by the collapse of the Soviet empire, but the view from China, where a communist party continues to rule, may lead in different directions. Although any attempt to discuss long-term trajectories of "civilizations" is typically denounced as essentialist, and the cultural construction of all political units and histories is emphasized in most contemporary scholarship, it is striking how, in East Asia, numerous political units/cultural constructions that predate the modern world system continue to play a critical role in structuring the space. Furthermore, these states, which have been successful in upgrading their status and economic position, have not wholeheartedly embraced the principles of modernity promoted by Western Europe. By looking at how China appears in these historically defined spaces and narratives, it is to be hoped that we can produce a richer picture than those who claim "the world is flat" or that capital now dominates a placeless, "smooth" "empire."

The North/South Divide

Notwithstanding Marxian predictions of a polarization between the workers of the world and the capitalists, the central struggle of the twentieth century was between the colonized world ("the global South") and the colonizing states ("the global north"), with the latter largely in retreat. This trend was given impetus by the experience of the Soviet revolution. Though made under the banner of socialism and defined by a worker's revolt, in the USSR *socialism* soon came to mean employing the state to speed up industrialization so the nation could better defend itself and reclaim its status. The Chinese revolution demonstrated the relevance of this idea to the decolonizing world. In the context of the Sino-Soviet split, the idea of revolution came more and more to mean the rebellion of Third World peoples against the constraints of their position in the world-system, although in the 1970s, as this attitude bore political fruit, the Soviet Union was better positioned than China to reap the harvest. Among other things, 1968 had marked an apparently definitive turning point, when antisystemic movements would be understood as grounded in the global South (the World Social Forum, which is in many ways a response to and divergence from the theory/practice of the old left, consolidates this understanding by always being held in the global South). Mao, along with Che Guevara and Ho Chi Minh, was a key icon of the moment, galvanizing a global generation of revolutionaries (by contrast European and U.S. new left figures tended to have a more limited regional appeal). In addition, the Chinese revolutionary experience, from Yenan through the Cultural Revolution, opened up a range of questions—about the relationship between political leadership and local knowledge, bureaucracy and socialism, rural and urban development—that remain highly relevant, even if these days they are rarely viewed through the optic of the Chinese experience. After the Cultural Revolution, China ceased to play a revolutionary role in the world, at times adopting reactionary positions in its conflict with the Soviet Union. It also famously opened up parts of its economy to world market forces, a dynamic typically associated with the rise of neoliberalism (see Harvey 2005).

But the success of China in employing this strategy complicates the narrative. Whereas neoliberalism is typically viewed as a setback for the global South, involving the resubordination of many states to U.S.-led global capital, it is difficult to view China in this way, given the foreign reserves and industries it has accumulated and the expanding reach of its foreign policy. Its ascension to the WTO notwithstanding, China does not presently appear subordinated to anyone. As the global South begins to regain its footing after twenty years,

China continues to have a role to play. Amid rising anger at U.S. unilateral military interventions and one-sided trade pacts, China is no longer the voice of uncompromising revolution. It now has real diplomatic and economic heft to throw into these struggles, however.

In its low-key, nonideological, cautious opposition to U.S. hegemony, one might describe China's strategy as "speak softly and carry a big stick." In this sense, China is a bigger stick in the arsenal of the global South than any in the last 500 years, including the Soviet Union, which never attained economic might to match its worldwide ideological appeal and empire building. It is relevant here to note that although the United States has continued a (post) colonial European pattern of blending asymmetrical economic negotiations, empire building, and humanitarian lectures in its relations with the global South, China has largely eschewed the use of its military in pursuit of its global economic interests. Instead, it has attempted to negotiate practical deals with southern states to access resources, also avoiding advice about democracy, gender relations, human rights, and so on. This effort may signal the construction of a world market that would supersede the collection of colonial empires that has constituted the modern world-system (whether the construction of such a world market would ultimately be ecologically viable is, however, another question).

There is another way in which the story of China is likely to continue to be intertwined with the story of the global South—as a potential model for how to distribute a limited amount of economic wealth among a large population. Presuming China is not able to consistently maintain the breakneck levels of growth seen over the last fifteen years and that the core states (United States, Europe, Japan) manage to grow at even very moderate rates (both presumptions seem realistic), it will be many decades, if ever, before China is able to catch up to the core states in terms of GDP per capita. As a result, the political question China will face for the indefinite future is how to manage scarcity, using the limited economic resources accumulated to secure a social peace and ensure that large portions of the population are not marginalized. Furthermore, if only a portion of the predictions about peak oil or global warming are true, China will have to address major ecological crises with its limited resources. Since most of the other southern states are likely to face similar issues, the successes and failures of China will become highly relevant to their situations, much more so than the experiences of the wealthy countries with their smaller populations but larger access to and command over world resources. It also speaks volumes about the difference between China and the core states that although travelers from China to Africa (and more generally the global South) are almost exclusively drawn from the professional class (either visiting for work or leisure), China has exported thousands of small shop owners, who live among the general population, "some even sleep in their stalls at outdoor markets, ready to open the shop at dawn" (Kurlantzick 2007: 10).

The East/West Divide

By *the East/West divide*, I mean the broad separation between the portion of Gunder Frank's world-system defined by Greek and Roman Empire building (and later Islam) and that portion in which China constitutes "the middle of the Earth." The Western half of the system has been characterized by two processes. First, it has failed to produce a stable, centralized form of rule. Instead, there have been repeated collapses into a state of all against all. In Europe, beginning around the fourteenth century, this began to have beneficial effects in terms of competitively spurring the development of military technology and economic growth. Second, this region has produced monotheistic creeds organized around sacred books with expansionist tendencies. Christianity, with its sharp divide between believers and nonbelievers (even as it was open to the universal conversion of the latter) and its powerful sense of historical time, eventually became wedded to the militaristic tendency and was synergistically involved in the conquest of the non-Western world. Christianity gave way to the Enlightenment, which secularized many Christian beliefs, producing a division between enlightened moderns and backwards traditionalists and replicating the belief that history progresses toward an end, here the universal reign of reason (or later, socialism).

The crucible of the modern world system was western Europe in the sixteenth century. War and ideological conflict were a crucial part of the landscape then, and although things eventually settled down, order in Europe repeatedly broke down, typically climaxing in a total war with ideological overtones, compounded by state breakdowns and revolutions. The ideas that emerged out of these periods—Protestantism, republicanism, socialism—all had global ramifications, and although their most dramatic moments are in the past, they remain unresolved narratives in the present. Although socialism and, more generally, Enlightenment ideologies, were secularized, they possessed a strong continuity with the past and a belief that the world could be organized according to universal principles, patterns of thinking that might be considered endemic to Western thought going back to the early Christians at least.

One might argue that the repeated appeal to abstract universals was rooted in the repeated failure of Europe to unify. The slide into chaotic total wars inspires intellectuals to remove themselves from the quotidian and espouse universalisms. This is the argument that Stephen Toulmin makes about Descartes and Talcott Parsons—one wonders if it could be extended further back in time (Toulmin 1990). By now, however, universalisms have themselves produced sufficient chaos that there is deepening skepticism about their utility. In the arc traced by David Harvey in *The Condition of Postmodernity*, the dream of reason produced by the "time-space compressions" of the sixteenth through eighteenth centuries has been confounded by more recent collapsing of space through time (Harvey 1989). Beginning in the nineteenth century,

Western intellectuals and artists began to lose faith in Enlightenment verities. One consequence of that loss of faith was the embrace in the world of aesthetics of non-Western models. Is not this process now creeping through Western society in a more amorphous manner?

By now there is an entire library of popular works expounding on the parallels between Buddhist (and sometimes other Eastern) thought and the latest developments in physics and neurobiology (e.g., Zukav 1979). The essential point is that both (post)modern science and Buddhism emphasize the impermanence and illusory nature of reality. Buddhism (as well as other non-Western spiritualities, such as yoga, and popularized Eastern practices such as feng shui and Chinese medicine) offers the prospect of a spiritualization of mind and body that does not repudiate scientific ways of understanding.[1] (Both Buddhism and yoga, furthermore, offer the "postmodern" option of embracing aspects of their practice without a full-fledged "conversion" typical of the faiths on the Western end of the Eurasian land mass.)

Another touchstone of the West has been individual rights, and of course, this continues to reverberate throughout the entire world. This tradition, too, predates the Enlightenment and to some extent has its roots in the power of monotheism to shatter all intermediate social ties between the believer and god. Although, following World War II, additional rights were announced in the UN Declaration of Human Rights, it cannot be said that they have gained much traction, either with Western leaders declaring their defense of "human rights," or with the nonstate human rights community epitomized by Amnesty International. Other rights traditions have developed in the East—notably a "moral economy"–style right to a fair share of the wealth enabling subsistence, a right that has been invoked from Mencius to Mao (Nathan, cited in Chun 2006: 141; Perry 2007). One wonders if this tradition of rights may resonate in the restructuring of the world-system, as Western versions of human rights seem increasingly restricted to a cosmopolitan middle class while the rest of humanity is consigned to chaos, second-class forms of citizenship, incarceration, and so on (it is of course the case that such a critique can be launched at contemporary China as much as anywhere and that assertions of Eastern conceptions of rights will be targeted at the current regime). "Asian values" have already been invoked by the Singaporean and Malaysian regimes to counter the critiques of Western human rights organizations and emphasize the role of family and community in East Asian development. This was more of an effort to claim a little space for these regimes than to reconstruct a global ideology. I am suggesting that as East Asia becomes more powerful economically, there is likely to be global interest in East Asian ideologies (although the general principle implicitly invoked by "Asian values"—that different parts of the world have rights to ground themselves in different traditions—may also prove increasingly relevant).

Western Europe conquered nearly the entire world and positioned itself at the peak of the status hierarchy of the modern world. It thus became the site of emulation by all those wishing to change their position on the hierarchy. This facilitated global enthusiasm for secularism, republicanism, and even socialism (simultaneously a road to emulation and a critique of Western modernity). Whether a new, Eastern-centered world system will be so precipitously hierarchical is not clear. If it is not, the motivation to adapt Eastern practices and beliefs would likely be less powerful. Nevertheless, both for the reasons described above—because they may address some elements of the contemporary world better than Western answers—and because of the economic rise of the East, Eastern practices and beliefs are likely to increase in prestige. For the medium term, the West has a great deal of confidence borne of its lengthy spell at the top of the world. It has developed globe-spanning "hard power" (U.S. military) and "soft power"' (media, human rights organizations, U.S.-trained political elites, etc), institutions to produce a relatively coherent "civilizational" project to impose on the world. Any "Easternization" process is far less coherent and assertive. But one wonders whether the Eastern tortoise will eventually pass the Western hare.

The Empires and the Colonized World of the Periphery

A different way of approaching the question can be found by taking seriously a comment made by Wallerstein to the effect that the most difficult/unruly zones of the global South have been those that had only limited colonization by the West. These zones include Russia, most of East Asia, and the Middle East. Another way of putting this is that, if colonization is the primary mode of integration into the modern world-system, these areas were only capitalist in a limited sense before they began their respective quests for modernity in earnest in the twentieth century. This is another way of putting the familiar notion that Russia and China skipped (or attempted to skip?) the capitalist phase before embarking on socialism. Although Marxists fully absorbed a stage-oriented approach to history—adding a new twist to the march from backward tradition to liberal modernity by declaring the latter (capitalism) simply a new obstacle to historical progress, which could only be fulfilled through socialism—for these empires on the periphery of the system, socialism was one way toward modernity, and considering the alternatives (semi-peripheral capitalism), perhaps the best way to ensure their continued sovereignty and revitalize their geopolitical importance. Ironically, by embracing the futuristic ideology of socialism, the "backward" East threw the West on the defensive, and the ostensibly hypermodern United States became more vocal in defense of religion and various feudal remnants around the world. But the dissolution of Cold War ideology does provide space to more soberly analyze the civilizational heritage of these zones, which might be integrated into a revamped modernity.

It should be noted that the end of the Cold War did not end the salience of the distinction between colonized parts of the periphery and those that entered the modern world-system as weakened empires. This is not only because in the former Ottoman lands (relatively quiescent during most of the twentieth century) the Islamic heritage has proven to be a potent ideological counter to neoliberal consumerism but is also more widely true.

Consider the geography of the World Social Forum. The first three forums were held in Porto Alegre, Brazil. Later forums have been held in Mumbai, India; Caracas, Venezuela; Bamako, Mali; Karachi, Pakistan; and Nairobi, Kenya. These sites suggest a distinct geography that somewhat belies the global nature of the forum and the claim that "we are everywhere." As noted above, the forum deliberately is located in the global South to symbolize its contrast with the North-dominated World Economic Forum, although there is considerable participation from North America and Europe. But it is also striking that the geography of the sites of the forum echoes the geography of the colonized zones of the world—Latin America, Africa, and South Asia. There have been no World Social Forum events in Russia, China, or the Middle East. There have been national forums in Russia and Turkey, relatively modest affairs in the social forum world (in line with the modest level of left activity in these states). And there has been a Mediterranean Social Forum, conceptualizing a Braudelian commonality between southern Europe and the Middle East. But the center of gravity of the movement has been first and foremost Latin America, and then South Asia and Africa. Of course, were a World Social Forum event to be held in China, it would face real challenges given the illiberal political climate (although we should note that a women's conference sponsored by the UN was held in Beijing in 1995). It would face similar, probably less drastic, difficulties in Russia, whereas a World Social Forum held in the Middle East would have to directly confront the weakness of anything resembling a traditional left in that region as compared to the strength of Islamist ideologies.

But perhaps these "difficulties" are simply a different way of stating the main dynamic, namely that the three regions in question have civilizational resources that can limit the impact of neoliberalism, resources deprived from the colonized world. Neoliberalism was largely a project to remove any barriers to the pillage of national economies by finance capital and to remake citizens as consumer/entrepreneurs. The state of indebtedness developed in the 1970s set the groundwork, and ideologically, neoliberalism was invigorated by the collapse of the USSR and the larger communist movement. It triumphed over nearly the entire world, but in highly uneven ways. For example, the United States, its ideological/military center, was able to bend the rules to allow for the continuation of military Keynesianism. Continental Europe never as enthusiastically embraced the program as the UK.

The evolution of neoliberalism in the three former-empire regions is striking. Russia wholeheartedly adopted shock therapy, with perhaps the most disastrous results anywhere, but the project was short-lived; without a major revolt from the populace, under Putin the state backed away from the neoliberal precipice. China is often seen as a key player in the rise of neoliberalism, but the Chinese state largely stayed in control of the process, avoiding the punitive measures meted out by international institutions (China's ascension to the WTO is perhaps an exception). Over the last few years, it appears that China, too, is backing away from the more dogmatic elements of neoliberalism, again without a coherent political left force demanding it do so. Finally, in the Middle East, although a number of pro-U.S. rulers have embraced neoliberal formulations, the strength of political Islam has limited the assertion of hegemony by a transnational consumer class, with the partial exception of a handful of spaces such as Beirut and Dubai. On the other hand, the postcolonial world has seen the rise of more deeply entrenched transnational elites and a seemingly inescapable web of negotiations binding them into the neoliberal program (although the hard-fought pink tide in Latin America is certainly fraying that web). This provides the context for the grassroots and civil society movements that constitute the World Social Forum. The geography of the World Social Forum strikingly inverts the geography of the communist movement, to which China and Russia were so central. Surely this has something to do with the significance of states to each project. Communist revolutionaries wanted to seize state power, and these fading empires provided relatively strong turf to do so. By contrast, the "movement of movements" often talks of civil society, horizontal solidarities, and other nonstate ideologies.

On the other hand, there is at least the prospect that there may be some convergence between the "movement of movements" and the former empires, particularly if, as seems likely, the latter continue to adopt self-protective measures. The success of the Chavez regime has clearly reopened debate (until recently dominated by anarchistic tendencies) about the possible virtues of state power in the quest for social justice (Wilpert 2007). In addition, the empire-building efforts of the Bush administration have alerted the movements to the continued salience of geopolitics. If China lends heft to the struggles of the global sSuth for economic justice, it also strengthens an emergent coalition against the approach of "regime change" (as does Russia). In this context, some of the "bottom-up" experiences of the Chinese Revolution (the only twentieth-century revolution, it is worth noting, to claim the heritage of the Paris commune [see Chun 2006: 139–140]) may be reclaimed as part of the history of the "movement of movements." Some sort of fusion of the bottom-up sensibility with the virtues of historically strong states seems likely.

Conclusion

A shift in economic power from the West (indeed, from the North Atlantic Protestant communities of the West) to the East cannot help but have significant cultural consequences. The historical geographies that have defined the context for contemporary China will continue to be of significance, even as the world enters into what may be a period of greater uncertainty. That the rise of China is embedded in the narrative of the resistance of the global South, that it is an old empire that has reinvented and modernized itself through socialism and by maintaining a strong state, and that it is nestled in Eastern traditions of nonsingular identities, collective rights, and a relatively stable interstate system will have consequences. It would be overreaching to identify precisely what those consequences will be; however, efforts to orient oneself with the goal of reconstructing the world-system will be flawed if they are not taken into consideration.

Note

1. Immanuel Wallerstein suggested that Gandhian nonviolence also qualifies as a (mostly) Western adoption of an Eastern practice. I would add that its appeal is not unlike Buddhism, as it breaks down the gap between actor and action so characteristic of the West and now causing increasing alienation.

References

Chun, Lin (2006) *The Transformation of Chinese Socialism*. Durham, NC: Duke University Press.
Friedman, Thomas (2005) *The World Is Flat: A Brief History of the 21st Century*. New York: Farrar, Straus, and Giroux.
Hardt, Michael, and Antonio Negri (2000) *Empire*. Cambridge, MA: Harvard University Press.
Harvey, David (1989) *The Condition of Postmodernity: An Enquiry into the Origins of Cultural Change*. Cambridge, MA: Blackwell.
——— (2005) *A Brief History of Neoliberalism*. New York: Oxford University Press.
Kurlantzick, Joshua (2007) "Beijing Envy." *London Review of Books* 29, no. 13, July 5, pp. 9–11.
Nathan, Andrew (1985) *Chinese Democracy*. New York: Knopf.
Perry, Elizabeth (2007) Keynote Address at PEW Conference, St. Lawrence University, Canton, New York, May 12.
Stark, Rodney (2005) *The Victory of Reason: How Christianity Led to Freedom, Capitalism, and Western Success*. New York: Random House.
Toulmin, Stephen (1990) *Cosmopolis: The Hidden Agenda of Modernity*. New York: Free Press.
Wilpert, Gregory (2007) *Changing Venezuela by Taking Power*. New York: Verso.
Zukav, Gary (1979) *The Dancing Wu Li Masters: An Overview of the New Physics*. New York: Morrow.

5

THE ROLES OF CENTRAL ASIAN MIDDLEMEN AND MARCHER STATES IN AFRO-EURASIAN WORLD-SYSTEM SYNCHRONY[1]

Thomas D. Hall, Christopher Chase-Dunn, and Richard Niemeyer

Introduction

Our argument is that various Central Asian states were one of many important links between East and West Asia over the last two and half millennia. Furthermore, their linking role seems to have attenuated this synchrony somewhat. Research has demonstrated an East/West synchrony in growth and decline of the population sizes of largest cities from 500 BCE to 1500 CE in West Asia and those in East Asia (Chase-Dunn and Manning 2002). There is a similar synchrony in the territorial sizes of the largest empires. Though separated by 4,000 miles, these empires and cities were dancing in time for 2,000 years. The cities and empires in South Asia *appear*, however, to march to a different drummer. This could be an artifact of poor data, as suggested by Andrey Korotayev. This synchrony involves more than the many exchanges reviewed by Sorenson and Johannessen (2006). Such synchronization strongly suggests that there has been some sort of systemic interaction. Yet, research in population ecology indicates that even relatively "minor" exchanges of "luxury" or "prestige" goods can provide such links (Turchin and Hall 2003; Hall and Turchin 2007).

Scholars have long pointed to the importance of Central Asia as a corridor of communications, trade, and the diffusion of religions and technologies across the Silk Roads for more than two millennia. In particular, many note the important roles of steppe nomads in these linkages (Barfield 1989; Chase-Dunn and Hall 1997: chap. 8; Christian 1994, 2000; Frank 1992; Hall 2005; Kradin 2002; Kradin, Bondarenko, and Barfield 2003; Lattimore 1940; Liu and Shaffer 2007; Mair 2006; Sherratt 2006; Teggart 1939).

Such connections and synchronizations are major mechanisms that link erstwhile isolated ancient world-systems. Ancient world-systems have different boundaries for bulk goods networks, political/military networks, prestige goods networks, and information networks. Furthermore, semiperipheral societies often play vital roles in transformations of ancient world-systems. Finally, the linkages of these formerly isolated and largely independent world-systems into a single Afroeurasian-wide world-system played a vital role in the development of the modern capitalist world-system (Chase-Dunn and Babones 2006; Chase-Dunn and Hall 1997).

For this analysis we define Central Asia as the territory between the eastern edge of the Caspian Sea (E53) and the old Jade Gate near the city of Dun Huang (E95), north of latitude N37 (the northern edge of the Iranian Plateau, the northern part of Afghanistan, and the southern edge of the Tarim Basin [see Guang-da 1996]), and south of the steppe transition to forest and tundra. This includes deserts, mountains, and grasslands or steppes.

David Christian traces Central Asian history since the Paleolithic with an emphasis on the continuing importance of the ecology and geography. Big game hunting was followed by the emergence of sedentary or short distance pastoralism, then by the emergence of long distance pastoralism. This is a story of radical adaptation to a challenging environment. Exchanges between farmers and pastoralists have very deep roots in Central Asia that predate the earliest written observations from the agrarian civilizations. Central Asians or Eastern Europeans domesticated horses as early as the fourth or third millennium BCE. Use of horses increased labor productivity. Greater mobility permitted the formation of nomadic polities, probably before most of the historically known ones. These early steppe pastoralists were the probable transmitters of technologies, languages, shamanic practices, and diseases across Eurasia (Christian 1994, 2000; see too Mair 2006).

Large confederations of steppe nomads probably emerged on the eastern steppe, where rainfall is less (Christian 2000: 198). This is a process analogous to other instances of conquering polities emerging from semiperipheral regions in ecologically marginal areas. What is unusual about Central Asia is that instead of semiperipheral marcher states these are peripheral marcher states (Chase-Dunn and Hall, 1997: chap. 5). In Central Asia nomadic peripheral societies undergo a special kind of state formation and then occasionally conquer agrarian civilizations. In world historical comparison this is unusual. Whereas peripheral peoples are often raiders, they rarely settle and form classes and states that subsequently create a core-wide empire. Central Asian nomadic states did not develop an institutionalized elite who appropriated food and other products from commoners. Rather, they were nearly pure cases of a tributary mode of accumulation in which the peasant and artisan classes of adjacent agrarian civilizations substituted for a domestic working class (Kradin 2002; Hall 2005).

Thomas Barfield (1989, 1991) adds nuances to this scenario in his discussion of an oscillation between an "outer frontier" and an "inner frontier" strategy. The outer frontier strategy consisted of nomadic pastoralist raids on border cities and demands for tribute payments against threats of future raiding. Raiders avoided occupying Chinese land. They expected that destroyed cities and towns would be rebuilt. The leader of a steppe confederacy used the booty from the raids to subsidize current followers and to garner more alliances (Barfield 1989: 49ff). The inner frontier strategy is a variant of the semiperipheral marcher process. The weaker party in a conflict among steppe khans seeks an alliance with a local agrarian warlord in China, who is eager to use "barbarians against barbarians" (Barfield 1989: 63ff). The steppe leader uses goods from the warlord to gain followers. Both grow strong together. The steppe leader then usually either himself becomes an agrarian lord or reverts to an outer frontier strategy.

Barfield argues that large steppe confederacies usually cycle synchronously with the rise and fall of the large sedentary agrarian states that they raid. This is because the ability of a steppe khan to hold his coalition together is based on success in extracting tribute to reward confederates. This strategy works best when there is a large and productive agrarian state to extort. If a large steppe empire emerges during a "time of troubles" for the agrarian core, it is unable to extract large quantities of surplus and is likely to fall apart itself. These cycles are one hypothesized mechanism of the systemic linkages between East and West Asia.

Figure 5.1 shows evidence for East/West synchrony in city and empire sizes. David Christian argues that "the political history of Inner Eurasia shaped the rhythms not just of Inner Eurasia but of the entire Eurasian world-system" (1994:182). In this account we focus on the ways Central Asian peoples helped to synchronize city and empire growth/decline phases across Afroeurasia.

Possible Explanations

Climate change might affect regions synchronously by causing growth and decline of agricultural productivity that in turn affects cities and empires. Perhaps because South Asia is nearer the equator, its climate change history

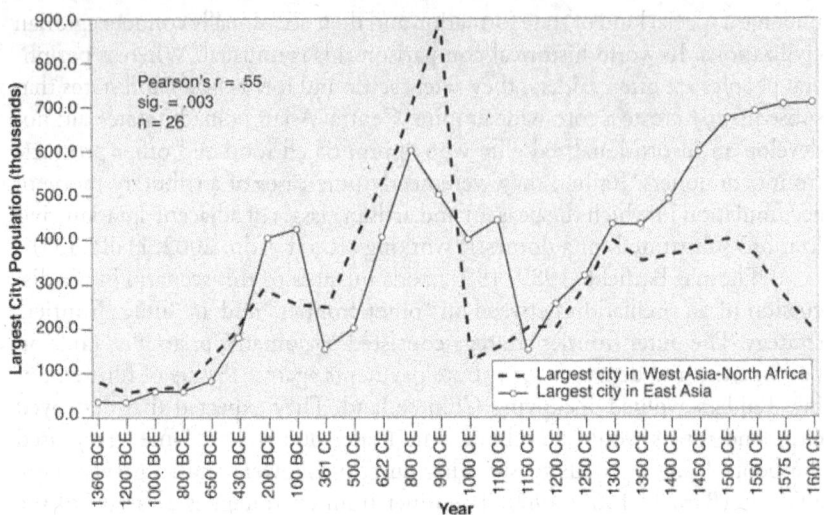

Figure 5.1 Largest Cities in East and West Asia

is different from that of East and West Asia, and this might explain why its growth/decline pattern is different. So far we have not found any indication that climate changes instigated or reinforced the synchronization of East/West growth/decline phases. Yet an article in the *New York Times* (Blakeslee 2006) reports evidence of a major comet impact circa the time of biblical Noah, about 4,800 years ago, in the Indian Ocean. This impact may be the source of many myths of a great flood. More germane to the discussion here, this would be precisely the type of event that might reset cyclical processes in South Asia, knocking it out of synchrony with the reset of Afroeurasia.

But climate could play other roles. Steppe nomads were very sensitive to minor fluctuations in temperature and rainfall. Slight changes can have major effects on the critical lambing season. A late frost can force a group to seek other sources of food, either through raiding or amalgamation (Cribb 1991). This, in turn, could have influenced nomadic military campaigns and thus both cities and agrarian empires in the East and West Asia.

These approaches conceptualize climate change as an exogenous variable. But it is also possible that city and empire growth changes the local climate. Population growth and the development of complex civilizations change the environment through deforestation, soil erosion, and the construction of large irrigation systems. These changes can affect local rainfall and temperatures. Thus, climate change may also be endogenous. Ruddiman (2005) reports strong evidence of the effects of human farming on climate, possibly retarding the onset of the most recent ice age, which is now contributing to global warming. An important aspect of Ruddiman's findings is that such climatic effects may go back 5,000 years or more (see also Chew 2001, 2007).

Another explanation for synchrony could be cycles of Central Asian migrations that impacted agrarian civilizations in the East and the West (Thompson 2005). Additional factors could include epidemic diseases that spread across Afroeurasia killing large numbers of people in cities, for example the Black Death (bubonic plague) in the thirteenth century (McNeill 1976). Perhaps earlier pandemics (e.g., the plague of Justinian, etc.) caused the synchrony.

Finally, it is also possible that two systems that are cycling independently can become synchronized if they are both reset by simultaneous, but largely accidental, shocks. This is the known as the "Moran Effect" in population ecology. This can happen more readily with cycles of relatively constant period. But even for irregular cycles, or even cyclically chaotic processes, such resets can last for a few cycles. For cycles which are of 300- or 600-year durations, a few cycles encompass a large swath of history (Turchin 2007; Turchin and Hall 2003; Chase-Dunn, Alvarez, and Pasciuti 2005a, 2005b). Figure 5.2 depicts these explanations of East/West synchrony.

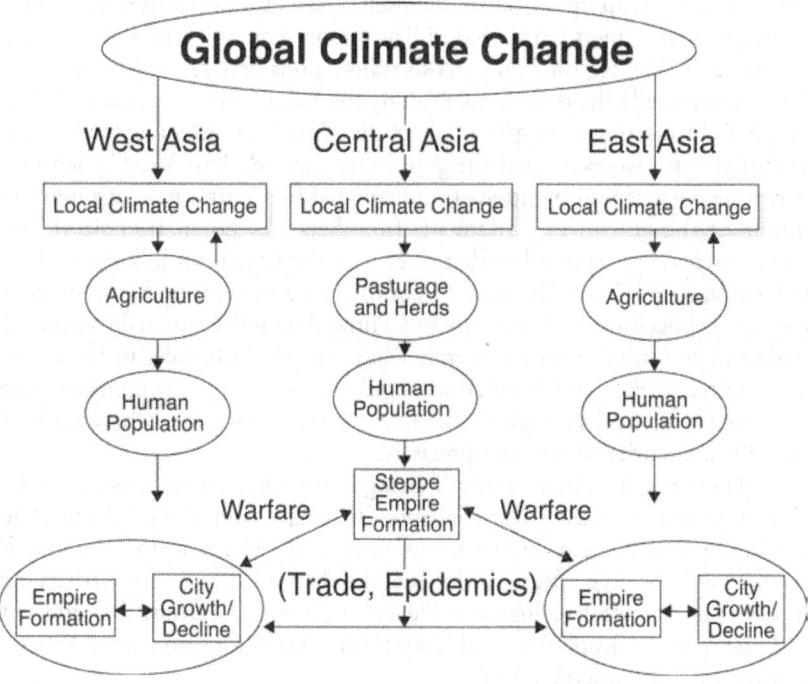

Figure 5.2 An Inventory of Possible Causes of East/West Synchrony

David Christian suggests that the causal path from Central Asian state formation, through trade intensification, to the rise of large agrarian cities and empires in the East and West, is that ecological exchanges were often as important as, or more important than, civilizational exchanges. Beckwith (1991) has documented the crucial role of steppe pastoralists in supplying horses to various Chinese dynasties. The rise of a large steppe confederacy allowed the horse trade to flourish, brought more silk and other metallic goods into the hands of pastoralists, and fueled the Silk Road trade. The original basis of the Silk Roads was the local interaction between steppe pastoralist nomads and oasis farmers and settlement dwellers in Central Asia itself.

Christian describes the early emergence of "transverse routes" across which steppe nomads and oasis agriculturalists were exchanging bulk goods as well as some prestige goods. He says: "Thus the evidence shows that the transverse routes were not just tacked on to the arterial routes. They were older than the arterial routes, and were always integral to the functioning of the Silk Roads" (Christian 2000:9). Local bulk goods, exchange networks among oasis farmers, and steppe nomads within Central Asia came into existence before the emergence of long-distance prestige goods camel caravans. The long shift from semisedentary horticulture and stock-raising to fully nomadic pastoralism was never complete. Di Cosmo (2002) shows that nomadic steppe pastoralists themselves sometimes planted temporary crops and that farmers continued to live among them in certain areas of the steppe lands. The regional bulk goods transactions between pastoralists and farmers, especially the oasis farmers along the Silk Road routes, expanded to supply caravansaries as long-distance trading increased. In an earlier version of this chapter we examined the possibility that the East/West synchrony may have been caused by interaction mediated by Central Asia through the timing of the growth of settlements (numbers and population sizes), the rate of increase of reported trade routes, and the formation of large polities in Central Asia (Chase-Dunn et al. 2006). The argument is that periods of growth and decline of settlements in Central Asia reflect intensifications of trade and communications that might have carried influences to the agrarian empires in East and West Asia. Population sizes of settlements may be estimated from archaeological and documentary evidence, whereas other variables are harder to measure precisely.

There may be other causes of changes in settlement size besides trade. Climate change, especially desertification, may have complicated effects. The shifting of river courses, drying up of oases, and changes in the amount of rainfall can have large effects on the sizes and the very existence of settlements in desert climes. Archaeological evidence suggests that earthquakes affected some settlements (Korjenkov et al. 2003). State formation also affects the sizes and growth rates of settlements.

Central Asia, Capitalist City-States, and World-System Evolution

What are the implications of Central Asian historical change for understanding the evolution of modes of accumulation, especially capitalism? During the Bronze and Iron Age expansions of the tributary empires, a new niche emerged for states that specialized in the carrying trade among the empires and adjacent regions. Sometimes these city-states specialized in trade and production of commodities for exchange, and domestic merchants and production capitalists controlled them. The expansion of trade and communications networks facilitated the growth of empires and vice versa. The emergence of agriculture, mining, and manufacturing production of surpluses for trade gave conquerors an incentive to expand state control into distant areas. The apparatus of the empire was itself often a boon to trade. The specialized trading states promoted the production of trade surpluses, bringing peoples into commerce over wide regions, and thus they helped to create the conditions for the emergence of larger empires and commercialization.

The interaction of capitalist city-states in Central Asia with pure tributary states of the steppes may have produced interesting and unique institutional forms. Some of the groups, such as the Soghdians, became trade diasporas, handling the carrying trade for the cities of emergent territorial states in Central Asia. Some groups, such as the Türks and Oighurs, transformed their economic roles to take advantage of opportunities presented by social change in Central Asia. The Türks were originally a mining and metal-working caste of mountain and forest people within the Juan-Juan steppe nomad empire who rebelled and established their own huge steppe states (Sinor and Klyashtorny 1996). Later the Oighurs shifted to become urban trading people in the oasis cities of the Silk Roads.

In short, increases in trade over the Silk Roads gave rise to new social forms and provided a means for spreading knowledge of those forms.

Findings on Central Asia

In order to explore these possibilities we took the data from Rein Taagepera's (1978, 1997) study of the expansion and contraction of large polities over the past 5,000 years of human history. In its original form, empire sizes were coded at specific time points according to their availability, and as a result, these temporal gaps were not conducive to the comparison of trends across regions. To overcome this limitation, we recoded Taagepera's original data to the nearest decade and linearly interpolated the missing data points. For example, if Taagepera reported an empire as having an area of 2 square megameters (Mm^2) in 323 CE, we coded the data as 2 Mm^2 in 320 CE (see Table 5.1).

Table 5.1 Example of How Empire Data Were Coded

Decade Reported by Taagepera	Empire Size Reported by Taagepera	Decade Coded for in the Data Set	Empire Size Coded for in the Data Set
323 CE	2 Mm²	320 CE	2 Mm²
326 CE	3 Mm²	330 CE	3 Mm²
No decade reported	No size reported	340 CE (interpolated)	4 Mm² (interpolated)
349 CE	5 Mm²	350 CE	5 Mm²

Although this solution addressed the problem of missing data, it created a new problem involving an artificially inflated number of cases. Because levels of significance are sensitive to sample size, this limited our ability to accurately interpret the statistical significance of our results. Our solution to this problem is to use only cases in which at least one of the empire sizes represented an actual score reported by Taagepera for the computation of statistical significance levels. As an example consider Table 5.2. Assume that the coded values for the size of the largest Western Empire in 250 CE, and the largest Eastern and Central Empire sizes in 280 CE, all represent real values reported by Taagepera. Given our coding rules, only the Western, Eastern, and Central Empire sizes for the years 250 CE and 280 CE would be considered in the Pearson r correlation analysis. In other words, the real area of the largest Western Empire in 250 CE would be compared with the interpolated values of the largest Eastern and Central Empires in 250 CE, and the real values for the largest Eastern and Central Empires in 280 would be compared with the interpolated Western Empire value. Because all of the empire values coded for years 240 CE, 260 CE, 270 CE, 290 CE, and 300 CE are interpolated, those time points are not included in our calculation of significance levels.

Once the data set was created, a Pearson r test was performed. As can be seen in Table 5.3, there is a positive relationship between the rise and fall of

Table 5.2 Selection of Empire Data (Taagepera Data Indicated)

Decade (CE)	Western Empire Size	Eastern Empire Size	Central Empire Size
240	2.3	1.1	.33
250	2.4	1.3	.35
260	2.5	1.5	.47
270	2.6	1.6	.56
280	2.4	1.7	1.2
290	2.3	3.0	2.0
300	2.3	3.1	3.0

Table 5.3 Pearson r Correlations Between Eastern, Western, and Central Empire Sizes

N = 99	Largest Western Empire Size	Largest Central Empire Size
Largest Eastern Empire Size		
Pearson r Correlation	.349 (.323)	−.386 (−.329)
Sig. (2-Tailed)	.000 (.001)	.000 (.001)
Largest Central Empire Size		
Pearson r Correlation	−.236 (−.199)	
Sig. (2-Tailed)	.019 (.050)	

Note: Values in parentheses are the partial correlations controlling for year.

Eastern and Western Empires (r = .349, sig. at .000) and a negative relationship between the rise and fall of Eastern and Central Empires (r = −.386, sig. at .000). There is also a negative relationship between the rise and fall of Western and Central Empires, with a Pearson r value of −.236 that is significant at the .019 level. Because the time frame of our analysis covers several centuries, we next performed a partial correlation that controlled for time to detrend the data (see the estimates in parentheses in Table 5.3). Although all of the relationships still hold, the level of significance of the Western Empire/Central Empire correlation is now just barely significant at the .05 level.

In order to better isolate the specifics of the relationships involved, a partial correlation was performed between two of the regions controlling for the third. As can be seen in Tables 5.4 and 5.5, the Western/Eastern and Eastern/Central correlations remain significant and are of a similar strength. The relationship between the Largest Western Empire and the Largest Central Empire is no

Table 5.4 Partial Correlation Between Eastern and Western Empire Sizes, Controlling for Central Empire Size and Year

N = 96 (95)	Largest Western Empire Size
Largest Eastern Empire Size	
Pearson r Correlation	.287 (.279)
Sig. (2-Tailed)	.004 (.006)

Table 5.5 Partial Correlation Between Eastern and Central Empire Sizes, Controlling for Year and Western Empire Size

N = 96 (95)	Largest Central Empire Size
Largest Eastern Empire Size	
Pearson r Correlation	−.384 (−.286)
Sig. (2-Tailed)	.001 (.005)

longer significant. Once again, we also controlled for year to detrend the data, and these values are reported in parentheses.

Again, these findings could be artifacts of data problems. It appears that when Central Asian empires are getting bigger, East Asian empires are getting smaller. This would seem to contradict Barfield's (1989) claim that steppe confederacies and sedentary states rise and fall in tandem. Barfield's claim is about pastoral confederacies, however, not local states. That some steppe confederations occasionally became states, albeit briefly, renders these associations problematic. Hence, the apparent contradiction. We also find that the east-west synchrony is smaller when we control for the rise and fall of Central Asian empires, but it does not go away completely.

We need to explore this analysis further. Two key problems may originate in coding decisions. First, which empires are considered part of East Asia and Central Asia? For purposes of our analysis, it may be better to code as Central Asian all empires that are in, or largely in, steppe regions. Second, we should examine whether the results differ if we divide Central Asian empires into sedentary-agricultural and largely pastoral. This second issue is very complex, since steppe confederacies, when large, often built or connected with existing sedentary agricultural cities. The classic example, of course, is the Mongol capital of Karakorum. But this happened with other confederacies. We need to remain cognizant of differences among sedentary states, city-states, pastoral empires or confederations, and amalgams that are alliances among these different types of polities. We discuss this further in our conclusions.

Conclusions

Central Asian peoples were much more than simple conduits for interaction between the great agrarian civilizations of East and West Asia. They played contradictory roles in synchronizing various cyclical processes in East and West Asia—at time strengthening the synchrony, at other times attenuating it. At this stage of investigation it appears that states, especially the marcher states, played a different role than pastoral steppe confederacies. Clearly, further investigations are necessary. Still, these findings do point out why broad brush studies might yield weak or contradictory results. This, incidentally, further underscores a general finding that states play vastly different roles in world-systems than do nonstate societies.

Extreme climatic and geographical conditions repeatedly inspired Central Asian peoples to develop modes of subsistence and institutional structures that had huge consequences for world history. Consideration of these and various alliance and steppe confederations suggests that much of world history may have been distorted by an overly narrow conception of empires as agrarian and sedentary and by the failure to consider the importance of pastoral empires.

We do not yet have a firm answer as to which of the possible explanations for East/West synchrony is the most important. Recent discoveries about comets (Blakeslee 2006), climate (Chew 2007; Ruddiman 2005), and work on synchrony (Turchin and Hall 2003; Hall and Turchin 2007) all suggest a satisfactory explanation will most likely combine many different factors and interactions.

Narratives of waves of migration and incursions such as provided by Thompson (2005) correspond fairly well with the growth/decline phases of East and West cities and empires. But the only quantitative indicators we have been able to find for Central Asia suffer from flaws that make it difficult to affirm or deny the role of trade fluctuations (see Chase-Dunn et al. 2006).

In order to test the explanations for East/West city and empire synchrony we need quantitative data over the relevant time period and in the relevant regions for settlement and empire sizes, climate change, epidemic diseases, migrations, trade, and warfare. The trade route data are useful in providing lists of Central Asian settlements to be studied. Our future work will focus on the largest of these and will assemble estimates of settlement sizes and network structures.

It may well be, as our preliminary findings suggest, that the East-West correlation is weakened by consideration of Central Asian empire fluctuations. If we return to Barfield's narrative discussions (1989), however, and keep in mind discussions of the nature of Central Asian confederations (see especially Kradin 2002; see also Kradin, Bondarenko, and Barfield 2003; Hall 2005), another interpretation of those data is possible.

When steppe confederacies weaken, due to decline in China, pastoralists may turn to the Central Asia states, statelets, and city-states both to supply agricultural and craft goods and to dispose of surplus animals and animal products. If so, then Central Asian empires would, in fact, expand as East Asian empires declined. When China, and East Asian empires in general, strengthened, pastoralists, via the outer frontier strategy, would likely have returned to associations with those empires, withdrawing or abating relations with Central Asian empires, states, or city-states for more robust suppliers.

Now, if this is the case, then two issues are clarified. First, the synchronizing mechanisms we suggest above are indeed responsible for East-West correlations. Second, this would give some insight into why South Asia dances to a different tune. These kinds of connections are far weaker across the mountain barriers. South Asian states are not viable alternatives to either East or Central Asian states as suppliers of agricultural and craft goods.

Finally, we need to develop more robust accounts for how all the factors listed above—climate change, epidemic diseases, migrations, trade, and warfare—shaped these processes. All of these factors shaped the degree of urbanization, the volume and velocity of trade, and relative dependence on pastoral versus agrarian resources. Central Asian pastoralists, as we and many others cited above have noted, were extremely flexible and adaptable and adjusted their ways of making a living rapidly to changing circumstances.

We also need to employ analyses with different coding schemes to discover how sensitive our findings are to coding decisions. As with the original East-West synchrony discovery, correlations that are robust with respect to coding and data issues suggest much more confidence in the overall findings. Findings that fluctuate with data and coding decisions would indicate that there are factors and processes that are not sufficiently theorized nor sufficiently precisely and accurately measured. This, in turn would suggest a need to reexamine the narrative histories to discover the relevant factors and processes. But, it is ever so with empirical research on historical processes.

Regardless of the specific details of further research, we are confident that the vital role of Central Asia and Central Asians in the development of all of Afroeurasia will remain important and yield further insights into the processes of world historical evolution.

Note

1. This chapter is one of the products of a National Science Foundation–sponsored project on "Measuring and modeling cycles of state formation, decline and upward sweeps since the Bronze Age": http://irows.ucr.edu/research/citemp/citemp.html, SES-057720. An earlier version was presented at the Society for Cross-Cultural Research, February 21–24, 2007 San Antonio, Texas.

References

Barfield, Thomas J. 1989. *The Perilous Frontier: Nomadic Empires and China.* Cambridge, MA.: Blackwell.

———. 1991. "Inner Asia and Cycles of Power in China's Imperial Dynastic History." Pp. 153–182 in Gary Seaman and Daniel Markes (eds.), *Rulers from the Steppe: State Formation on the Eurasian Periphery.* Los Angeles, CA: Ethnographic Press, Center for Visual Anthropology, University of Southern California.

Beckwith, Christopher I. 1991. "The Impact of the Horse and Silk Trade on the Economies of T'ang China and the Uighur Empire." *Journal of the Economic and Social History of the Orient* 34:2:183–198.

Blakeslee, Sandra. 2006. "Ancient Crash, Epic Wave." *New York Times,* November 14, 2006, Science Section.

Chase-Dunn, Christopher, Alexis Alvarez, and Daniel Pasciuti. 2005a. "Power and Size: Urbanization and Empire Formation in World-systems." Pp. 92–113 in C. Chase-Dunn and E. N. Anderson (eds.), *The Historical Evolution of World-Systems.* New York: Palgrave

———. 2005b. "World-systems in the Biogeosphere: Three Thousand Years of Urbanization, Empire Formation, and Climate Change." Pp. 311–332 in Paul S.

Ciccantell, David A. Smith, and Gay Seidman (eds.), *Nature, Raw Materials, and Political Economy.* Research in Rural Sociology and Development, vol. 10. London: Elsevier.

Chase-Dunn, Christopher, and Salvatore Babones. 2006. *Global Social Change: Comparative and Historical Perspectives.* Baltimore: Johns Hopkins University Press.

Chase-Dunn, Christopher, and Thomas D. Hall. 1997. *Rise and Demise: Comparing World-Systems.* Boulder, CO: Westview.

Chase-Dunn, Christopher, Thomas D. Hall, Richard Niemeyer, Alexis Alvarez, Hiroko Inoue, Kirk Lawrence, Anders Carlson, Benjamin Fierro, Matthew Kanashiro, Hala Sheikh-Mohamed, and Laura Young. 2006 "Middlemen and Marcher States in Central Asia and East/West Growth/Decline Phases." IROWS Working Paper no. 30. Available at http://www.irows.ucr.edu/papers/irows30/irows30.htm

Chase-Dunn, C., and E. Susan Manning. 2002. "City Systems and World-systems: Four Millennia of City Growth and Decline." *Cross-Cultural Research* 36:4:379–398. Available at http://irows.ucr.edu/research/citemp/ccr02/ccr02.htm

Chew, Sing C. 2001. *World Ecological Degradation: Accumulation, Urbanization, and Deforestation 3000 B.C.–A. D. 2000.* Walnut Creek, CA: Altamira Press.

———. 2007. *The Recurring Dark Ages: Ecological Stress, Climate Changes, and System Transformation.* Lanham, MD: Altamira Press.

Christian, David 1994 "Inner Eurasia as a Unit of World History." *Journal of World History* 5:2:173–211.

———. 2000. "Silk Roads or Steppe Roads? The Silk Roads in World History." *Journal of World History* 11:1:1–26.

Cribb, Roger. 1991. *Nomads in Archaeology.* Cambridge: Cambridge University Press.

Di Cosmo, Nicola. 2002. *Ancient China and Its Enemies: The Rise of the Nomadic Power in East Asian History.* Cambridge: Cambridge University Press.

Frank, Andre Gunder. 1992. *The Centrality of Central Asia.* Comparative Asian Studies no. 8. Amsterdam: VU University Press for Center for Asian Studies Amsterdam (CASA).

Guang-da, Zhang. 1996. "The City-states of the Tarim Basin." Pp. 281–302 in B. A. Livitsky, Zhang Guang-da, and R. Shabini Samghabadi (eds.), *History of the Civilizations in Central Asia*, vol. 3. Paris: UNESCO.

Hall, Thomas D. 2005. "Mongols in World-System History." *Social Evolution & History* 4:2 (September):89–118.

Hall, Thomas D., and Peter Turchin. 2007. "Lessons from Population Ecology for World-Systems Analyses of Long-Distance Synchrony." Pp. 74–90 in Alf Hornborg and Carole L. Crumley (eds.), *The World System and the Earth System: Global Socioenvironmental Change and Sustainability Since the Neolithic.* Walnut Creek, CA: Left Coast Books.

Korjenkov, Andrey, Karl Baipakov, Claudia Change, Yury Peshkov, and Tamara Saavelieva. 2003. "Traces of Ancient Earthquakes in Medieval Cities Along the Silk Road, Northern Tien Shan and Dzhungaria." *Turkish Journal of Earth Sciences* 12:241–261.

Kradin, Nikolay N. 2002. "Nomadism, Evolution, and World-Systems: Pastoral Societies in Theories of Historical Development." *Journal of World-Systems Research* (Fall):368–388. Available at: http://jwsr.ucr.edu/index.php.

Kradin, Nikolay N., Dmitri M. Bondarenko, and Thomas J. Barfield, eds. 2003.

Nomadic Pathways in Social Evolution. The Civilization Dimension Series, vol. 5. Moscow: Russian Academy of Sciences: Center for Civilizational and Regional Studies.

Lattimore, Owen. 1940. *Inner Asian Frontiers of China.* New York: American Geographical Society.

Liu, Xinru, and Lynda Norene Shaffer. 2007. *Connections Across Eurasia: Transportation, Communications, and Cultural Exchange on the Silk Roads.* New York: McGraw-Hill.

Mair, Victor H., ed. 2006. *Contact and Exchange in the Ancient World.* Honolulu: University of Hawai'i Press.

McNeill, William H. 1976. *Plagues and People.* Garden City, NJ: Anchor Books.

Rosen, Staffen. 1999 "The Sino-Swedish Expedition to Yar-tonguz in 1994." Pp. 59–72 in Mirja Juntunen and Birgit N. Schlyter (eds.), *Return to the Silk Routes: Current Scandinavian Research in Central Asia.* London: Kegan Paul.

Ruddiman, William F. 2005. "How Did Humans First Alter Global Climate?" *Scientific American,* March, pp. 46–53.

Sherratt, Andrew. 2006. "The Trans-Eurasian Exchange: The Prehistory of Chinese Relations with the West." Pp. 30–61 in Victor H. Mair (ed.), *Contact and Exchange in the Ancient World.* Honolulu: University of Hawai'i Press.

Sinor, D., and S. G. Klyashtorny. 1996. "The Turk Empire." Pp. 327–348 in B. A. Livotsky, Zhang Guang-da, and R. Shabani Samgjabado (eds.), *History of Civilizations of Central Asia,* vol. 3, *A.D. 250 to 750.* Paris: UNESCO.

Sorenson, John L,. and Carl L. Johannessen. 2006. "Biological Evidence for Pre-Columbian Transoceanic Voyages." Pp. 238–297 in Victor H. Mair, *Contact and Exchange in the Ancient World.* Honolulu: University of Hawai'i Press.

Taagepera, Rein. 1978 "Size and Duration of Empires: Systematics of Size." *Social Science Research* 7:108–127.

———. 1997. "Expansion and Contraction Patterns of Large Polities: Context for Russia." *International Studies Quarterly* 41:475–504.

Teggart, Frederick J. 1939. *Rome and China: A Study of Correlations in Historical Events.* Berkeley: University of California Press.

Thompson, William R. 2005. "Eurasian C-wave Crises in the First Millennium B.C." Pp. 20–51 in C. Chase-Dunn and E. N. Anderson (eds.), *The Historical Evolution of World-Systems.* New York: Palgrave.

Turchin, Peter. 2007. "Modeling Periodic Waves of Integration in the Afroeurasian World-System." Unpublished paper (9th draft).

Turchin, Peter, and Thomas D. Hall. 2003. "Spatial Synchrony Among and Within World-Systems: Insights from Theoretical Ecology." *Journal of World-Systems Research* 9:1(Winter):37–64. Available at: http://jwsr.ucr.edu/index.php.

PART TWO
Asian Struggles

6

DICTATORSHIP AND DEVELOPMENT IN CHINA
THEIR IMPACT ON THE WORKERS OF THE WORLD

Robert K. Schaeffer

Introduction

Since 1978, the dictatorship in China, assisted by governments and global institutions in the core, has adopted policies that have enabled it to acquire a global, comparative advantage in low-wage labor. This development has disadvantaged workers in the core, the semiperiphery, the periphery, and in China itself. This chapter examines the role of dictatorship in the development of China.

Since 1978, the Communist Party dictatorship in China has adopted developmentalist policies that have helped it secure a global, comparative advantage in low-wage labor and promote rapid industrialization and development. The policies that made industrialization and development possible in China were not based on the "free-market" strategies associated with the Washington Consensus, or what Chris Chase-Dunn has called "ideological globalization" (Arrighi 2007: 185). They were instead based on the party's control of labor, technology, capital, monetary policy, and the state. Core states and private investors have helped the party consolidate power and pursue its developmentalist agenda by permitting China to reenter the interstate system and the world economy without requiring China to adopt the structural adjustment, privatization, and free-market policies required of other indebted or "reentry" states in the period of widespread democratization. Core states and global economic institutions have made an exception for China because, they argue, its reentry will enable firms in core states to capture Chinese markets; political and economic integration will eventually, inevitably promote democratization in China; and the import of low-wage goods from China will make it possible to maintain consumption levels in the core without increasing the wages of workers in the core.

But the industrial developmentalism associated with the rise of China has had adverse consequences for workers in the periphery, in the semiperiphery, in the core, and in China itself. To appreciate these developments, it is important first to analyze the developmentalist policies adopted by the regime in China.

Industrialization and Development?

After it took power in 1949, the Chinese Communist Party adopted policies designed to promote industrialization and development. During the first thirty years, from 1949 to 1978, the regime's industrialization policies did not result in appreciable development. But during the thirty years since 1978, industrialization in China resulted in significant economic development. As Arrighi (2007: 185) has argued, "industrialization" is not necessarily synonymous with "development," which he has defined as closing the income gap that separates the semiperiphery and the periphery from the core. If this is true, then why did industrialization in China fail to promote development during the first thirty years of communist rule but succeed during the next thirty years?

During the first thirty years, China, like many other states in the periphery and semiperiphery, promoted rapid industrialization. But because China did not have access to foreign investment, foreign aid, or foreign military assistance (except for a brief period of Soviet foreign and military aid during the Korean War), the import-substitutionist industrialization it practiced was more mercantilist-autarkic than most. The regime's effort to force the pace of industrialization during the Great Leap Forward in the late 1950s was a conspicuous failure. It disrupted agriculture, led to widespread hunger and acute famine in some regions, and contributed to the death of between 14 and 16 million people (Cross 1988: 101). During the 1960s, the regime continued to promote industrialization, though at a slower pace, and collectivized agriculture, which increased grain production from 195 million metric tons in 1957 to 304 million metric tons in 1978, a significant achievement that allowed China to feed the population, which grew from 574 to 962 million in this period, and to improve diets slightly (Shen 2004: 50).

At some cost, Chinese policies resulted in substantial industrialization. As Arrighi (2007: 190) has noted, China's percentage of GDP in manufacturing as a percentage of First World manufacturing doubled in this period, from 81.8 percent in 1960 to 165.8 percent in 1980. But Chinese industrialization in this period did not result in any real development. According to Arrighi (2007: 191), China's GNP per capita, as a percentage of First World GNP per capita, actually fell slightly, from 0.9 in 1960 to 0.8 in 1980.

Although agricultural development and industrialization in China did not result in much real development in this period, the party's mercantilist policies delayed China's reentry into the world economy until the late 1970s. This was important because it meant that China did not adopt the debt-financed development strategies common to other peripheral and semiperipheral states in the 1970s. This enabled it to avoid the ruinous structural adjustment programs imposed on most debtor states during the debt crisis of the 1980s (Schaeffer 1997: 226–245). As James Galbraith (2004) has written, "both China and India steered free of western banks in the 1970s and spared themselves the debt crisis." It turned out that Chinese mercantilism, which deferred its reentry into the capitalist world economy until the late 1970s, protected it from a ruinous development strategy. So even though industrialization in China did not contribute to significant economic development in the first period, it nonetheless created a manufacturing and agricultural infrastructure that could be reformed in the second period. "Without that foundation," one economist (Meisner 1999: 247) has argued, "the post-Mao reforms [of the late 1970s] would have had little to reform."

Although agroindustrial change in China did not result in appreciable development in the period between 1949 and 1978, domestic reform and foreign assistance in the period after 1978 resulted in rapid agricultural and industrial growth and substantial development.

When Deng Xiaoping took power in 1978, he instituted several "reforms"—which he described as "crossing the river by groping for stepping stones"—while at the same time maintaining "controls" over important parts of the economy and political life. Although the "reforms" have received considerable attention, less attention has been paid to the role of "controls" in Chinese development.

Deng introduced three important reforms. First, the regime abandoned policies that had encouraged population growth and introduced a strict, one-child policy, which was enforced by close surveillance of child-bearing households, widespread sterilization and abortion, and a system of economic penalties for noncompliance. These steps dramatically slowed the pace of population growth.

Second, the regime abandoned its collective approach to agriculture and leased public land to farm households, giving them an incentive to make independent production decisions and reap their benefits. The government increased the prices paid to farmers for produce delivered to the state and allowed farmers to sell food in excess of their quotas on the market for even higher prices. These reforms increased agricultural production from 305 million metric tons in 1978 to 407 million metric tons by 1984 (Selden 1983: 19).

Third, the regime borrowed money to invest in industry, permitted foreign investors to build factories to manufacture goods for export, devalued the currency to make these goods cheap in overseas markets, and allowed Chinese entrepreneurs to set up businesses that could produce goods for the domestic market. Using foreign loans totaling $40 billion during the first decade of reform and foreign investment amounting to $28 billion, the regime expanded and modernized its manufacturing base (Segal 1992: 183). The rapid growth of Chinese exports, which grew from $9.7 billion in 1978 to $52 billion in 1989, enabled the regime to repay foreign loans and avoid the debt crises common to other peripheral and semiperipheral states in this period (Shirk 1993: 48).

But even though the regime altered its approach to population, agriculture, and foreign capital, it maintained its control of technology (using technological transfer or theft to secure foreign technology for technologically deficient domestic industries), capital, monetary policy (keeping the yuan unconvertible and undervalued), and labor. The regime's control of labor was a key component of the regime's developmental project.

In China, the dictatorship has long used policies designed to control labor supplies and suppress wages. The government's residential permit system (*hukou*), which designated where people could live and work, was established in 1955 to control and allocate the labor supply (Chan 2004: 229–230; Solinger 1999). It was designed primarily to prevent workers in rural areas from moving to urban areas. During the 1980s, as the government and foreign investors expanded industry in urban areas, the demand for labor increased (Guthrie 2006: 209–213). The regime allowed rural workers to migrate to the cities to meet demand, but kept the *hukou* system intact, so that migrant workers were treated like illegal immigrants in their own country. Migrant workers could not lay claim to the legal protection provided workers with residential permits and work assignments, could not claim the minimum wage, could not obtain food rations or any of the health and pensions benefits associated with legal employment, could not, until recently, send their children to school, and could be arrested and "deported" to the countryside if they complained about working conditions, petitioned the government for redress, or demanded higher wages (Yardley 2004a; Gilboy and Heginbotham 2004: 257; Eckholm 2004).

The regime's labor-control policy, which allowed massive migration to occur but kept it illegal, created a huge reserve army of labor, now estimated at between 90 and 114 million workers, and a bifurcated labor force (Yardley 2004b; Gilboy and Higenbotham 2004: 260). Urban workers with residency and work permits are allowed to work for foreign investors and domestic entrepreneurs in the export-manufacturing sector, for low wages. Illegal migrant workers are not permitted to work for foreign investors, and they labor instead for Chinese employers for even lower, less-than-legal wages. This policy keeps labor supplies plentiful and keeps down wages, both because it makes labor plentiful and because the large illegal labor force suppresses the wages of legal workers, just as it does in the United States.

But although the government's policies, which combined "reforms" and "controls," produced significant development in the 1980s, they also created problems, primarily inflation, which is a discriminatory economic process. Rising food prices associated with agricultural reform, and rising rents associated with rural-to-urban migration, increased prices for urban workers, both legal and illegal, who could not raise their wages to keep pace. Inflation in China reached double-digit rates in 1985 and rose 28 percent in 1989 (Naughton 1989: 270; Kristof 1989).

When students rallied at Tiananmen Square in the spring of 1989, they were joined by urban workers who were disadvantaged by inflation and economic reform, creating a *minjung* or student-worker movement that challenged the Communist Party's control of the state (Schaeffer 2005: 196–197). The destruction of the student-labor coalition in Tiananmen Square enabled the party to reassert its control over labor, which meant that labor costs and political demands could be contained. The reassertion of dictatorship in China came at a time when other peripheral and semiperipheral countries in Asia and around the world were democratizing, leaving China as one of the world's few remaining dictatorships. At this juncture, foreign investment in China surged, emptying out of semiperipheral states in Asia and then from other peripheral, semiperipheral, and core states around the world. In the decade after Tiananmen Square, foreign investors poured $339 billion into China, and by 2000 directed one-half of all foreign direct investment into the country (Zheng 2004: 4, 6; Pottinger and Kyne 2004). It was this dual development—the party's reassertion of control over labor and the fortuitous demise of labor-controlling dictatorships around the world—that enabled China to secure a global comparative advantage in low- and lower-wage labor in the years after Tiananmen Square.

It is also important to recognize that the regime's developmentalist policies were not alone responsible for its success. Core states, primarily the United States, played a key role in assisting Chinese development and making its policies efficacious.

The United States and Chinese Development

U.S. officials invited and facilitated China's reentry into the interstate system and the capitalist world economy without requiring the regime to adopt political reforms or the kind of free-market, Washington Consensus policies imposed on other indebted (countries in Latin America and Africa) or reentry (countries in Eastern Europe and the former Soviet Union) states during the period of global democratization.

The United States facilitated the admission of the regime into the United Nations, secured it a permanent seat on the Security Council, and recognized its sovereignty over Taiwan, which was thrown out of the United Nations, without demanding any political reforms or concessions on its part. Contrast this to the treatment of apartheid regimes in Rhodesia and South Africa, or communist regimes in Cuba, North Vietnam, and North Korea during this period. After Tiananmen Square, U.S. officials decided not to punish the regime for slaughtering 2,600 people and arresting thousands more, but instead allowed private investors to transfer technology and invest heavily in the regime. In the late 1990s, the United States helped China gain admission to the World Trade Organization despite widespread evidence of on-going labor and human rights violations, patent and technology theft and piracy, government subsidies in manufacturing and illegal dumping and, perhaps most important, without relinquishing control of its monetary policy, which keeps the yuan unconvertible and undervalued.

It is remarkable that core states did not use reentry as an opportunity to impose structural adjustment on China, as they did for almost every other indebted, democratizing, and reentry state. But why did the United States and other core states make an "exception" for China?

Initially, President Richard Nixon invited China to reenter the interstate system to undermine the Soviet Union and end Chinese support for North Vietnam during the war in Vietnam. For Chinese leaders, abandoning their North Vietnamese allies was a small price to pay for U.S. recognition and for the U.S. decision to abandon Taiwan, a long-time U.S. ally.

Later, U.S. officials welcomed reform in China because they believed it would enable U.S. firms to capture markets in China, a dream that dates back more than a century (Shenkar 2006: 103). The prospect of opening the Chinese market, with one billion consumers, to U.S. agricultural and industrial goods has provided a key rationale for not demanding reforms or concessions from the regime. The irony is that U.S. policymakers and investors have been slow to realize that the regime has taken steps to prevent the capture of China's domestic market by foreigners. They have done so by allowing domestic firms and state-run enterprises to employ lower-wage "illegal" migrant workers so they can undercut labor costs in foreign-run firms, by providing domestic firms with below-market interest rates on loans so they can obtain capital more cheaply than foreign firms, by creating excess capacity and driving down prices and profit margins so foreign firms cannot compete in domestic markets, by transferring foreign technology to domestic firms or allowing them simply to steal technology so that foreign firms lose their technological advantages, by discouraging domestic retailers from displaying or selling foreign-made goods, and, an important point, by keeping the currency undervalued so that domestic firms have a price advantage over more expensive foreign imports (Lardy 2002: 89; Gottschang 1992: 271). Moreover, in recent years, "tastes in China are also changing to the detriment of American companies ... not because of anti-Americanism but because of Chinese nationalism," one businessman in China observed (Bradsher 2005b: C4). As a result of these policies, it has been very difficult for foreign firms to capture the markets they expected to conquer when China "opened" its doors to foreigners (Rhoads and Hutzler 2004).

U.S. officials and economists have also argued that China need not adopt serious political reforms as a condition for reentry because participation in the capitalist world economy would eventually and inevitably lead to democratization in China. "While democratic reform may not in all cases be an inevitable outcome of economic reform, it is, at this point, an inevitability in China," one economist wrote in 2006 (Guthrie 2006: 303).

Optimism about the inevitability of democratization in China has been undeterred by the facts. The early period of reform, and the student-worker movement it engendered, led to the violent suppression of the prodemocracy movement by the regime and the consolidation of its power, with massive support from foreign investors. In the nearly twenty years since Tiananmen Square, the Communist Party has grown stronger, not weaker (Kahn 2007). The party can now plausibly claim that economic growth and development in this period was due to its sound economic policies and astute leadership, rather than admitting that it was dictatorship, supported by foreign capital, and the widespread collapse of dictatorships elsewhere that made it possible for it to deliver its legal and illegal workforce to domestic and foreign capitalists at the lowest possible prices.

An analysis of democratization in other peripheral and semiperipheral states since 1978 suggests that dictatorships fell not because they promoted economic growth, but because they experienced economic crisis (Schaeffer 1997). Given this pattern of democratization, it is difficult to see why China would democratize in the absence of any significant economic crisis.

Of course, workers in urban areas and peasants in rural areas have protested the regime's policies and practices in the years since Tiananmen Square (Perry and Goldman 2007). One might make the argument that widespread grassroots protest might, eventually, contribute to democratization in China. But if one looks at grassroots movements in other countries, grassroots political protest is usually effective only where its power is decentralized. In the United States, the civil rights, environmental antitoxics, and antinuclear power movements were effective, in large part, because they confronted local authority, not the power of central government authorities (Schaeffer 1999: 201–203). In the Chinese context, it is difficult to imagine that local grassroots groups can accomplish what a broad-based coalition in Tiananmen Square could not achieve—a decisive weakening of central power authority and a devolution of power to wider political constituencies or successors. Indeed, Elizabeth Perry and Merle Goldman (2007: 2) have warned that "China's current grassroots political reforms could actually help forestall rather than facilitate the advance of formal democracy at the national level."

In recent years, U.S. policymakers have argued that it is not necessary to demand political or economic concessions from China because Chinese exports have made it possible to maintain or increase levels of consumption in the core without increasing wages because low-priced manufactured goods reduce the cost of consumer goods for U.S. workers. This rationale is what might be called the Wal-Mart strategy. The problem with this rationale is that outsourcing jobs to China results in job loss in the United States, which weakens consumer demand in the United States.

These different political and economic considerations persuaded policymakers in the United States and in other core countries to make an exception for China and allow it to reenter the interstate system and the capitalist world economy without adopting either "democratization" or "structural adjustment" as a price for its admission. This seems shortsighted and unfair to all the other countries that were required to pay a high price for participation. It also suggests that core states exempted China because it did *not* democratize. The pattern of investment flows suggests that investment surged into China at a time when dictatorship was being consolidated in China but was being abandoned elsewhere, a development that might be described as capital flight from democratizing states. This should not be surprising, given the fact that Wallerstein has argued that the capitalist world economy has always combined "free" and "coerced" forms of labor and "democratic" and "despotic" forms of government in the same, unitary world-system.

The Workers of the World

The developmentalist policies adopted by the regime in China and promoted by core states have had an adverse impact on workers in the periphery, the semiperiphery, and the core and in China itself.

The Periphery

Many countries in the periphery have large supplies of poor workers who earn about what Chinese workers earn, sometimes even less. India, for example, has a huge supply of low-wage labor, many of whom speak English. But except for a small sector of English-speaking service jobs, which employ about two million people, India has been unable to attract much foreign investment. Between 1990 and 2000, India received only $4 billion in foreign investment, despite the introduction of market-reform policies and the availability of a huge supply of low-wage labor, whereas China received eighty-five times as much investment (Rai 2004).

Investors in the core prefer China not simply because it has low-wage workers but also because the dictatorship promises to keep wages low. In democratic peripheral countries such as India, workers can migrate freely, change jobs, and organize collectively to demand higher wages and better benefits and working conditions. That is exactly what they have done in the English-speaking outsourcing and technology service sector: "Entry level salaries in the software industry [in India] have been rising by an average of 10 to 15 percent in recent years" (Sengupta 2006: A6).

Because wages can and do rise more easily in democratic peripheral states than they can in a dictatorship, foreign investors have preferred to employ low-wage workers in China. The expansion of foreign investment in China has allowed it to expand the production of industrial and agricultural goods that are also made by other peripheral states and to capture market shares at their expense. In the case of textiles, the expansion of Chinese textile exports has come at the expense of "the developing and especially the least-developed economies that will be hard pressed to find alternative venues for growth and employment" (Shekar 2006: 105).

The expanded production of tea in China has likewise caused "alarm in other developing countries that depend on growing tea, like India, Sri Lanka, Indonesia, Bangladesh, Kenya, Malawi, and Zimbabwe" because Chinese supplies will lower prices and capture markets and displace millions of people who depend on this crop for their livelihood. In Sri Lanka, for example, tea production, which is one of the world's most labor-intensive crops, helps feed nearly one-tenth of the population (Bradsher 2005c: A1).

Many of the peripheral states in Asia—India, Bangladesh, Sri Lanka, Indonesia, Malaysia, Thailand—are at least nominal democracies (though there have been recent military coups in Bangladesh and Thailand). When they compete with China for foreign investment and export markets, they are at a disadvantage because they are democratic. But there are other peripheral states in Asia and Africa that are also dictatorships, like China, which means they can offer low-wage workers on terms much like those in China. The problem for them is that dictatorships in these states earlier tried to use debt to promote development and, when it failed, were forced to adopt structural adjustment policies. As a result, government spending fell and their infrastructure substantially deteriorated. The poor quality of infrastructure in these dictatorships is a deterrent to investors and raises the real cost of producing goods, low wages notwithstanding.

The Semiperiphery

States in the semiperiphery have also lost manufacturing industries and jobs to China in recent years. During the 1970s and 1980s, one-party states such as

South Korea, Taiwan, and Mexico built up export manufacturing industries, generically *maquiladoras,* to supply goods to core countries, principally the United States. But in the late 1980s, regimes in South Korea and Taiwan slowly began to democratize, holding elections and opening them to participation by opposition parties, as Mexico did a decade later. When they did, foreign and domestic investors, who expected democratization to lift the decades-long ceiling on wages, moved their manufacturing industries to China, where the government's suppression of worker protest at Tiananmen Square imposed a new ceiling on wages in China. In South Korea and Taiwan, the capital flight from democratizing semiperipheral state to consolidating dictatorship in China was first apparent in industries that produced footware, toys, games, and sporting goods. In 1987, when the democratization process began, the United States imported 60 percent of these goods from South Korea and Taiwan, and only 5 percent from China. But by 1991, two years after Tiananmen Square, imports from South Korea and Taiwan had fallen to 30 percent, whereas import from China had risen to 30 percent, and by 1999, the United States imported 90 percent of these goods from China and only 5 percent from South Korea and Taiwan (Lardy 2002: 52). A similar shift affected personal computers in the late 1990s. During the 1990s, "tens of thousands of firms in Taiwan shifted operations across the strait to the mainland," largely because they were "lured by Chinese wages that [were] a fifth of those in Taiwan" (Bradsher 2005a: W1). Business in Taiwan invested $100 billion in China during the 1990s. As a result, economic growth in Taiwan slowed from 6 percent annual growth in GDP in 1990 to 0 percent in 2001, and unemployment tripled (Dean 2004; Bradsher 2005a).

The same process occurred in Mexico. During the 1990s, "Mexico lost nearly half a million manufacturing jobs and 500 maquiladora manufactures" to China, where workers earned one-quarter of the wages paid to Mexican workers (Fishman 2004: 50). Mexico lost another 287,000 jobs, mostly in telephone equipment, household appliances, and electric assemblies between 2000 and 2003, as part of "an exodus of factories ... to China" (Malkin 2002: W1; Shenkar 2006: 111). This latter shift occurred during a period of "democratization" in Mexico, when the Institutional Revolutionary Party (PRI) lost control of the presidency to an opposition party.

The Core

Between 2000 and 2006, the United States lost more than three million jobs, or one-sixth of its manufacturing jobs, as a result of automation and outsourcing, primarily to China (Greenhouse 2007; Shenkar 2006: 133). A similar process is also underway in Japan, where domestic firms are "relocating plants to China" (Barboza 2006).

The low wages that dictatorship in China can provide are an important reason why businesses in the core outsource jobs to China. But exchange rates also play an important role. The regime in China keeps the yuan pegged to the dollar at a rate that makes its exports cheaper than they would if exchange rates were set by market forces. The regime has been able to deflect U.S. demands to appreciate the yuan by threatening to sell its large stock of U.S. treasuries—worth $1 trillion in 2007 (Yardley and Barboza 2007). If it did, U.S. officials would have to raise interest rates to cover its huge budget deficits, a move that would trigger a recession and increase unemployment in the United States. Faced with this prospect, U.S. policymakers would rather let U.S. businesses outsource jobs to China and blame it on "globalization" than raise interest rates, cause a recession, and take the blame for growing unemployment in the United States.

For Japan, the appreciation of the yen against the dollar-yuan (the yuan is fixed in relation to the dollar) has meant that imports from China have become even cheaper, which has encouraged Japanese business to manufacture and import goods from China.

China

The developmentalist policies adopted by the regime and sanctioned by states in the core have had adverse economic and political consequences for workers in China. In economic terms, the regime's labor-control policy discriminates against rural migrant workers, who receive lower pay than their "legal" brethren and who often have their wages garnished or withheld by their employers to hold them in place. They receive none of the public economic benefits—housing, health care, pensions—that legal urban workers receive (French 2007). To accommodate the growth of cities and provide land for housing and industrial construction, the government has seized land from rural farmers, displacing 70 million farmers during the 1990s (Yardley 2004a). For legal, urban workers, the huge army of migrant labor has suppressed wages and raised urban rents (Barboza 2005).

The government's expansionary policies, fueled by massive amounts of foreign investment, have kept inflation rates high, from 6 to 10 percent annually, which discriminates against both rural and urban workers who cannot increase their wages at the same rate. The regime has virtually abandoned its once-universal health care system, which reduced infant mortality from 200 per 1,000 live births to 34 and increased life expectancy from 35 to 68 years between 1952 and 1982 (French 2006). By 2006, 80 percent of the population was uninsured and ill treated (French 2006).

Although China has made economic gains, measured in per capita income, most workers have not gained. As one group of economists has noted, "One of the world's most egalitarian societies in the 1970s, China in the 1990s became one of the most unequal countries in the region and among developing countries generally. This retreat from equality has thus been unusually rapid"

(Riskin, Remwei and Shi 2001: 3). The regime defends growing inequality by arguing, like Kuznets, that it is a temporary phenomena. "Let some get rich first," officials argued in the early days of reform (Riskin, Remwei, and Li 2001: 18). More recently, they have argued that inequality would lead, in a series of stages, to eventual equality: "Prosperity to some, to most, then to all" (Knight and Song 2001: 120). But thirty years into the reformist project, inequality is still increasing and the first stage has now become a permanent condition.

Chinese developmentalism has also disadvantaged workers in political terms. It has enabled the regime to consolidate domestic political power and enhance its stature within the interstate system. For Chinese workers, this means that the regime can deny migrants their rights as citizens; deprive legal and illegal workers of human rights; and subject them to an arbitrary legal system that practices widespread torture, according to the UN Commission on Human Rights, and annually imposes the death penalty on 10,000 people (Kahn 2005b). Although Chinese workers have a constitutional right to petition the government for redress, petitioners are "as likely to be harassed, kidnapped, jailed or tortured as they are to have their complaints adjudicated by a higher authority" (Kahn 2005a: A12).

The inability of workers to engage in a meaningful political process has meant that the regime has been able to consolidated its political power and, significantly, expand its economic power by creating a new bourgeoisie, which comprises largely Communist Party cadre. This class transformation, much like those described by Wallerstein during the English and French "revolutions," where the aristocracy became bourgeoisie, has made it possible for the elite to capture most of the benefits associated with industrialization and development in China.

References

Arrighi, Giovanni. 2007. "Globalization and Uneven Development." In *Frontiers of Globalization Research: Theoretical and Methodological Approaches*, ed. Ino Rossi, pp. 185–202. New York: Springer-Science.
Barboza, David. 2005. "China Builds Its Dreams, and Some Fear a Bubble." *New York Times*, October 18.
———. 2006. "Some Assembly Needed: China as Asia Factory." *New York Times*, February 9.
Bradsher, Keith. 2005a. "After an Exodus of Jobs, a Recovery in Taiwan." *New York Times*, March 19.
———. 2005b. "Made in U.S., Shunned in China." *New York Times*, November 18.
———. 2005c. "Read the Tea Leaves: China Will Be Top Exporter." *New York Times*, October 11.
Chan, Kam Wing. 2004. "Internal Migration." In *Changing China: A Geographical Appraisal*, ed. Chiao-min Hseih and Max Lu, pp. 229–242. Boulder, Colo.: Westview.

Croll, Elisabeth J. 1988. "The New Peasant Economy." In *Transforming China's Economy in the Eighties,* ed. Stephan Feuchtwang, Athar Hussain, and Tehierry Pairault, pp. 77–100. London: Zed Books.

Dean, Jason. 2004. "China Raises Economic Heat on Taiwan." *Wall Street Journal,* July 27.

Eckholm, Eric. 2004. "How's China Doing? Yardsticks You Never Thought Of." *New York Times,* April 11.

Fishman, Ted C. 2004. "The Chinese Century." *New York Times Magazine,* July 4.

French, Howard W. 2006. "Wealth Grows, but Health Care Withers in China." *New York Times,* January 14.

———. 2007. "China Strains to Fit Migrants into Mainstream Classes." *New York Times,* January 25.

Galbraith, James. 2004. "Debunking the Economist—Again." Available at http://www.salon.com/opinion/feature/2004/03/22/economist/print.html

Gilboy, George J., and Eric Heginbotham. 2004. "The Latin Americanization of China?" *Current History* (September), pp. 256–261.

Gottschang, Thomas R. 1992. "The Economy's Continued Growth." *Current History* (September), pp. 268–272.

Greenhouse, Steven. 2007. "A Unified Voice Argues the Case for U.S. Manufacturing." *New York Times,* November 5.

Guthrie, Doug. 2006. *China and Globalization: The Social, Economic, and Political Transformation of Chinese Society.* New York: Routledge.

Kahn, Joseph. 2005a. "Chinese Abused for Complaints, Study Concludes." *New York Times,* December 9.

———. 2005b. "Torture Is 'Widespread' in China, U.N. Investigator Says." *New York Times,* December 3.

———. 2007. "China's Leader Vows to Uphold One-Party Rule." *New York Times,* June 27.

Knight, John, and Lina Song. 2001. "Economic Growth, Economic Reform, and Rising Inequality in China." In *China's Retreat from Equality,* ed. Carl Riskin, Zhao Renwei, and Li Shi, pp. 84–122. Armonk, N.Y.: M. E. Sharpe.

Kristof, Nicholas. 1989. "China Erupts." *New York Times Magazine,* June 4.

Lardy, Nicholas R. 2002. *Integrating China into the Global Economy.* Washington, D.C.: Brookings Institution.

Malkin, Elisabeth. 2002. "Manufacturing Jobs Are Exiting Mexico: Business Leaders Try to Stop the Exodus of Factories to China." *New York Times,* November 5.

———. 2004. "A Boom Along the Border." *New York Times,* August 26.

Meisner, Maurice. 1999. "China's Communist Revolution: A Half-Century Perspective." *Current History* (September), pp. 243–248.

Naughton, Barry. 1989. "Inflation and Economic Reform in China." *Current History* (September), pp. 269–272.

Perry, Elizabeth J., and Merle Goldman. 2007. "Introduction: Historical Reflections on Grass Roots Political Reform in Contemporary China." In *Grass Roots Political Reform in China,* ed. Elizabeth J. Perry and Merle Goldman. Cambridge, Mass.: Harvard University Press.

Pottinger, Matt, and Phelim Kyne. 2004. "Beijing Restrains Growth in Loans but Raises Risks." *Wall Street Journal,* July 14.

Rai, Saritha. 2004. "India Market Falls on Jitters After Election." *New York Times*, May 15.
Rhoads, Christopher, and Charles Hutzler. 2004. "China's Telecom Foray Squeezes Struggling Rivals." *Wall Street Journal*, September 9.
Riskin, Carl, Zhao Remwei, and Li Shi. 2001. "Introduction." In *China's Retreat from Equality*, ed. Carl Riskin, Zhao Renwei, and Li Shi, pp. 3–22. Armonk, N.Y.: M. E. Sharpe.
Schaeffer, Robert K. 1997. *Power to the People: Democratization Around the World*. Boulder, Colo.: Westview.
———. 1999. "Success and Impasse: The Environmental Movement in the United States and Around the World." In *Ecology and the World-System*, ed. Walter L. Goldfrank, David Goodman, and Andrew Szasz. Westport, Conn.: Greenwood Press.
———. 2005. *Understanding Globalization: The Social Consequences of Political, Economic, and Environmental Change*. 3rd ed. Lanham, Md.: Rowman and Littlefield.
Segal, Gerald. 1992. "The Challenges to Chinese Foreign Policy." In *The Reform Decade in China: From Hope to Dismay*, ed. Marta Dassu and Tony Saich, pp. 162–192. New York: Columbia University.
Selden, Mark. 1983. *The Political Economy of Chinese Development*. Armonk, N.Y.: M. E. Sharpe.
Sengupta, Somini. 2006. "In a Twist, Americans Appear in the Ranks of Indian Firms." *New York Times*, October 17.
Shen, Jianfa. 2004. "Agricultural Growth and Food Supply." In *Changing China: A Geographical Appraisal*, ed. Chiao-min Hseih and Max Lu, pp. 47–64. Boulder, Colo.: Westview.
Shenkar, Oden. 2006. *The Chinese Century: The Rising Chinese Economy and Its Impact on the Global Economy, the Balance of Power, and Your Job*. Upper Saddle River, N.J.: Wharton School.
Shirk, Susan L. 1993. *The Political Logic of Economic Reform in China*. Berkeley: University of California Press.
Solinger, Dorothy. 1999. *Contesting Citizenship in Urban China: Peasant Migrants, the State, and the Logic of the Market*. Berkeley: University of California Press.
Yardley, Jim. 2004a. "Farmers Being Moved Aside By China Real Estate Boom." *New York Times*, December 8.
———. 2004b. "In a Tidal Wave, China's Masses Pour from Farm to City." *New York Times*, September 12.
Yardley, Jim, and David Barboza. 2007. "China Is Forming Agency To Invest Foreign Reserves." *New York Times*, March 10.
Zheng, Yongninan. 2004. *Globalization and State Transformation in China*. Cambridge: Cambridge University Press.

7

CHINA, ASIA, AND LABOR STANDARDS AFTER THE 2005 MULTI-FIBER ARRANGEMENT

Robert J. S. Ross

Introduction: South-South

In the early part of this decade, Ross and Chan (2002) and Chan and Ross (2003) argued that much of the competition for the markets in manufactured goods of the global North was South-South—competition for market share among peripheral and semiperipheral economies. This chapter examines the effects of the dramatic 2005 change in the rules of the world textile and apparel trade to assess the Chan and Ross and other predictions about the end of quantitative national ceilings—the Multi-fiber Arrangement (MFA)—on clothing exports to rich country markets.

The MFA expired on January 1, 2005. It had provided for quotas—quantitative country by country (and item by item) ceilings on exports of textiles and clothing from lower-income countries to the EU and the United States. The quotas that are broadly referred to as the MFA refer to the original 1974 exception and supplement to the Uruguay round of General Agreement on Tariffs and Trade (GATT) negotiations. When the World Trade Organization was formed, the MFA was moved into the WTO agreement and retermed the Agreement on Textiles and Clothing (ATC). According to the ATC (universally referred to as MFA), the national quotas of exports to the United States and to the EU were to grow, item by item, at a steady rate each year, and as well, rising numbers of all items were to be quota-free. By January 2005 all textile and clothing items were to be released from quota constraints (World Trade Organization 2007).

As the end of the MFA drew near in 2004, observers of the world textile and apparel trade feared that a dramatic surge of Chinese exports would accelerate a labor standards "race to the bottom" of unprecedented dimensions. (Appelbaum 2004, 2005; Chan and Ross 2003; Clean Clothes Campaign 2004a, 2004b; Foo and Bas 2003) Using the Mexico versus China competition for the U.S. apparel market as their model, Chan and Ross (among many others) forecast that the existing "race to the bottom" in labor standards would be accelerated because of China's combination of rural labor surplus and a dictatorial labor regime that suppressed labor costs.

A Strange Protectionism: The MFA

There is no small irony in the reversal of the global discourse on the MFA/ATC. A trade agreement that had been characterized by developing country governments, neoliberal economists, and progrowth nongovernmental organizations (NGOs) as "protectionist" and a sign of core nation raw power had now, paradoxically, become the symbol of a regime of positive globalization. (See, e.g., Oxfam 2004; Hudgins 1985; Raghavan n.d.; Yearman and Gluckman 2005) If it was protectionist, it was unusually ineffective. In the course of a generation the United States (and less so the EU) voluntarily gave up one of its largest industries. In the United States apparel employment fell by 842,000 from 1974 to 2002; according to a somewhat different classification of U.S. industries, from 1990 to 2006 apparel jobs fell from more than 900,000 to just under 240,000. Whichever time series one chooses, the United States lost more than one million jobs in combined textile and apparel production after 1974, about 65 percent of the combined industries.[1] If that was protectionism, it was but a slender reed.

Throughout the Cold War period—and after—the United States used apparel production and then MFA quota as an anti-Communist and counterrevolutionary alliance-making tool (cf. Rosen 2002) in the Cold War and in the Central American civil wars.[2] In the process, EU and U.S. quota distributions made the provisioning of textiles and apparel to the world export market the most globalized industry in the world.

As the end of the quota regime approached in January 2005, the global discourse about the MFA changed from one that emphasized its protectionist and rent-seeking structure to a discourse in which the MFA/ATC was understood as having spawned a true globalization of the textile and clothing industries. As each country with an expanding clothing or textile industry reached the limits of its quota, apparel brands and retailers in the older industrial countries of the global North sought suppliers in yet other low wage/low cost regions. By the eve of quota termination, as of 2004, eighty-nine different countries exported at least $10 million in clothing to the United States (calculated from Office of Textile and Apparel [OTEXA] 2007). Small countries (and their advocates) and those whose costs of production were higher than China's worried—at length—that they would lose market share to China or even be eliminated entirely from the U.S. and EU clothing supply chain.[3]

A High Stakes Game Even Though the Rag Trade Is Cheap

The stakes involved in quota elimination were high on many dimensions. There were about 20 million jobs in the global textile and clothing complex in 2005, and at least 7.5 million of these were clothing workers. (Rosen 2005:7) Drawn into the global supply chain by the scanning functions of the big brands' managers, numerous low-income countries saw this venerable industry as the start of hoped-for industrialization. Heavy reliance on textile and clothing exports was the poignant result for many. Table 7.1 is a list (compiled by the United Nations Conference on Trade and Development [UNCTAD]) of the twenty countries most dependent on textiles and clothing as a fraction of their total exports in 2003.

In the run-up to the expiration of the MFA there were numerous projections of the effect of the end of the quotas. One projection from the American Textile Manufacturers Institute predicted that China would obtain about 75 percent of the U.S. clothing and textile market (American Textile Manufacturers Institute 2003, 2004). A somewhat more refined study, presenting a broadly accepted view of the structure of the global apparel trade, was commissioned by UNCTAD and put forward by Appelbaum (2004) and Appelbaum, Bonacich, and Quan (2005). This body of work predicted, indeed, that China would loom large in the emerging structure of world apparel trade. But the Appelbaum study also proposed underlying structural trends: (1) concentration of national sourcing as the end of quotas "released" investors to move toward a smaller number of low-cost platforms; (2) increasing power of retailers with "price-making" power in an oligopolistic market; and (3) some remaining advantages of geographic proximity, for example, for Mexico. At the time that Chan and Ross were writing—the early 2000s—China and Mexico held roughly equal shares of the U.S. import market—about 15 percent each. Because of the North American Free Trade Agreement (NAFTA) treaty, there was no quantitative ceiling on Mexico's apparel exports to the United States but there was a ceiling on Chinese exports.

During the first few months of 2005, with no quotas, the surge of apparel imports from China to the United States was as least as large as expected—blowing the proverbial barn doors off their metaphoric hinges. In response the

Table 7.1 Exporters That Are Highly Dependent on Exports of Apparel and Textiles, 2003 (percentage share of total merchandise exports)

Economy	Apparel	Textiles	Total
Cambodia[a]	84.3	1.08	5.3
Haiti[b]	82.2	1.98	4.1
Bangladesh	75.9	7.3	83.3
China, Macao SAR	71.0	11.7	82.8
Pakistan	22.9	47.5	70.3
Lesotho[b]	65.3	5.0	70.3
Mauritius	52.9	4.1	57.1
Sri Lanka	51.7	3.3	55.0
Tokelaua	13.0	40.5	53.4
Nepal	34.6	16.4	51.0
Dominican Republic[b]	41.5	1.7	43.3
Lao People's Democratic Republic[b]	41.6	0.2	41.8
Tunisia	37.0	3.7	40.7
Albania	34.3	0.3	34.6
Morocco	32.4	1.5	33.9
FYR Macedonia	30.0	3.1	33.1
Madagascar	31.1	1.4	32.5
Turkey	21.1	11.1	32.2
Maldives	32.0	0.0	32.0
Fiji	26.8	1.2	28.0

Source: United Nations Conference on Trade and Development 2005.
[a] As of mid-2005 a senior Cambodian official put the clothing fraction of total exports at 93 percent (Siphana 2005: 2).
[b] Includes estimates by the UNCTAD secretariat.

United States and the EU resorted to clauses in China's WTO accession agreements that gave them the right to restrain Chinese imports (to allow orderly market adjustments) through the end of 2008. These partial restraints were implemented but the actions did not restrain all categories Chinese exports of clothing and in the meantime all other countries' quotas expired.

As a result of the MFA expiration, even though China's exports were still partially restrained, the world apparel market was in a previously unparalleled largely "free" state. An examination of the resulting structure of clothing imports to the United States allows an examination both of previous predictions and, as well, of underlying structures.[4]

Chinese Surge and Domination

In the first instance, the Chinese (PRC) share of apparel imports to the United States by dollar value jumped from $8.93 billion in 2004 to $18.5 billion in

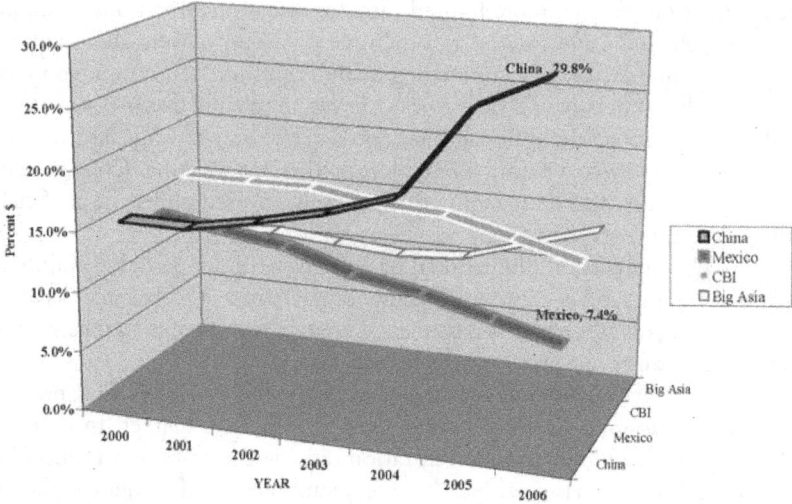

Figure 7.1   Shares of U.S. Apparel Imports

2006. The total Chinese (PRC and Hong Kong) proportion of the value of clothing imports to the United States went from 15.7 percent in 2000 to 29.8 percent in 2006 (Office of Textile and Apparel [OTEXA] 2007). In almost direct proportion, Mexico's market share of imports dropped from 14.7 percent to 8.8 percent in dollar value of exports to the United States in this period. Mexico's market share loss was an absolute (not inflation corrected) loss of $1.3 billion in exports of clothing. The closest competitor to Mexico for U.S. market share in 2006 was Indonesia, whose share grew to 5.1 percent of the value of the U.S. clothing import market. Indonesia was part of a group of "Big Asia" clothing exporters that increased drastically its U.S. import share: Indonesia, India, Bangladesh, and Vietnam collectively went from around 10 percent to 13.6 percent of the import market from 2000 to 2006. See Figure 7.1.

In sum, the predictions that Chinese producers would overwhelm their competitors for the U.S. market proved true—and they gained total market share even during the period when certain categories of their imports were put under "standby restraints." Whether Chinese clothing exports will reach 75 percent of U.S. apparel imports, or 50 percent of world exports—as some predicted—remains to be seen.

Concentration

The post-MFA projections of the world apparel trade envisioned a market where the concentrated buyers—the retailers and brands of the global North—would focus their orders on a more limited number of national locations of suppliers. (Appelbaum 2004 inter alia) When national quotas were abolished, the logic of both a factor cost minimizing analysis and internal transaction costs dictated that orders would flow toward fewer contractor factories that could fulfill, for example, the (full package) needs of the brands while also meeting their rigorous low-cost requirements. The predictions were that fewer national locations would meet these requirements than were used under the artificially dispersed regime of the MFA.

Although part of 2005 and all of 2006 were under partial restraints on Chinese imports, other countries were not so restrained. A global analysis of the restructuring of import shares is thus a moderately fair test of the concentration thesis. As it turns out, it is moderately accurate.

One convenient metric for the concentration thesis involves using national sources of imported clothing as analogues to firms in a market. In that case we can examine a four-firm concentration ratio as a test of the concentration thesis. In 2004, the last year before the expiration of all MFA quotas, the top four national suppliers to the U.S. import market (counting the PRC and Hong Kong as one entity) accounted for 38 percent of all U.S. apparel imports by value. In 2006 the top four accounted for just under 47 percent—an increase in concentration of 22 percent. Such a rapid increase in an analogue national market of firms would be almost without precedent. The top ten national sources of U.S. clothing imports in 2004 accounted for 57 percent of the market; in 2006, they accounted for 66 percent (Office of Textile and Apparel [OTEXA] 2007).[5] In 2004, 89 countries exported at least $10 million of clothing to the United States. In 2006, 78 countries exported at least $10 million of clothing to the United States. Alternatively, in 2004, 24 countries had at least a 1 percent share of the U.S. import market ($648 million); this was unchanged in 2006.

About the concentration thesis, the evidence appears to support the following conclusions. First, there has been concentration of national sources of imported clothing. Second, there are still many (small) suppliers who have not been crowded out by the big Asian exporters, and fully two dozen (the same number as in 2004) who reach the 2006 2 percent threshold—$716 million.

China indeed dominated the newly (almost) deregulated world clothing market with absolute dollar gains compared to Mexico's losses and Indonesia's moderate gains. Overall the changes when disaggregated also have regional and labor standards stories within them.

Regional Shift

The shift from higher-cost providers to lower-cost providers creates a strongly regional picture of the changes. As Figure 7.1 showed, the Central American and Caribbean exporters covered under the Caribbean Basin Initiative (CBI) umbrella lost significant market share to the large Asian producers—Indonesia, India, Bangladesh, and Vietnam.[6]

The cluster of smaller Central American and Western Hemisphere countries (with three exceptions) lost market share, whereas all of the low-wage Asian exporters gained, and the middle-income and higher-income Asian countries (Malaysia, Taiwan, and South Korea) lost market share. Restraints were replaced on Chinese exports only in the latter half of 2005—so for most of that year the Chinese exporters rapidly gained share in relation to all competitors. Yet, in the global chess game, Bangladesh, where officials and business spokespersons feared they would lose to the Chinese, gained even more from other—perhaps Western Hemisphere—competitors. Bangladeshi exports to the United States increased by about 20 percent from 2004 to 2005 and then another 23 percent from 2005 to 2006. For the Bangladeshi economy this was no small matter; clothing composed almost a 78 percent share of its 2005 merchandise exports (Heron 2007). Figure 7.2 shows that in the Western Hemisphere, the only exporting nations who gained share from 2004 to 2006 were Nicaragua, Haiti, and Peru. Nicaragua increased its clothing exports to the United States by 48 percent between 2004 and 2006; Haiti increased its exports by 39 percent. The other distinction shared by these two countries is that they are two of the three lowest per capita income economies in the Western Hemisphere and have correspondingly low wages.[7] The CBI nations as a whole declined $1.1 billions in current dollar exports of clothing to the United States in the 2004—2006 period—almost 12 percent. This is reflected in the ranking of the top twenty importers to the United States, as shown in Table 7.2. Comparing the top twenty

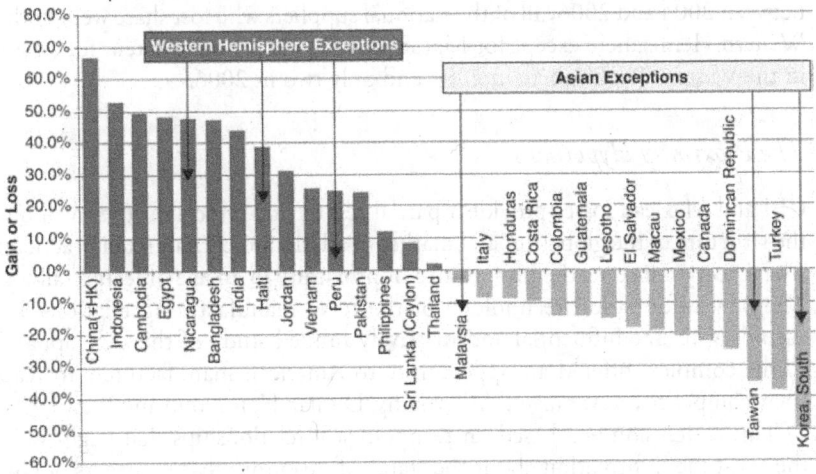

Figure 7.2   Winners and Losers

Table 7.2 Top Twenty Importing Countries, 2004 and 2006

2006 Rank	(Losers in Italics)	2004 Rank	
1	China(+HK)	1	China(+HK)
2	Mexico	2	Mexico
3	Indonesia	3	Honduras
4	Vietnam	4	Vietnam
5	India	5	Indonesia
6	Bangladesh	6	India
7	*Honduras*	7	Dominican Republic
8	Cambodia	8	Bangladesh
9	Philippines	9	Guatemala
10	Thailand	10	Korea, South
11	Sri Lanka (Ceylon)	11	Thailand
12	*Guatemala*	12	Philippines
13	*Dominican Republic*	13	El Salvador
14	Pakistan	14	Sri Lanka (Ceylon)
15	*El Salvador*	15	Taiwan
16	Italy	16	Canada
17	Jordan	17	Macau
18	*Canada*	18	Cambodia
19	*Macau*	19	Italy
20	*Taiwan*	20	Turkey
Cumulative Share	86.10%		81.00%
Number of Top Ten in Western Hemisphere	2		4

between 2004 and 2006, all of the national suppliers who lost share were in the Western Hemisphere except for Macao and Taiwan; of the top ten, four were in the Western Hemisphere in 2004 and only two in 2006.

The Proximity Hypothesis

CBI and Mexican losses provide a partial test of one important theory about the structure of the global apparel market in relation to current retail practices. That theory concerns the importance of proximity in an age of lean retailing. The new information technology of the retail-manufacturing relationship, according to one influential and massively funded study of the U.S. apparel textile complex, offered an opportunity to American manufacturers to reap "new competitive advantages."(Abernathy, Dunlap Hammond and Weil 1999: 1) This conclusion was based on technological relationships that begin with the real-time information about the status of inventory that managers obtain from bar code scanners at checkout counters. The scanner reports the specifics (color, size, etc.) of garments sold, by the hour, day, week, month, season or year. A manager can thus discern the level of inventory on hand in stores and warehouses and know to a day or so when to reorder and which styles and variants are succeeding. This information retrieval capacity allows shrinkage in the amount of inventory on hand (thus conserving capital) and it reduces the reorder cycle from months to weeks. The Abernathy group thought (and they continue to hope against the data—see Mukherjee 2005 and Weil 2006) that the shortened reorder cycle would give American or Central American suppliers supply chain advantages for the U.S. market.

In the eight brief years since Abernathy et al. mailed in their manuscript (1998–2001) the American apparel industry has lost 400,000 jobs (639,000 to 238,000)—63 percent of the industry. (Calculated from U.S. Department of Labor, Bureau of Labor Statistics 2007) Having deserted the U.S. proximity hypothesis (Mukherjee 2005) the Harvard Center for Textile and Apparel Research (re)placed its hope on North and Central American proximity. Mexico's fading grasp on the jeans market seems a weak prop for the theory.

The increasing perfection of Asia to North America logistics has made China and India much closer than they once were relative to Mexico or the Caribbean. Western Hemisphere suppliers are hanging on by thin threads of turn-around time and cheap labor. The former is, it turns out, thinning all the time; and the existence of even ostensibly democratic regimes in the Western Hemisphere would seem to be in some tension with long run viability in the race to the bottom.

Is There a Race to the Bottom?

Despite the restraints on the Chinese import stream through the end of 2008, it appears that predictions of Chinese domination of the textile and clothing markets are well sustained. Supplier consolidation has occurred but not yet to the largest extent imagined by the pre-2005 projections. Regional shift has occurred as anticipated, favoring low-wage Asian suppliers, including Bangladesh, India, Pakistan, Cambodia, and even Vietnam (which is still constrained by certain quotas because it is not yet in the WTO). Lurking behind much concern about the end of the ATC was the broad question of labor standards.

Systematic data about labor conditions are extremely difficult to attain, especially since actual industrial practices are much worse than even inadequate national laws. In China, for example, there is a small consultancy industry that teaches factory managers how to keep multiple sets of books, including one to show to U.S. corporation social auditors to convince them they are following Chinese labor law. (Roberts and Engardio 2006) The corporate oriented Fair Labor Association and the more independent auditor Verité, in addition to a *Business Week* investigation, found that in China, and in most export factories elsewhere, majorities of firms fail to pay national minimum wages or overtime (for the United States, see Ross 2004) Therefore only notional use could be made—even in principle—of official wage statistics. Anecdotes about poor conditions or abusive treatment, although abundant in the textile and clothing businesses, do not allow a fully systematic comparison to shifts in production. There are, however, some ways to discern the pattern in quantitative and relevant qualitative terms.

In the first instance, available data allow an answer to the question of whether the U.S. import stream is becoming cheaper. The answer is yes. In inflation-corrected and in absolute terms, clothing and textiles have been costing importers less over the period 2000–2006—and the release of quota appears to have a relationship to the price decrease. Figure 7.3 uses a standard measure of clothing volume, square meter equivalents, to measure the inflation-corrected cost of clothing imports to the United States from 2000 to 2006.[8] It shows declining cost in each year and a very sharp decline from 2001 to 2002 and from 2004 to 2005. The first sharp decline—7.3 percent—was one in which large numbers of clothing items were released from MFA quotas as part of the ten-year gradual reduction in the total amount of clothing subject to quota. The second decline—7.1 percent—took place during the year in which China's imports were unrestrained from January through May (Office of Textile and Apparel [OTEXA] 2007).

There is additional inferential evidence that at least part of the source of the price declines is attributable to shifts in supplier locations. It seems fair to estimate that clothing workers' earnings, when compared cross-nationally, would be highly correlated to the levels of living and compensation in their respective nations. That is, it is likely that national differences in clothing and

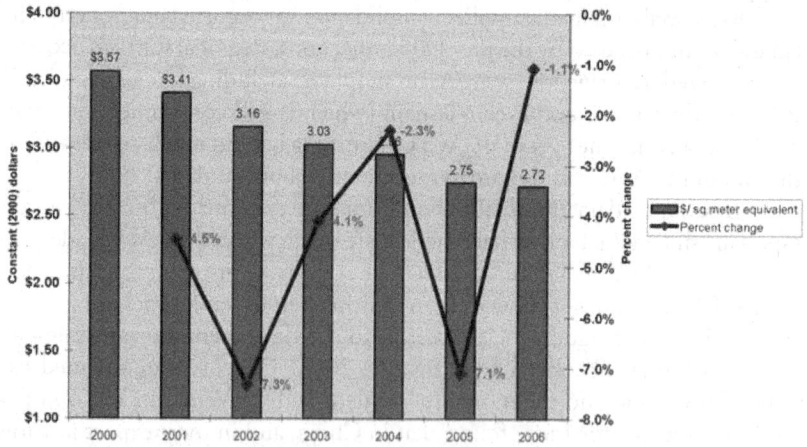

Figure 7.3 Dockside Cost/Square Meter Equivalent

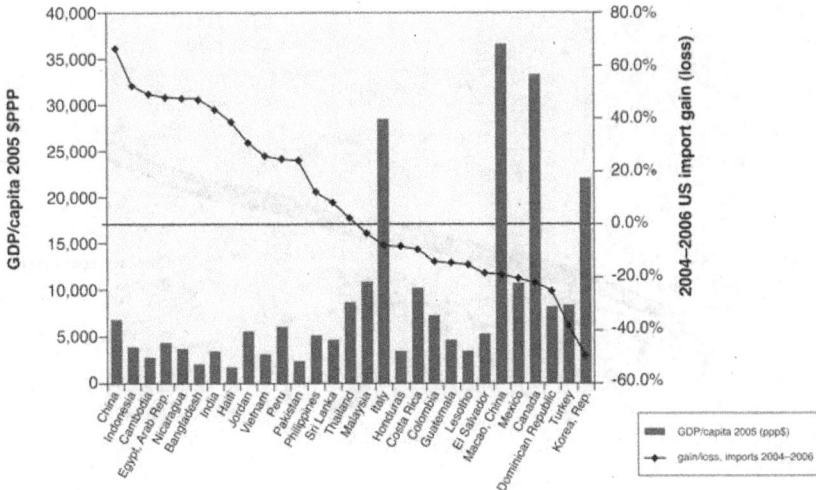

Figure 7.4   GDP/Capita and Percent Change in U.S. Apparel Imports

textile workers' wages bear a roughly similar relation to the economies in which they find themselves in many different countries. For example, in nations with very large rural labor surpluses and very low incomes, we would expect that although clothing factory workers would have higher levels of cash income than rural workers, they would have lower levels of wages than those in more capital intensive industries. Over a large number of nations we would then expect there to be a very high correlation between garment wages (and conditions) and overall levels of GDP/capita. If clothing sourcing, freed of quota restraint, were highly influenced by labor costs, then we would expect a nontrivial (negative) relationship between source shifting and GDP/capita. Figure 7.4 shows that lower GDP/capita (2005) is clearly related to higher gains in the U.S. import markets. The correlation is about –0.51.

Sharply declining prices of clothing imports implies either shifting sourcing decisions—which did occur—or declining cost of production including compensation to workers. In any case it may or may not result in lower retail prices. Over the last two decades the rapid replacement of domestic with imported sources of clothing has certainly resulted in lower retail clothing prices. Figure 7.5 shows that the Consumer Price Index for All Urban Consumers (CPI-U) increased almost ten times (9.6) as fast as the cost of apparel since 1987. The 2004–2006 period did not, however, show as sharp a decline at the retail level as it did at dockside. From 2004 to 2006, the retail cost of clothing declined a bit more than one-third as much as the dockside cost (–0.75 percent retail v. –2.1 percent FOB). The implication is that source shifting in the post-MFA world was a source of new profits for clothing retailers.[9]

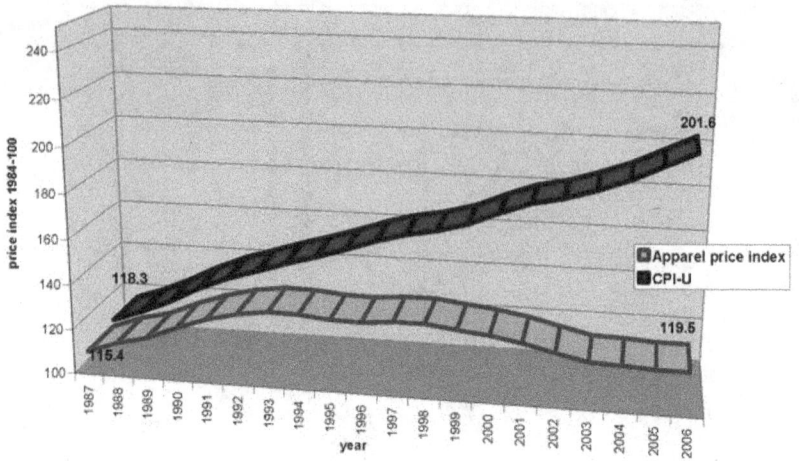

Figure 7.5 Apparel Price v. Consumer Price Index

Apart from the evidence of source shifting to lower-income countries and of lowered measured prices of imports to the brands and retailers, there is also qualitative evidence that buyers continued their generation-long evasion and suppression of unions and their reluctance to pay for worker improvements in pay or conditions.

The viewing-with-alarm pre-2005 documents about labor standards and the release from MFA quotas are numerous and commonplace. They tend to use the word "challenge"—as in the "challenge to maintain labor standards" or the "challenge to compete" in other industry-specific ways with Chinese or Indian competition. Without quantitative evidence for *heightened incidence* of worker abuse, there is nevertheless qualitative evidence of continued choice by buyers and producers to move employment away from more organized or conscious workers and toward places where workers are the most vulnerable. Here are some are some other types of indicators that the race-to-the bottom in labor standards is alive and well:

The Bangladesh Export Promotion Bureau web site, as of May 6, 2007, claimed under the heading "Production Oriented Labor Laws" that "Law forbids formation of any labor union in EPZs."[10] It noted the minimum (monthly) wages for apprentices/trainee as U.S. $22.00, but this appears to be the prevailing garment wage. ("Bangladesh EPZ" 2007; National Labor Committee 2006a). Although Bangladesh has long been a target of Western campaigners against child labor, the U.S.- based National Labor Committee (2006a) found 200–300 child laborers at a large factory producing for, among others, Hanes underwear and Puma. Bangladesh has gained market share in the post-MFA period.

After a more than a decade of struggle, most recently in cooperation with the United Students Against Sweatshops solidarity campaigns in 1998 and 2003, the BJ&B cap factory in Alta Gracia, Dominican Republic, owned by the Yupoong Company, a Korean multinational that is among the world's largest producers of sport caps, closed its unionized factory in December 2006 (Ross 2006). It left a few hundred workers without their legally entitled severance payments. Yupoong opened a Bangladesh factory in 2000 and has gradually moved employment out of its Dominican factory since then.

After a long struggle at the Kukdong/Mexmode factory in Mexico in 2003, workers gained a union contract, wage gains, and pledges for decent food and water. By 2005 they were unable to collect their contracted wage gain, and employment levels at the factory were drastically reduced (Ross 2006).

Despite a U.S.-Jordan trade agreement notable for its explicit inclusion of labor rights (White House 2000), Jordan-based factories aiming for duty-free no-quota access to the U.S. market used involuntary servitude among thousands of Bangladeshi workers in a number of factories (National Labor Committee 2006b). Despite Jordanian government intervention to address the worst abuses, human trafficking, forced overtime, 15-hour shifts, persistent minimum wage violations, and passport confiscations by employers continue to be used to exploit thousands of workers from Bangladesh and Sri Lanka as well as Jordanians (National Labor Committee 2007).

Cambodia is, as is Jordan, a signatory to a bilateral trade agreement with the United States that linked highly favorable clothing import quota to Cambodia's agreement to enforce core International Labor Organization (ILO) labor standards in its garment industry. This 1999 agreement includes ILO monitoring of labor conditions at factories. The international consensus is that this regime of labor law and monitoring did improve conditions in Cambodian garment factories (see, e.g., Marston 2007 and Siphana 2005; but see Wells-Dang 2002 for skepticism on the matter). The impending end of the MFA regime threatened to erode Cambodia's advantage in gaining access to the large U.S. market. Many analysts argued, though, that legal wages and other conditions were so low and permissive in Cambodia that even after the end of quotas Cambodia would actually gain market share as brand name buyers sought to share its good labor standards reputation. The warning flag was put up in 2004 when the leader of a Cambodian garment workers union was murdered as were at least two other union activists. Then Chey Mony, the brother of Chea Vichea, the slain leader, was "detained" and forced into exile. One inference: employers—with some official connivance—are seeing to it that official policies in favor of the right of association and of minimum labor standards will not push the costs of production beyond what they consider the threat of the China price ("Action: Justice Still Needed in Chea Vichea Murder Case" 2007).

Marston (2007) observes the removal of MFA quotas and the "race-to-the-bottom" problem in Cambodia this way:

[A] growing culture of fear, linked to the end of the quota system, has been used to ensure that garment workers remain docile in the face of new challenges. According to Alonzo Suson, Director of the American Center for International Labor Solidarity (ACILS), a non-profit organization with links to the AFL-CIO union federation in the United States, "The end of the MFA was used to put workers in line. [They're told] "Do more work, be conservative, don't ask for much, and don't rock the boat."

Although increasing international competition is a valid concern, it appears that it is often exaggerated and used as a threat to remind workers of the precariousness of their employment and to keep them from demanding better wages or improved working conditions.

Discussion: South-South

The end of the MFA regime continued but did not accelerate U.S. job loss in the apparel industry. Far from protecting the apparel industry, the MFA provided a long inevitable glideway to extinction. Enmeshed in a supply network where the global labor reserve can be mobilized for pennies an hour, remaining U.S. apparel workers are at serious risk of sweatshop conditions themselves (Ross 2004). The basic shifts in apparel sourcing brought about by the end of the MFA have heightened the South-South competition among suppliers in low-income peripheral economies, however. In particular, the lower wages, and either lax labor law enforcement or outright repression, or both, have given Asian suppliers advantages over Western Hemisphere suppliers in the competition for the U.S. market.

Since the MFA expired there has been a more or less predicted shift in world apparel export production. This shift included a large component of higher wage to lower wage motion that in turn entailed relative gains to Asian sources and losses for Western Hemisphere producers. The cost of clothing also continues to decline. This is the result of source shifting and possibly also a product of deterioration in workers' conditions.

As things now stand, the world's working class in labor-intensive manufacturing has at its center the Asian and in particular the Indian and Chinese working classes. Richard Freeman has pointed out that the entry of China, India, and the former Soviet bloc has doubled the global labor pool, bringing about 1.47 billion workers into the competitive mix. In the process, Freeman estimates the capital to labor ratio has been cut by 55–60 percent (Freeman 2005). It is here, in Asia, that what is now called the "China price" the lowest dependable product price for a commodity—will be determined.[11]

In the meantime, the 87,000 officially counted protests in China in 2005 (there may have been many more) exceeded the 74,000 of 2004 (Lum 2006).

All around the world, much depends on whether that number rises and what the Chinese government will do about it.

Notes

1. See the U.S. Department of Labor Current Employment Survey SIC (Standard Industrial Classification) statistical series compared to the NAICS (North American Industry Classification System) series at www.bls.gov.

2. This suggests the summary slogan: beating Communists with brassieres (in the interests of etiquette, we might pass over it; in the interests of entertainment, we will not).

3. A Google search for the words *Multifibre Arrangement* and *2005* produced 75,000 hits on April 28, 2007.

4. U.S. imports of clothing were about 28 percent of the world total in 2005; Among the twenty-five EU members of that period imports were about 44 percent. Extracted from the WTO trade database: http://stat.wto.org/StatisticalProgram/WSDBViewDataPrintableVersion. aspx?Language=E&TOPIC=MT&SUBTOPIC=CO&PAGEINDEX=1&ROWSCNT=30&STARTYEAR=2001&ENDYEAR=2005&MSTR_QUERY_TYPE=PRINT . This investigation is focused on the U.S. data.

5. Compare these concentration ratios to the 2002 Economic Census, which shows transportation equipment: top 8: 52 percent; apparel: top 8: 21.3 percent(United States Census 2002)

6. CBI includes twenty-four Central American and Caribbean countries: Antigua, Aruba, the Bahamas, Barbados, Belize, British Virgin Islands, Costa Rica, Dominica, Dominican Republic, El Salvador, Grenada, Guatemala, Guyana, Haiti, Honduras, Jamaica, Montserrat, Netherlands Antilles, Nicaragua, Panama, St. Kitts and Nevis, St. Lucia, St. Vincent and the Grenadines, and Trinidad and Tobago.

7. Honduras is comparable to Nicaragua in GDP/capita when using purchasing power parity (PPP) dollars.

8. The Office of Textile and Apparel (OTEXA) (2007) database reports clothing imports by SME (square meter equivalents) and by dollar value. It thus permits simple division: dollars/SME.

9. Although retail clothing prices went down 0.75 percent, the CPI-U went up 6.7 percent—a difference of 7.5 percent

10. In fact the U.S. State Department *Human Rights Report* notes that a new law allows Workers' Associations, but these may not have affiliation with unions outside the Export Processing Zones.

11. The China price is not only about labor costs, for the Chinese market is among the least regulated markets, and thus it has the smallest time lost in permitting and other such matters.

References

"Action: Justice Still Needed in Chea Vichea Murder Case." 2007. Labour Behind the Label. Available at http://www.labourbehindthelabel.org/content/view/157/115/1/0/. Accessed May 9, 2007.

American Textile Manufacturers Institute (ATMI). 2003. *The China Threat to World Textile and Apparel Trade.* Washington, D.C. Available at http://www.ncto.org/quota/china.pdf. Accessed April 30, 2007.

———. 2004 *Update Number 3: The China Threat to World Textile and Apparel Trade.* Available athttp://www.ncto.org/newsroom/china0904.pdf. Accessed April 30, 2007.

Appelbaum, Richard. 2004. *Assessing the Impact of the Phasing-out of the Agreement on Textiles and Clothing on Apparel Exports on the Least Developed and Developing Countries.* Center for Global Studies, University of California, Santa Barbara, Year 2004 Paper 05. Available at http://repositories.cdlib.org/isber/cgs/05. Accessed December 12, 2006.

Appelbaum, Richard P., Edna Bonacich, and Katie Quan. 2005. "The End of Apparel Quotas: A Faster Race to the Bottom?" Center for Global Studies. Paper 2. February 5. Availalble at http://repositories.cdlib.org/isber/cgs/2. Accessed March 1, 2009.

———. 2005. *The End of Apparel Quotas: A Faster Race to the Bottom?* Global and International Studies Program, University of California, Santa Barbara. Year 2005 Paper 35. Available at http://repositories.cdlib.org/gis/35. Accessed December 12, 2006.

"Bangladesh EPZ." 2005. Export Promotion Bureau, Bangladesh Ministry of Commerce. Available at http://www.epb.gov.bd/bangladesh_epz.html. Accessed May 7, 2007.

Chan, Anita, and Robert J. S. Ross 2003. "Racing to the Bottom: International Trade Without a Social Clause." *Third World Quarterly* 24, no. 6: 1011–1028.

Clean Clothes Campaign. 2004a. The Phase-out of the Multifiber Arrangement, SOMO Bulletin on Issues in Garments and Textiles no. 5, April. Available at http://www.cleanclothes.org/publications/04-04-somo.htm. Accessed December 12, 2006.

———. 2004b. Trade and Investment Agreements, SOMO Bulletin on Issues in Garments and Textiles no. 4, February. Available at http://www.cleanclothes.org/publications/04-02-somo.htm. Accessed December 12, 2006.

Foo, Lora Jo, and Nikki Fortunato Bas. 2003. "Free Trade's Looming Threat to the World's Garment Workers," Sweatshop Watch Working Paper, October 30. Available at http://www.sweatshopwatch.org/global/index.html. Accessed December 12, 2006.

Freeman, Richard. 2005. "China, India, and the Doubling of the Global Labor Force: Who Pays the Price of Globalization." *The Globalist.* June 3. Available at http://hussonet.free.fr/freeman5.pdf. Accessed May 7, 2007.

Heron, Tony. 2007. "Small States and The Politics of Multilateral Trade Liberalisation." Paper prepared for the Small State Capacity Building Workshop, University of Birmingham, UK, April 4–5, 2007. Available at www.polsis.bham.ac.uk/research/Heron.pdf. Accessed April 19, 2007.

Hudgins, Edward L. 1985. "Why Limiting Textile Imports Would Hurt Americans." Heritage Foundation, Backgrounder no. 458. Available at http://www.heritage.org/Research/TradeandForeignAid/upload/87488_1.pdf. Accessed April 27, 2007.

Lum, Thomas. 2006. *CRS Report for Congress: Social Unrest in China.* Order Code RL33416. Congressional Research Service. Available at http://www.fas.org/sgp/crs/row/RL33416.pdf. Accessed May 7, 2007.

Marston, Ama. 2007. *Labor Monitoring in Cambodia's Garment Industry: Lessons for Africa.* Realizing Rights; the Ethical Global Initiative. Available at http://www.reports-and-materials.org/Marston-Labor-Monitoring-Cambodia-1-May-2007.pdf .Accessed May 9, 2007.

Mukherjee, Andy. 2005. "Latin American Flow Means Few Jobs in U.S. Saved by Anti-Asian Embargo." *Los Angeles Business Journal.* Available at http://findarticles.com/p/articles/mi_m5072/is_1_27/ai_n8709334. Accessed June 6, 2007.

National Labor Committee. 2006a. *Train Wreck for Corporate Monitoring at the Harvest Rich Factory in Bangladesh.* Available at http://www.nlcnet.org/article.php?id=195. Accessed May 7, 2007.

———. 2006b. *U.S.-Jordan Free Trade Agreement Descends into Human Trafficking and Involuntary Servitude.* Available at http://www.nlcnet.org/article.php?id=10. Accessed May 7, 2007.

———. 2007. "U.S.-Jordan Free Trade Agreement: Progress on Worker Rights, but Much Remains To Be Done." March 30. Available at http://www.nlcnet.org/article.php?id=241. Accessed March 1, 2009.

Office of Textile and Apparel (OTEXA). 2007. "U.S. Imports of Textiles and Apparel" Database. International Trade Administration, United States Department of Commerce. Available at http://otexa.ita.doc.gov/scripts/tqads1.exe/catpage. Accessed March 1, 2009.

Oxfam. 2004. *Stitched Up: How Rich-country Protectionism in Textiles and Clothing Trade Prevents Poverty Alleviation.* Briefing paper 60. Available at http://www.oxfam.org.uk/what_we_do/issues/trade/bp60_textiles.htm. Accessed April 27, 2007.

Raghavan, Chakravarthi. N.d. "Barking Up the Wrong Tree: Trade and Social Clause Links." Third World Forum. Available at http://www.twnside.org.sg/title/tree-ch.htm. Accessed April 27, 2007.

Roberts, Dexter, and Pete Engardio. 2006. "Secrets, Lies, and Sweatshops." *Business Week,* November 27. Available at http://www.businessweek.com/magazine/content/06_48/b4011001.htm. Accessed May 1, 2007.

Rosen, Ellen Israel. 2002. *Making Sweatshops: The Globalization of the U.S. Apparel Industry.* Berkeley: University of California Press.

Rosen, Howard. 2005. Labor Market Adjustment to the Multi-Fiber Arrangement Removal. MFA Forum. Available at http://www.mfa-forum.net/downloads/mfa-forum_labour_market_adjustment.pdf. Accessed on March 1, 2009

Ross, Robert J. S. 2004. *Slaves to Fashion: Poverty and Abuse in the New Sweatshops.* Ann Arbor: University of Michigan Press.

———. 2006. "A Tale of Two Factories: Successful Resistance to Sweatshops and the Limits of Firefighting." *Labor Studies Journal* 30, no. 4 (Winter): 1–21.

Ross, Robert J. S., and Anita Chan. 2002. "From North-South to South-South: The True Face of Global Competition." *Foreign Affairs* 81, no. 5: 8–13.

Siphana, Sok. 2005. "Labour Standards, Social Labels, and Company Standards: Example of Cambodia." Paper prepared for Economic and Social Commission for Asia and the Pacific conference, "Weaving the Fabric of Regional Cooperation for a Competitive Garment Sector," June 1–2, 2005, Beijing, China. Available at http://www.unescap.org/tid/mtg/tradenv_s5.pdf. Accessed May 6, 2007.

United Nations Conference on Trade and Development. 2005. *TNCs and the Removal of Textiles and Clothing Quotas.* New York: United Nations.

United States Census Bureau. 2002. *Economic Census. Manufacturing-Subject Series. Concentration Ratios.* Available at http://www.census.gov/prod/ec02/ec0231sr1.pdf. Accessed April 19, 2007.

Weil, David. 2006. "Lean Retailing and Supply Chain Restructuring: Implications for Private and Public Governance." Paper prepared for conference "Observing Trade: Revealing International Trade Networks," Princeton Institute for International and Regional Studies, Princeton University. Available at http://www.princeton.edu/~ina/gkg/confs/weil.pdf. Accessed June 6, 2007.

Wells-Dang, Andrew. 2002. "Linking Textiles to Labor Standards: Prospects for Cambodia and Vietnam." Policy Report, Foreign Policy in Focus. Available at http://www.fpif.org/pdf/reports/PRtxt-labor.pdf. Accessed May 9, 2007.

White House. 2000. "United States and Jordan Sign Historic Free Trade Agreement." Press release. Available at: http://clinton4.nara.gov/WH/new/html/Tue_Oct_24_163554_2000.html. Accessed May 7, 2007.

World Trade Organization (WTO). 2007. "Textiles Monitoring Body (TMB): The Agreement on Textiles and Clothing." Available at http://www.wto.org/english/tratop_e/texti_e/texintro_e.htm. Accessed on May 2, 2007.

Yearman, Keith, and Amy Gluckman. 2005. "Falling Off a Cliff." *Dollars and Sense*. September/October. Available at http://www.dollarsandsense.org/archives/2005/0905yearman.html. Accessed 27 April 2007.

8

AQUACULTURE COMMODITY CHAINS AND THREATS TO FOOD SECURITY AND SURVIVAL OF ASIAN FISHING HOUSEHOLDS

Wilma A. Dunaway and M. Cecilia Macabuac

Because commercial aquaculture has been touted to be one of the most important solutions to world hunger, the World Bank and the International Monetary Fund stimulated the expansion of the "Blue Revolution" throughout Asia, Africa, and Latin America in the 1980s and 1990s. Although shrimp comprises less than 1 percent of global fisheries output, it is the most valuable seafood product in international trade. Consequently, prawn farming has proliferated in poor countries since 1975 (Barraclough and Finger-Stich 1996). Despite increased commercial outputs, less fish and seafood is now available to peripheral populations, and malnutrition and hunger are on the rise in those countries engaged in export aquaculture (Yoshinori 1987). After 1975, the Philippines expanded its commercial aquaculture until it rose to be one of the world's most important shrimp exporters. Since 1989, however, the Philippines has been a *food extractive enclave* in the bust stage of export-oriented aquaculture and commercial fishing. This study analyzes the impacts of that boom-to-bust process on subsistence fishing households and describes the inequitable strategies through which women have struggled to cope with economic and ecological crisis.

Target Area and Methods of Research

To support its export production agendas in agriculture, fishing, timbering, and mining, the Philippine government targeted the island of Mindanao (see Map 8.1) for extensive exploitation of natural resources in the late 1980s. Eleven provinces were targeted for rapid development of prawn farms, and the government privatized mangroves and offered tax abatements to entice investments from multinational corporations. Rapid expansion of prawn farming put new massive strains on the resources that had historically supported subsistence fishers. Before commercial aquaculture, 770,000 small-scale fishers were critical to the national food supply because they produced two-fifths of the country's fish output. These subsistence producers fish within 3 miles of coasts and sell most of their catches for local consumption. After expansion of shrimp ponds, the total annual output of these small fishers dropped by 80 percent, endangering local food security (JEP ATRE 2004).

We selected for our study the Panguil Bay area of northern Mindanao, which was targeted for rapid aquaculture development. Between 1982 and 1991,

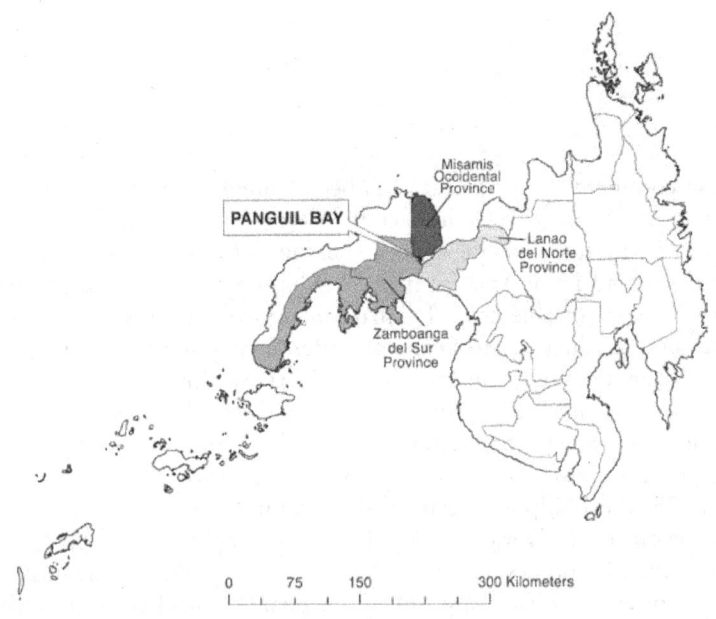

Map 8.1   Island of Mindanao, the Philippines

shrimp ponds expanded 18 percent annually, tripling the area utilized by export aquaculture in just a decade (Naawan School of Fisheries 1991). Surrounding the bay are seventy-six communities that support more than 450,000 people (Loquias 1990–1991), including nearly 10,000 households that engage in small-scale fishing, prawn farming, or seaweed cultivation (Israel et al. 2003). The typical Panguil Bay fisher is a thirty-nine-year-old male who has helped to support a household of five through seasonal fishing for 30 years (JEP ATRE 2004). More than 70 percent of Panguil Bay adults have 6 years or less of elementary education, and a majority of women are illiterate or nearly so (Israel et al. 2003). Thus, Panguil Bay households are typical of the conditions that face a majority of Filipino artisanal fishing families. Even though this area was assessed by the government to be the richest shallow water fishing ground in Mindanao, it is now a fishery in severe crisis, and it exhibits one of the highest poverty and unemployment rates in the country. Well before 1990, export shrimp farming had reached the bust stage in Panguil Bay, and most of the corporate ponds had ceased operations or decreased production. Presently in these coastal villages, a day's catch fetches an average income of less than $1 a day, situating these families among the world's poorest (Asian Development Bank 2005: 60–61).

With the help of local NGOs and fishery officials, we selected three communities that permitted case studies of the impacts of three forms of aquacultural production on subsistence fishing. Located in the town of Kapatagan, the Lapinig community was involved in aquaculture as early as 1957 and now has corporate fishponds that employ intensive harvest techniques. Located in Tangub City, the Silanga community experienced a shrimp boom in the 1970s but now has only small-scale fishponds. Located in Ozamis City, the San Roque community specializes in seaweed gardening. Over a one-year period in 2005 and 2006, numerous interviews and focus groups were conducted with fishery, local government, and NGO officials. Focus groups were conducted in each of the villages to permit subsistence fishing women to identify problems facing their families. To pinpoint household transformations, inequalities, and survival strategies, we conducted in-depth interviews in the local dialect with husbands and wives in twenty-six subsistence fishing households. In addition, our research has been richly informed by the research of Philippine feminists (e.g., Arnado 2003, Illo and Polo 1990, Israel-Sobritchea 1987, Noralsco 1987, Pineda-Ofreneo 1985) whose household analyses rarely appear in U.S. or European libraries and are largely ignored by Western feminists.

Impacts of Aquaculture on Subsistence Fishing Households

To maximize profits, capitalists must exploit as many "costless" social and natural conditions as possible. Thus, capitalists shift to society, to the culture, to the ecosystem, and to human laborers most of the real costs of commodity production (Dunaway 2001). If households and nature did not absorb so many externalities from commodity chains, the global production process could not endlessly accumulate the capital that is essential to capitalist economic growth (Wallerstein 1999). According to Jacinto (2004: 9), export shrimp farming "is perhaps the most glaring example of social and environmental costs borne by small scale fishers and coastal communities so that consumers in developed countries can meet their increasing demand for cheap and affordable shrimp." Consequently, aquaculture commodity chains externalize to households and to nature most of the costs of production. As the food resources of Panguil Bay and the Philippines have been more deeply integrated into the global food commodity chains (McMichael 1994), export aquaculture has externalized four costs to subsistence fishing households: (1) loss of access to ecological resources, (2) deterioration of local livelihoods, (3) loss of food security, and (4) loss of social services.

Loss of Access to Ecological Resources

The country's intensive aquaculture has caused loss of biodiversity, salinization of agricultural lands and drinking water, destruction of coral reefs, and massive mangrove deforestation (*Philippines Environmental Monitor* 2000). The export prices of prawn and seaweed "do not reflect the true costs of producing fishery products as long as externalities are not made to 'show up' in the value chain. With social and environmental costs missing from the equation, what is actually expensive and wasteful become apparently cheap" (Jacinto 2004: 17). Every acre of an industrial shrimp farm destroys 200 acres of productive ecosystem. Shrimp ponds degrade the ecosystem so extensively that fish catches are lowered too far to provide a livelihood, forcing household members to migrate in search of employment. In addition to degrading the ecosystem, commercial aquaculture development has required the elimination of common property rights and the reallocation of mangroves to monopolistic use of pond operators. "Mangrove forested areas in the Philippines have been steadily transformed from a common property resource, of multiple use and benefit to a large number of people, to a private good, of single use for shrimp ponds, whose benefits are narrowly channeled to the benefit of a select few" (Nickerson 1999: 279). The national government issued long-term leases assigning prawn pond owners sole control over mangroves and waterways. This land reform delegitimated traditional access of subsistence households to these forests and transformed fishers into unwelcome squatters around shrimp ponds (Primavera 1997). To make matters worse, the Philippine government does not provide safe public water systems in the areas where shrimp farms have expanded, so aquaculture pollutants threaten the water available for household use. Little wonder that diarrhea is a major cause of death around Panguil Bay. Forced to rely on rivers and canals for bathing and laundry, a large proportion of bay residents are infected with incurable, life-threatening *schistosomiasis* (World Health Organization 2000).

Filipino fishing women have been more negatively affected than men by these ecological changes. Female resource gatherers who have traditionally relied on mangroves, coastal waters, and rivers for subsistence and for livelihood must internalize the external costs associated with the elimination of community property rights. In addition to losing significant food resources and craft materials, women must now also work harder to secure fuel wood or charcoal for household cooking. Now that commercial prawn ponds have appropriated most of the waterways and mangroves, women have been pushed out of fishing and out of many of their traditional artisan crafts into marginal activities, such shell gathering or craft piecework on a putting-out basis. Males work in boats, whereas women are more directly exposed to diseases, pollutants, and parasites because they wade into water on a consistent daily basis to gather oysters, catch small fishes and crustaceans, or do laundry. In addition, environmental threats to water safety require females to assume increased caregiving responsibility for sickened family members.

Deterioration of Local Livelihoods

Despite the rapid expansion of commercial aquaculture and other export agendas, the Philippines presently has the lowest economic growth rate in Southeast Asia, and its foreign direct investment has declined to less than one-fifth of its 2002 level (Escobar 2004). Despite market-oriented economic reforms, the Philippine export structure is now less diversified and less industrialized than it was in 1980 (Lim and Montes 2002). More than half the GNP is now earmarked for external debt repayment (IBON Foundation 2005). The transformation of small-scale fishing and seaweed gathering into export-oriented aquaculture can be traced to structural adjustment policies imposed on the Philippines. During the decades that shrimp aquaculture has boomed and busted in the Philippines, the economic conditions facing families have steadily worsened. Devaluation of Philippine currency resulted in a 72 percent drop in the value of the peso. Subsequently, prices inflated at an average rate of 9.7 percent yearly while consumer prices rose as much as 27 percent in some years (Casino 2004: 1–2). Unemployment is rising owing to the loss of jobs after trade liberalization, and household incomes have steadily declined since 1995. Wealth and income have been increasingly concentrated into a few hands, and the Philippines now has a higher incidence of poverty than its Asian neighbors. Nearly half of all Filipino families struggle to survive on less than fifty-seven cents a day per person while the incomes of two-thirds fall below one dollar a day per person (Schelzig 2005). Little wonder that most Philippine citizens are convinced that their livelihoods have worsened, that the national economy is in crisis, and that there is widespread government corruption (IBON Foundation 2004).

In addition to these macrostructural trends, export-oriented aquaculture has externalized hidden costs to fishing households. Shrimp farming is grounded in short-term economic motives. In most instances, the prawn pond has a productive lifespan of only five to ten years. Abandoned after that, the dead resource can no longer be utilized for agriculture or resource-gathering activities (Naylor 2003: 886). On the one hand, export-oriented aquaculture has not generated long-term economic growth. On the other hand, the highest incidence of poverty occurs in those Philippine regions where prawn farming has expanded most rapidly (Jacinto 2004). Since shrimp farms require few workers, they have not generated new employment opportunities to offset the job losses their construction has caused. In fact, export-oriented shrimp cultivation has been a "rape and run industry" that decimates fifteen jobs for each it creates and destroys five to ten dollars of ecological and economic capital for every dollar earned through exports (Shiva 2000: 15). Most of the profits in the Philippine shrimp commodity chain accrue to multinational corporations, Philippine agribusinesses concentrated in Manila, and middlemen traders. Rural prawn ponds generate only a few below-subsistence jobs in their local communities, and urban shrimp processors pay low wages to their female labor forces. In fact, most fishing households derive no income from aquaculture, and the vast majority of fishers cannot afford to start a small aquaculture pond (Irz et al. 2004). While providing little income to local people, shrimp farms eliminate the ecological access that is required to support the fishing, agriculture, livestock raising, and handicrafts through which subsistence households earned a livelihood.

Loss of Food Security

Peripheral countries that specialize in export-oriented aquaculture have grown less and less food self-sufficient since the 1980s. Since 1993, Philippine seafood output has not kept pace with population needs, and there has been an annual shortfall of 600,000 metric tons. All over the country, household fish catches have declined to less than 1 kilo per day, reflecting the depletion of coastal resources (Aguilar 2002). Panguil Bay fishing households increasingly must compete in five ways with agroindustrial aquaculture for dwindling animal protein. First, massive outputs of prawn, fish, and seaweed are exported to rich countries. Second, two-thirds of the species swimming in rich-nation aquariums derives from the Philippines and Indonesia, and many of these endangered species once comprised part of the local food chain of fishing households. Third, massive levels of food fish and shellfish are fed to export prawn and fish. Because shrimp feeds contain about 30 percent fishmeal and 30 percent fish oil, intensive shrimp farming actually results in a net loss of fish protein (Naylor 2003: 883–884). One kilo of farmed shrimp must be fed 5 kilos of wild fish that would otherwise be available for the local food chain. While shrimp are being fattened for export through their consumption of natural protein, one-third or more of Philippine households suffer malnutrition, the highest incidence among small fisher families (Philippine Food and Nutrition Institute 2005). As one Philippine fisher puts it, "the shrimp live better than we do. They have electricity, but we don't. The shrimp have clean water, but we don't. The shrimp have lots of food, but we are hungry" (Environmental Justice Foundation 2003: 1). Fourth, massive levels of food fish are destroyed and wasted by shrimp producers. Every time a prawn farm opens its gates for seawater exchange or to flush out wastes, it destroys fish and shellfish that could be consumed in local food chains. When prawn farmers apply toxins, such as tea-seed, to eliminate "unwanted" fish that stray into the pond, they once again waste valuable nutrients and biodiversity (Primavera 1997). As a result of all these factors, the quantity and quality of protein resources in Panguil Bay waters have declined dramatically (*Philippines Environmental Monitor* 2000). At present, the average daily catch is only about 16 percent of the average daily catch in 1970 (Adan 2000).

Fifth, shrimp aquaculture threatens food security through loss of rice lands to prawn pond expansion or to salinization (Primavera 1997). While exporting high levels of sea-foods, the Philippines has become so dependent on grain imports that the country's agricultural sector now registers an annual trade deficit (IBON Foundation 2005). Since the expansion of export-oriented aquaculture has diminished the Philippines' rice production (Primavera 1997), the country now imports a higher percentage of rice for consumption even as domestic consumer prices have steadily risen (Cabanilla 1997). With far fewer fish to sell, many families cannot afford rice, so they substitute cornmeal that can be purchased at about 60 percent of the cost of rice.[1] Since the mid-1980s, the diet of Philippine fishing households has been increasingly limited to a few vegetables, small amounts of fish, and cornmeal or rice (when it can be afforded), with protein missing from many meals and on many days (Philippine Food and Nutrition Institute 2005, Pineda-Ofreno 1985). One fisher wife rationalized why she buys 1 kilo of corn per meal when money is short. When food rations are inadequate, "corn is preferred over rice," she explained in a field interview, "because it makes us feel fuller."

The substitution of corn for rice is a hidden externalized health cost for fishing households. Rice contains small amounts of fat, dietary fiber, calcium, phosphorous, potassium, sodium, Vitamin B_1, Vitamin B_2, and niacin, in addition to 11 percent of the average daily requirement of protein. In sharp contrast, diets high in corn cause the body not to absorb iron efficiently, including the high iron levels in fish. In a country in which iron deficiency anemia is problematic, cornmeal like that which is increasingly consumed by poor Philippine households has "practically no food value" and actually can cause health problems. In addition to providing unhealthy levels of sugar and empty carbohydrates, high consumption of corn and fish with few supplementary vegetables and fruits will lead to deficiencies in calcium, Vitamin A, phosphorus, copper, niacin, amino acids, Vitamin K, Omega$_3$ fatty acids, boron, and magnesium (International Rice Research Institute 2003). Although Panguil Bay fisher wives market their husbands' dwindling fish catches in local markets at low prices, they must in turn take that low income and purchase expensive food imports. Income from small fish sales cannot cover the cost of imported rice and salt that have been heavily centralized under the control of a few wholesalers and retailers (Szanton 1972). As one fishing wife observed:

> Now we spend less and less on foods and buy only necessities.... Household expenses usually exceed the family's income.... We rarely have fish.... Meat is rarely served.... When they wake up in the morning, the children open all our pots and often find them empty. There are days when we do not earn even a single centavo (Illo and Pineda-Ofreneo 2002: 152).

In fact, workers in *food extractive enclaves,* such as Panguil Bay and the Philippines, are the hungriest, most malnourished people in the world; these are the agricultural and fishing households that cultivate and process food for the rest of the world. At the end of the twentieth century, the richest fifth of the world consumed nearly half of all meat and fish, the poorest fifth only 5 percent (Shiva 2000). Protein-energy malnutrition, iron deficiency anemia, iodine deficiency, and Vitamin A deficiencies are typical of the countries that export high levels of shrimp and fish (World Health Organization 2001). At least one-third of the Filipino population is now chronically malnourished. In a country that produces iron-rich fish for export, per capita food consumption has declined dramatically. Because most Filipino diets lack adequate levels of fruits, green vegetables, fats and oils, cereals, poultry, and meats, deficiencies of iron, iodine, calcium and Vitamin A are common (Philippine Food and Nutrition Institute 2005). In 2003, nearly one-third of the families in Northern Mindanao lacked sufficient income to provide food for their households, and nutritional deficiencies are a major cause of death in this area (Philippine National Statistical Coordination Board. 2003). More than one-third of Northern Mindanao children are underweight and underheight. Two of every five Northern Mindanao children are stunted, and another 8 percent suffer from *miasma* (wasting). Iron deficiency anemia occurs in 20 percent of Northern Mindanao children and about one-third of pregnant and lactating women. Because they are iodine deficient, one-third of Northern Mindanao residents are at risk of goiter or impaired cognitive and motor development. Iodine is a very crucial nutrient during pregnancy, since deficiencies can cause brain damage in the fetus, low birth weight, premature labor, and increased prenatal or infant mortality. Two-fifths of Northern Mindanao children and one-quarter of the pregnant women are Vitamin A deficient, placing them at risk of blindness (Philippine Food and Nutrition Institute 2005). Despite the nutritional risks, the Philippine Food and Nutrition Institute now threatens the food security of infants by recommending a cheaper baby formula that contains a half cup of corn and a half cup of soy (Philippine Food and Nutrition Institute 2005).

Loss of Social Services

In the wake of structural adjustment agreements to shift public funds into economic growth agendas, the Philippine government has made cuts in three public services that have hit fishing households especially hard. First, health care delivery has been privatized and decentralized to the local level, leaving rural communities with inadequate medical personnel. Fishers suffer a higher mortality rate than any other occupation in the Philippines, and females in these communities are at higher risk of dying during their child-bearing years than other Filipino females (Philippine Census Bureau. 2004). Two of every five pregnancies is problematic or life-threatening, and the life expectancy of a Northern Mindanao woman is four years less than that of her male counterpart (Philippine National Statistical Coordination Board 2003). Despite their health crises, fishing communities have been left with a shortage of health care personnel. Two factors have been at play to cause a health care crisis in communities such as Panguil Bay. Even though the Philippines trains 2,000 doctors and 10,000 nurses annually, the country exports the vast majority of these new professionals to the United States and the Middle East (DeBrun and Elling 1987). To exacerbate this "brain drain," three-quarters of the country's doctors are concentrated in urban centers. As a result, a majority of rural Filipinos, such as fishing households, must rely on minimally trained nurses, traditional herbalists, and birthing attendants. Most likely, the lack of prenatal and postnatal care accounts for the high incidence of maternal mortality, infant low birth weight, and newborn deaths from blood poisoning of the umbilical cord stump (Philippine Department of Health 2002).

Family planning is the second public service sector that has been eliminated from fishing communities. Rather than point to the country's neoliberal export agenda as the underlying cause of ecological degradation and dwindling natural resources, current public fishery management policy places the blame for food shortages and environmental degradation on "overpopulation" in fishing communities (JEP ATRE 2004). Even though most of the population growth in fishing communities has resulted from the inmigration of displaced agricultural workers, public policy posits "responsible parenthood for sustainable development" to be the solution to food insecurity. While pressuring females to lower birth rates, the Philippine government has gutted family planning services over the last decade.[2] Because of national budget cuts to meet structural adjustment goals and to speed privatization of health care, in early 2005 local centers discontinued their free family planning services. More than half of the wives in fishing households who had relied on free contraceptive methods, such as Depro-Provera, birth control pills, intrauterine devices (IUDs), tubal ligations, and condoms, are left without affordable family planning mechanisms (Ardales 1981). Currently, the Philippines government is being funded by a USAID project aimed at helping the country to privatize its health care system, by transforming

> from a free contraceptive delivery system to a sustainable and commercial delivery model. The program promotes contraceptive products, builds and expands the market and harnesses the active participation of the private commercial companies to ensure the future of family planning.... Efforts are concentrated on increasing the usage of oral contraceptive pills and injectable contraceptives and expanding the market for these (USAID 2005).

Not only does the USAID program eliminate free services, but it also shifts the country's family planning strategy away from male condom use and places full responsibility on women for controlling population growth. In a country in which few women ever see a doctor before, during, or after a pregnancy, the NGO associated with this program offers "discounts" on vasectomies and tubal ligations, surgical procedures that are far out of the economic reach of a vast majority of the poor fishing couples (USAID 2005).

Public schooling is the third service that has been negatively impacted in rural areas. Even though their children's schooling is often beyond their economic means, these parents still prioritize it among their basic survival expenses, second only to food. They cannot afford the 40 percent of educational costs that have been gutted from the Philippines national budget by structural adjustment policies, however. Even though there are no outright fees for attending the public schools, there are frequent expenses for "school projects" and "contributions." One mother of three elementary graders explained during a field interview that "there are always required contributions, like to buy a floormat for the classroom." Since there is no hope of accumulating these added expenses from fishing, women assume responsibility for generating extra income to cover children's schooling through nipa thatching, sale of salted fish or oysters, or production of crafts for the informal sector.

Household Transformations and Inequalities

In the Philippines, four extrahousehold structural changes have dramatically compromised fishing household composition and survival options.

1. Local food production systems have been structurally integrated into world capitalist commodity chains.

2. National development policies have privatized the commons, eliminated public funding of social services, and privileged a small elite of export-oriented capitalists.
3. Export-oriented extractive industries have depleted and degraded ecological resources.
4. The boom-to-bust cycle of commercial aquaculture has left fishing households with fewer survival options than they had before this economic growth agenda.

In order to overcome the shortfalls that have resulted from loss of ecological resources, elimination of livelihood options, and the externalized costs of export-oriented aquaculture, subsistence fishing households have been forced to restructure themselves.

Judging from the frequency with which they focused on the topic, the widening of women's work represents their most dramatic transformation. The widening and deepening of capitalism engenders dramatic shifts in productive systems and in the transformation of laborer households. Crises and shortages generate revised definitions of the appropriate responsibilities of women within and outside the household.

> These changes, however, do not mean that old forms of the asymmetric sexual division of labor are abolished or replaced by egalitarian ones. They are only redefined according to the requirements of the new production system.... Because of the preservation of the asymmetric division of labor between the sexes in the ongoing processes, these changes do not lead to greater equality between women and men of the pauperized classes, but, rather, to a polarization between them. The social definition of women as housewives plays a vital role in this polarization (Mies 1982: 5).

Although the wife's burden of unpaid household labor remains unchanged, her income-earning and resource-pooling activities outside the household must increase to overcome shortages.

Widening of Women's Work Portfolio

Panguil Bay women describe a greater intertwining of household-based labors and market labors. For these women who often produce marketable commodities or services in their homes, there is not a line of demarcation between household and market-related labors. In short, fisher wives are both *semidomesticated* and *semiproletarianize*d (Mies 1982: 15) because of their widening portfolio of diverse household and extrahousehold labors and of unpaid and income-earning pursuits. Panguil Bay fisher wives reported that their extrahousehold labors have increased since the 1970s, but their husbands have not increased their contributions to unpaid household labor. Females spend hours every day gathering food and fuel resources from the mangroves and the water, processing those resources into edible meals or marketable goods, and cooking without electricity. Traditionally, wives have played several key roles in supporting the fishing work of husbands and older sons, including preparation of provisions for fishing trips, marketing fish, net repairs, securing credit and paying debts related to fishing, and help with boat repairs (Abregana 2000). About one-third of wives assist males directly with fishing (Oracion 2001), but several of the wives have broadened their roles in fishing in nontraditional ways, so that they are now using boats to collect fish from stationary platforms or to fish alone.

In addition to these unpaid labors, women have expanded their *income-earning* and *income-substituting* activities. Globally, the Philippines is unique in the degree to which males dominate the informal sector. Even though they are not as deeply embedded in the informal sector as males, women are still far more likely to earn income from informal sector activities and putting out systems than from waged jobs (United Nations 2000: 122). Women produce and sell crafts, livestock, and dried oysters and fish; operate small stores; and trade in fish in the informal sector. Because of the limited waged and informal sector opportunities, Panguil Bay women routinely engage in *casualized* labor through cottage industries and putting out systems. Traders and regional agents provide inputs from which women produce marketable commodities on a piecework basis, such as roof shingles thatched from nipa trees or wooden jewelry and baskets. Fishing women have double or triple work burdens that combine unpaid household labor with waged labor, informal sector vending, home-based industries, illegal activities, and services (e.g., laundry, herbalist, midwife). "What they cannot buy because they do not have cash, they collect or produce themselves" (Pineda-Ofreneo 1985: 2–3) Because wives are now engaged in new forms of income-earning labor, fewer of them are marketing male fish catches and making daily household purchases. Thus, husbands now exert greater decisionmaking control over daily expenditures. This transformation represents a dramatic shift in power relations within households in which wives have traditionally managed family budgets.

Some Western feminists (e.g., Atkinson and Errington 1990) celebrate "the relative economic equality" of men and women in the Philippines, but Panguil Bay fishing wives do not agree with their idealizations. Philippine society culturally constrains women to prioritize child rearing and household maintenance while simultaneously economically and ecologically limiting their capacities and opportunities to fulfill that role. "If you just count on the earnings of your husband," one fisher wife observed, "it is not enough" (Eder 1999: 114). Despite wives' diverse labor portfolios inside and outside household, their income-earning pursuits remain marginalized, low-paid, and sometimes stigmatized. Moreover, a woman faces the contradictory pressures to remain a "respectable housewife" and to undertake whatever income-earning work is necessary to sustain her household. When our interviewees described themselves as *housewives,* they reconstructed traditional social expectations to encompass with that term whatever efforts they undertook for the benefit of their households. Most women in fishing households must do some form of income-generating or income-substituting labors while managing child care and household maintenance without male assistance. Fisher wives are caught in the contradictory situation of simultaneously meeting household needs and of staying within rigid social conventions about appropriate women's work roles. To overcome this cultural conflict, fishing wives appeal to the Filipino cultural ideal of "sacrificial motherhood." As Afshar and Agarwal (1989: 1) have observed:

> Under the banner of this idealised, heroic nurturance a truly womanly woman is enjoined to do anything, to make any sacrifice, for the sake of household welfare, for the sake of her husband, and especially for the sake of her children.... However much the ideal is invoked to justify female passivity and subordination, it can also be invoked to justify activity, particularly to justify the potentially deviant and compromising behaviour involved in working outside the home. Taking up employment is frequently defined, both by working women and their families, as a form of female sacrifice for family well-being.

In the face of this *feminization of responsibility,* fisher wives take on additional income-earning tasks to cover unexpected costs related to children' schooling or health care. As a result of their broadening portfolio of labors, women estimated they are now working three to four hours more per day (about a 20 percent increase since 1980). Panguil Bay fisher wives report that they juggle the contradictory pressures between unpaid household labors and market-related work by reducing personal sleep and leisure.

Household Subsidization of Export Aquaculture

At the same time that fishing wives are widening their work portfolios to insure household survival, they are also providing hidden subsidies to commercial aquaculture. Integration of subsistence fishers into export commodity chains has not pulled their households out of poverty. Instead, that small group who are drawn into the waged labor force are

> located in household structures in which the work on this new "export-oriented activity" formed only a small part of the lifetime revenues.... In this case, other household activities which bring in revenues in multiple forms can "subsidize" the remuneration for the "export-oriented activity," thereby keeping the labor costs very low (Hopkins and Wallerstein 1987: 777).

At every point in a commodity chain, households subsidize capitalists' low wages in order to sustain the laborers who produce the commodity. Those waged laborers who make contributions to the prawn or seaweed export sectors do not earn a living wage that is sufficient for the reproduction of the household unit. Her husband's aquaculture income was "never enough," one Lapinig housewife explained during an interview. "I have to work in order for the family to survive. I bear the hardship because we could not depend solely on a monthly salary which is actually less than what we need to purchase household essentials." In fact, the hidden inputs of households are preconditions for the productivity of household members who engage in external waged labor required to produce the goods that are traded in the world economy (Dunaway 2001). In reality, *nonwaged* labors generate the bulk of household resources and subsidize the accumulation of profits within the commodity chain (Mies 1986, Salleh 1997).

Peripheral households subsidize commodity chains through low-paid, nonwaged direct inputs (such as harvesting wild fish for prawn feeds) into the production process. Such household-based labor generates market commodities or informal sector inputs into the export production process, but such labor—especially that of women—has typically remained socially invisible and has received below-market prices (Mies 1986). Women and households subsidize the shrimp commodity chain through several forms of invisible labor and hardship. Women make hidden inputs into the shrimp commodity chain at four levels other than waged labor. First, the biological reality of women's lives is sexual and reproductive; thus, mothers make their first subsidy to capitalism through the bearing and raising of successive generations of laborers. Despite its dependency upon this natural female contribution, however, capitalism has externalized laborer reproduction outside the realm of the economic. Second, the household is the site in which women undertake unpaid labor for those members who are waged laborers. By keeping production costs lower, women's hidden inputs subsidize the production process throughout the commodity chain, thereby keeping consumer prices lower and profits higher. A third way in which fishing wives subsidize prawn commodity chains is through their informal sector activities. When they produce low-priced crafts (such as baskets) or provide nonwaged services (such as packing, transport, or trading) that support the export process, they are integrated directly into the commodity chain. Their contributions remain poorly remunerated, however, and socially invisible. There is a fourth more deeply hidden way in which women subsidize the commodity chains in which their households are situated. The subsistence inputs of women and households at one node may subsidize other nodes of the commodity chain. In effect, the commodity chain structures a network in which laborers and consumers at higher nodes exploit households and women at lower nodes. The low wages, malnutrition, and degraded ecosystems of fishing households keep the global prices of shrimp low, permitting the distant consumer to avoid the real costs of production and to pay cheap prices for this luxury food. While the Panguil Bay fisher wife and her children go lacking in essential protein and iron, the Japanese middle-class housewife and her offspring eat an abundance of her hidden sacrifices and neither pay for nor acknowledge them.

Intrahousehold Inequalities

Fishing women are disadvantaged not only by structural changes outside their families but also by their inequitable households. Unpaid household labor is gender-bifurcated in fishing households. Even though fishing women are responsible for an inequitable share of non-income-generating labor and fishing help to males, fewer than one-third of husbands assist regularly in household work. Since 1985 wives have averaged fifty-one hours weekly of unpaid household labors and assistance with male fishing, whereas husbands have provided only fifteen hours of unpaid household work (Pineda-Ofreneo 1985).

> [W]hen women take on outside economic responsibilities, their supposedly primary responsibility in the household is not diminished.... The amount of time devoted to relatively fixed economic and social responsibilities more than doubled when the demands of housework and family were added to the time spent at paid work. Yet husbands were not inclined to do their share; husbands of employed women reported little more involvement in housework than husbands of unemployed women (Eviota 1986: 203).

Many scholars (e.g., Miraleo 1992) have idealized the degree to which Philippine rural women autonomously control household budgets, but Panguil Bay fishing wives do not agree. "I was supposed to be in charge of the money," one fisher wife complained," but there was no money" (Eder 1999: 113). As Dwyer and Bruce (1988: 235) explain:

> [The wife's] control is largely illusory, for she has no financial autonomy. The pool she manages must cover unavoidable expenditures. In addition, husbands do not withdraw from the scene after delivering their contribution; rather they exercise several mechanisms of control. Most important ... a husband makes sure that "his" money is spent to cover basic family needs as well as his desired level of personal consumption.

Fishing spouses often disagree about how household income and resources should be utilized. On average, most must be allocated for food, water, household tools, and dwelling maintenance, with less than 10 percent available for medical and school expenses. "Even if 92 percent of all Filipino wives hold the purse string," argues Philippine feminist Carolyn Israel-Sobritchea (1987: 91), "there is not much power that goes with it.... While more women in the lower classes keep the money and share with their husbands the right to manage such resources, these powers do not mean much when there is barely enough money to meet household needs."

According to one fisher wife, she and her husband argue more about how money will be spent. "I have to concentrate on basic needs," she explained. "With three kids in school ... there is very little left for other basic needs.... We no longer buy clothes. We recycle old ones.... We have to indoctrinate the children on the value of economizing and prioritizing needs" (Illo and Pineda-Ofreneo 2002: 115). In this context of children going without, women perceive male drinking, smoking, and gambling as unnecessary drains on household resources (Oracion 2001: 9). Panguil Bay wives report that disagreement over the amount of husbands' pocket money is the main cause of quarreling and domestic violence. Some women complained that their husbands utilized as much as one-quarter of household budget for their pocket money. Fishers do not just use money for entertainment and leisure, however, for they must also repair and reinvest in equipment and pay fees associated with their occupation. Consequently, productive expenditures to support the male livelihood that is central to household food and income are often in conflict with household survival needs. In these circumstances, husbands often make independent decisions regarding expenses to cover equipment or fishing loans, leaving it to wives to locate household essentials without an adequate income pool. When women cannot stretch the family budget to cover husbands' demands, they are often the targets of domestic violence, a problem that has continued to escalate throughout the 1990s (Illo and Pineda-Ofreneo 2002).

It is doubtful that we should consider fishing households as "pooling" fully or equitably the income or resources of all members, for males and females secure and control separate funds and often divide financial responsibilities (Eder 1999: 114). Moreover, husbands and wives prioritize spending goals differently, and fishing households commonly exhibit gender-specific expenditures. According to one Panguil Bay wife, women spend "all their earnings on the consumption of the family," but husbands expect to have weekly funds for leisure activities at a level that is not available to their wives. Although men accept responsibility for covering costs of fishing and minimal daily food, women assume responsibility for household and children's expenses.

> At issue is not simply the ways in which women's income is used, but the degree to which men and women differ in taking personal spending money from their earnings. Though the specifics of women's consumption responsibilities vary..., it is quite commonly found that gender ideologies support the notion that men have a right to personal spending money, which they

are perceived to need or deserve, and that women's income is for collective purposes (Dwyer and Bruce 1988: 5–6).

Panguil Bay mothers are aware that children are at greater risk of malnutrition in lean fishing seasons if the women have no independent income. "Cash controlled by women is usually spent by them on family needs, that by men more on personal needs. Not surprisingly, therefore, the daily nutritional shortfalls of children ... are found to be related more closely to the mother's employment than the father's (Agarwal 1988: 89).

In addition to inequalities and power struggles over household budgets, the greater workload of fisher wives has not insured them greater or equal access to crucial needs, such as food or health care. Protein and caloric intake of women is far below that of males (Philippine Food and Nutrition Institute 2005), and women's ailments are ignored until they reach a critical stage (Philippine Department of Health 2002). Lack of access to adequate food is not the only nutritional problem for fishing households, for food is distributed inequitably within households. The most malnourished members of fishing households are mothers, with greater amounts of nutrients going to fathers and teenaged sons (Noralsco 1987). Among our Panguil Bay women interviewees, women reported eating less in order to feed young children. When one pregnant mother's food supply is running low, she loses her appetite, so "the children can eat more."

Conclusion

In line with world-systems analysts (Smith and Wallerstein 1992; Dunaway 2001), neo-Marxist feminists (Mies 1986) and ecofeminists (Salleh 1997; Mies and Shiva 2001), this study views the household as the basic unit for the material and nonmaterial labors that are essential to reproduce and maintain the work force that is essential to the persistence of the capitalist world economy. Because its members are underpaid in that capitalist system, the household is the unit that makes laborer survival possible through resource pooling and distribution (Smith and Wallerstein 1992; Dunaway 2001). Because full proletarianization into waged workers would increase the cost of production and lower profits, the capitalist world-system has structured a controlling mechanism by which the demands of workers for increased compensation can be restrained. That mechanism is the *semiproletarianized* household that is now the dominant mode worldwide (Wallerstein 1983). In such households, "the wages paid to those members engaging in wage-labor activities can be reduced below the level of household reproduction because the household supplements this income with its other income-generating activities" (Wallerstein 1995: 5–6).

Consequently, it is not through waged labor that women are most inequitably exploited; it is through the *self-exploitation* (intensification of personal labor) of their nonwaged and unpaid coping strategies in *semiproletarianized* households. To provide household basic needs, women juggle an ever-widening work portfolio, in order to have a security net that provides a "hedge against failures in any one component of their survival package" (Illo and Polo 1990: 109–10). As fishing households become more deeply integrated into the global food chain both as exporters and importers, self-exploitation becomes their only alternative. As one fisher observed, "it is solely your body that earns a living.... If you rest, you will have nothing to eat" (Ledesma 1982: 171). In the face of the loss of ecological resources that once supported their livelihoods, poor Philippine fisher households have developed an uneasy and inequitable array of coping strategies that includes

- doing without and eating less
- self-provisioning rather than market purchases
- increased self-exploitation: more fishing, more activity in informal sector, more gathering by women
- new household resource allocation (changes in intrahousehold division of resources)
- expanding or restructuring credit or debts
- increased reliance on family and neighborhood networks
- migration to find work
- removing children from school and putting them to work
- fosterage (shifting children to kin household with more resources)
- more extensive resource exploitation (e.g., dynamite fishing)
- selling or pawning household assets or fishing equipment
- stealing

One Filipino described this ever expanding workload this way:

> A bird wakes up at dawn and immediately flies about looking for food.... The bird spends his days doing this. The next day is the same. Me, too. I wake up and scurry around looking for food and work wherever I can find it ... becoming dizzy trying to keep my family alive. By evening, I'm tired and weak. At dawn, I have to be up again doing the same, like the birds (Kerkvliet 1983: 51).

Notes

1. At 2005 prices, corn (27 cents per kilo in U.S. dollars) and rice (44 cents per kilo in U.S. dollars) were more expensive in the Philippines than in the United States.

2. One element of the privatization of family planning is the funding of the FriendlyCare Foundation (www.friendlycare.com.ph), whose mission is to "promote responsible parenthood for sustainable development."

References

Abregana, Betty C. 2000. "Women and Children in Coastal Communities." *SUAKREM Newsletter* 2 (4). Available at http://su.edu.ph/suakcrem/vol2-4.htm.
Adan, E. Y. 2000. "The Impact of Economic Activities on Water Quality and Fish Production in Panguil Bay, Philippines." Ph.D. diss: University of the Philippines–Los Banos.
Afshar, Haleh, and Bina Agarwal, eds. 1989. *Women, Poverty, and Ideology in Asia: Contradictory Pressures, Uneasy Resolutions.* London: Macmillan.
Agarwal, Bina. 1988. *Structures of Patriarchy: State, Community, and Household in Modernising Asia.* London: Zed Books.
Aguilar, G. D. 2002. "Present and Future Role of the College of Fisheries and Ocean Sciences." Working paper, Institute of Marine Fisheries and Oceanology, University of the Philippines in the Visayas.
Ardales, Venancio. 1981. *Time Allocation and Fertility Behavior of Married Women in Fishing Communities of Iloilo, Philippines.* Singapore: Institute of Southeast Asia Studies.
Arnado, M. Janet. 2003. *Mistresses and Maids in the Philippines.* Manila: LaSalle University Press.
Asian Development Bank. 2005. "Poverty in the Philippines: Income, Assets, and Access." Available at www.adb.org.
Atkinson, Jane, and Shelly Errington, eds. 1990. *Power and Difference: Gender in Island Southeast Asia.* Stanford, CA: Stanford University Press.
Barraclough, Solon, and Andrea Finger-Stich. 1996. "Some Ecological and Social Implications of Commercial Shrimp farming in Asia." UNRISD discussion paper, Geneva. Available at www.unrisd.org.
Cabanilla, L. S. 1997. "Achieving Food Security in the Philippines: Some Critical Points to Consider." Working paper no. 97–01, University of the Philippines- Los Banos.
Casino, T. 2004. "Impact of the WTO on the Philippines." Available at www.ibon.org/other/wto-content/teddy.htm.
DeBrun, Suzanne, and Ray Elling. 1987. "Cuba and the Philippines: Contrasting Cases in World-System Analysis." *International Journal of Health Services* 17 (4): 681–701.
Dunaway, Wilma. 2001. "The Double Register of History: Situating the Forgotten Women and Her Household in Capitalist Commodity Chains." *Journal of World-Systems Research* 7 (1): 2–29.
Dwyer, Daisy, and Judith Bruce, eds. 1988. *A Home Divided: Women and Income in the Third World.* Stanford, CA: Stanford University Press.
Eder, James. 1999. *A Generation Later: Household Strategies and Economic Change in the Rural Philippines.* Honolulu: University of Hawaii Press.
Environmental Justice Foundation. 2003. *Smash and Grab: Conflict, Corruption, and Human Rights Abuses in the Shrimp Farming Industry.* London: Environmental Justice Foundation.
Escobar, Arturo. 1994. *Encountering Development: The Making and Unmaking of The Third World.* Princeton, NJ: Princeton University Press.
Escobar, Pepe. 2004. "The Philippines: Disgraceful State, A Five-Part Series." *Asia Times* (October 1, 2, 3, 4, 5).

Eviota, Elizabeth. 1986. "The Articulation of Gender and Class in the Philippines." Pp. 194–206 in *Women's Work: Development and the Division of Labor by Gender,* ed. E. Leacock and H. Safa. South Hadley, MA: Bergin and Garvey.

Hopkins, Terence, and Immanuel Wallerstein. 1987. "Capitalism and the Incorporation of New Zones into the World Economy." *Review* 10 (3/4): 763–780.

IBON Foundation. 2004. "Public Perceptions of Economy and Government." Available at www.ibon.org.

———. 2005. "IBON Feature: WTO at 10: A Decade of Burden for Poor Countries." Available at www.ibon.org.

Illo, Jeanne, and Rosalinda Pineda-Ofreneo. 2002. *Carrying the Burden of the World: Women Reflecting on the Effects of Crisis on Women and Girls.* Quezon City: University of the Philippines.

Illo, Jeanne, and Jaime Polo. 1990. *Fishers, Traders, Farmers, Wives: The Life Stories of Ten Women in a Fishing Village.* Quezon City: Ateneo de Manila University.

International Rice Research Institute. 2003. "Rice Fact Sheet." Available at www.knowledgebank.irri.org.

Israel, D., E. Adan, G. Carnaje, N. Lopez, and J. de Castro. 2003. "Analysis of Long Term Impact of Coastal Resource Management in the Philippines: The Case of Panguil Bay." Working paper, Bureau of Agricultural Research and Philippine Institute of Development Studies.

Irz, X. and J. R. Stevenson, A. Tanoy, P. Villarante, P. Morissens. 2004. "Aquaculture and Poverty—A Case Study of Five Coastal Communities in the Philippines." University of Reading: Department of International Development, Working Paper 4.

Israel-Sobritchea, Carolyn. 1987. "Gender Ideology and the Status of Women in a Rural Economy." Pp. 87–96 in *Essays on Women,* ed. Mary J. Mananzan. Manila: St. Scholastica's College.

Jacinto, E. 2004. "Research Framework on Value Chain Analysis in Small Fisheries." Working paper, Tambuyog Development Center.

JEP ATRE. 2004. "Panguil Bay: Forestry Resource Management Program: Inception Report for the Philippine Bureau of Fisheries and Aquatic Resources, Region 10." Uncirculated document.

Kerkvliet, Benedict. 1983. "Profiles of Agrarian reform in a Nueva Ecija Village." Pp. 43–64 in *Second View from the Paddy,* ed. A. Ledesma, P. Mahil, and V. Miralaco. Quezon City: Ateneo de Manila University.

Ledesma, Antonio. 1982. *Landless Workers and Rice Farmers: Peasant Subclasses Under Agrarian Reform in Two Philippine Villages.* Laguna, Philippines: International Rice Research Institute.

Lim, J. Y., and M. F. Montes. 2002. "Structural Adjustment Program After Structural Adjustment Program, but Why Still No Development in the Philippines?" *Asian Economic Papers* 1 (3): 90–119.

Loquias, Servilla. 1990–1991. "Environmental Issues and Constraints Related to Panguil Bay Coastal Management." *Northwestern Mindanao Research Journal* 15: 41–57.

McMichael, Philip. 1994. *The Global Restructuring of Agro-Food Systems.* Ithaca, NY: Cornell University Press.

Mies, Maria. 1982. "The Dynamics of the Sexual Division of Labor and Integration of Rural Women into the World Market." Pp. 1–28 in *Women and Development: The Sexual Division of Labor in Rural Societies.* New York: Praeger Press.

———. 1986. *Patriarchy and Accumulation on a World Scale: Women in the International Division of Labor.* London: Zed Books.
Mies, Maria, and Vandana Shiva. 2001. *Ecofeminism.* London: Zed Books.
Miraleo, Virginia. 1992. "Female-Headed Households in the Philippines." *Philippine Sociology Review* 40: 46–51.
Naawan School of Fisheries, Mindanao State University. 1991. "Resource and Ecological Assessment of Panguil Bay." Manuscript.
Nash, June. 1994. "Global Integration and Subsistence Insecurity." *American Anthropologist* 96 (1): 7–30.
Naylor, Rosamond. 2003. "Nature's Subsidies to Shrimp and Salmon Farming." *Science Magazine,* 282, 883–888.
Nickerson, Donna. 1999. "Trade-offs of Mangrove Area Development in the Philippines." *Ecological Economics* 28 (2): 279–298.
Noralsco, Cynthia. 1987. "The Woman Problem: Gender, Class, and State Oppression." Pp. 77–86 in *Essays on Women,* ed. Mary J. Mananzan. Manila: St. Scholastica's College.
Oracion, Enrique. 2001. "Filipino Women in Coastal Resources Management: The Need for Social Recognition." SMA Working Paper Series 2001-8, Sociology Department, Silliman University, Philippines.
Philippine Census Bureau. 2004. "Feature for 27 February 2004." Available at www.census.gov.ph.
Philippine Department of Health. 2002. "Philippine Health Statistics." Available at www.doh.gov.ph.
Philippine Food and Nutrition Institute. 2005. "Statistics." Available at www.fnri.dost.gov.ph.
Philippine National Statistical Coordination Board. 2003. "Poverty Statistics." Available at www.nscb.gov.ph.
Philippines Environmental Monitor. 2000. Manila: World Bank Group.
Pineda-Ofreneo, Rosalinda. 1985. *Women of the Soil: An Alternative Philippine Report on Rural Women.* Manila: Philippine Women's Research Collective.
Primavera, J. H. 1997. "Socio-Economic Impacts of Shrimp Culture." *Aquaculture Research* 28: 815–827.
Salleh, Ariel. 1997. *Ecofeminism as Politics: Nature, Marx, and the Postmodern.* New York: Zed Books.
Schelzig, K. 2005. "Poverty in the Philippines: Income, Assets, and Access." Asian Development Bank. Available at www.adb.org.
Shiva, Vandana. 2000. *Stolen Harvest: The Hijacking of the Global Food Supply.* Cambridge, MA: South End Press.
Smith, Joan, and Immanuel Wallerstein, eds. 1992. *Creating and Transforming Households: The Constraints of the World-Economy.* Cambridge: Cambridge University Press.
Szanton, Maria C.B. 1972. *A Right to Survive: Subsistence Marketing in a Lowland Philippine Town.* University Park: Pennsylvania State University Press.
United Nations. 2000. *The World's Women: Trends and Statistics.* New York: Oxford University Press.
USAID-Philippines. 2005. "Provision for Wider Family Planning Options." Available at http://philippines.usaidgov/ophn_so3_ir2.dkt.php.

Wallerstein, Immanuel. 1983. *Historical Capitalism.* London: Verso Editions.
———. 1995. "The Modern World System and Evolution." *Journal of World-System Research* 1 (19): 55–68.
———. 1999. "Ecology and Capitalist Cost of Production: No Exit." Pp. 3–12 in *Ecology and the World System,* ed. W. L. Goldfrank, David Goodman, and Andrew Szasz. Westport, CT: Greenwood Press.
World Health Organization. 1997. "Water Pollution Control." Available at www.who.int.
———. 2000. "Water, Sanitation, and Health in Poor Countries." Available at www.who.int/docstore/water_sanitation_health/agride/ch4.htm.
———. 2001. "Nutrition in South-East Asia." Available at www.whosea.org.
Yoshinori, Murai. 1987. "The Life and Times of Shrimp: From Third World Seas to Japanese Tables." *AMPO Japan-Asia Quarterly Review* 18 (4): 2–9.

9

UTOPYSTICS AND THE ASIATIC MODES OF LIBERATION

GURDJIEFFIAN CONTRIBUTIONS TO THE SOCIOLOGICAL IMAGINATIONS OF INNER AND GLOBAL WORLD-SYSTEMS

Mohammad H. Tamdgidi

> Live content, with greed this world desire not.
> From the Time's "good and evil" free your lot.
> Hold the cup and caress a lover's hair.
> Like your days, they, too, will soon be naught.
> —Omar Khayyam, circa twelfth century AD

Introduction

Asian trajectories of mystical traditions significantly challenge the categories and paradigms associated with the world-systems perspective, particularly in the emerging field of utopistics (Wallerstein 1998) and its comparative/integrative variant "utopystics," which advocates cross-cultural explorations in utopia, mysticism, and science (Tamdgidi 2002b, 2006a, 2007b, 2008a, forthcoming [a] and [b]). Provocatively, the inner subjectivist, culturally determined, and enchanted modes of liberation informing Asian mysticisms in their diverse regional forms—such as esoteric fountainheads of Buddhism in East Asia, Hinduism in South Asia, and Islam and generally monotheism in West and Central Asia—subject world-systems analyses' global, politicoeconomic, and scientific/secular frameworks to critical scrutiny. As such, they can provide opportunities for fostering new conversations in favor of infusing the complex geographies of inner experience into the largely global and world-historical geographies of the world-systems perspective.

Marx developed, borrowing from Hegel, his rather derogatory concept of the Asiatic mode of production as one determined by the arid conditions thought to have characterized the landmass spanning West, South, Central, and East Asia, where the need for channeling water to cultivate the land necessitated the building of massive structures that in turn laid the economic basis for the rise of highly centralized states dominated by despots claiming godlike status. Such political and ideological superstructures, in turn, conditioned construction projects that further symbolized the centralized, godlike powers of the despots. Given the materialist, secular, atheist, antireligious, and orientalist frameworks shaping the classical Marxist view of the East and Asia, it was not surprising to note its minimal appreciations for the conceptual and intellectual innovations brought on, in religious form, by the often inaccessible and esoteric mystical traditions emergent from the region—traditions that were themselves often shaped in distinction from the more visibly dominant political, cultural, and economic milieu of the world-systems housing them.

An important attribute of what one may call the "Asiatic modes of liberation" characterizing the mystical traditions in the region has been their ascetic character. From a modernist point of view, such asceticism and world-escaping tendencies may appear backward, outdated, unrealistic, and unworkable as effective strategies for self-, let alone global, transformation—particularly in the context of a modern world-system and a world-systems analysis that perpetually call for dealing with the public issues arising from the everyday running of the capitalist world economy. One may also argue that, despite the escapist forms such ascetic mystical practices may have taken, however, they essentially contained an attribute regarding alternative modes of human liberation that is quite distinct from not only the dominant but even the oppositional and antisystemic, social diagnoses and prognosis found in the West. This has to do with the notion of property ownership that has occupied a central place in the Western and modern discourses on social organization and transformation.

Western discourses on the nature of the good society have often oscillated between arguments for private or collective property ownership; in the mystical traditions, in contrast, the possessive attitude toward things in the world (be they physical things, ideas, feelings, sensations, relations, or processes, etc.) and attachments to them, individual or collective, is the very factor that is problematized as being the source of much of the human suffering. One may choose to interpret this in the narrow sense of its implications in terms of asceticism and world-escaping behavior. But in a different vein, one may regard such a consideration in terms of the awareness of the limits the human propensity to habituation sets on the development and application of human creative powers to understand and transform the inner and broader human social landscapes.

The theoretical and methodological challenges facing such cross-cultural approaches to utopistics and world-systems analysis are intellectually exciting for those interested in developing sociological imaginations of historical world-systems—past, present, and emergent—characterized by simultaneous attention to the dialectics of inner personal and broader global and world-historical forces shaping the trajectories of world-systems. In this chapter I will draw upon G. I. Gurdjieff's (1872?–1949) hybrid teaching of synthesizing elements from diverse Asian mystical traditions in order to advance conceptual frameworks conducive to the understanding of the operational simultaneity of inner and global world-systems and the comparative/integrative pursuit of liberatory strategies in favor of a just global society. I will argue that enriching the world-systems perspective in favor of imaginative sociological approaches that take seriously the personal as well as the world-systemic discourses on and strategies for realistic historical alternatives to the modern world economy necessitate fruitful revisitations of the unit of analysis question in world-systems studies in favor of the adoption of not a singular unit but two-fold, dialectically conceived, micro/macro units of analyses of *inner* and *global* world-systems.

The Sociological Imagination and World-Systems Analysis

The sociological imagination, according to C. Wright Mills (1959), is characterized by the ability of the mind to relate one's personal troubles to broader public issues. More specifically, it requires its holder to consciously develop and integrate an understanding of one's *inner life* plus what Mills calls his or her "*external career*" (i.e., his or her interactions with others in everyday life) in terms of how they are shaped by the broader "social milieu," consisting of the nature and structure of the *present society* in which he or she lives and the *broader world-historical context* in which the particular and unique features of the present society may best be comprehended comparatively. Mills regards the employment of the sociological imagination as not simply a matter of choice, but a requirement that arises especially from the nature of the culture and society we live in today, and one that must be expected from all sociological endeavors that aim to tackle social problems in a way most conducive to bringing about their effective resolution. The sociology of self-knowledge as proposed and applied in my work (Tamdgidi [1997] 2005, [1999] 2002a, 2002b, 2004/2005, 2007a, forthcoming [a]) has been an effort to further exercise the sociological imagination with a particular emphasis—adopting a nonreductive causal modality of the self-society dialectic—on the exploration of the *investigator's own intra/interpersonal life* in relation to especially the *world-historical* scope of the sociological inquiry.

The world-systems perspective, from its inception, was characterized by several major attributes that have more or less endured throughout the decades and shaped the structures of knowledges produced in the field. These include its holism, its insistence on the primacy of economy, its reluctance to be rigidified into a theory, its Western scientific/secular character seeking to bridge with the knowledge produced in the humanities (hence, its self-characterization as a historical social science), and its concerns for bridging the true and the good, that is, a concern for developing a scholarship that is committed to social change in favor of a just global society.

In his brief but important 2000 essay titled "Where Should Sociologists Be Heading?" Immanuel Wallerstein called for efforts to erase five distinctions whose continuity in world-systems and generally sociological analyses have not borne fruitful results. Namely, he called for erasing the distinction between the studies of the past and of the present (a variant of what he also refers to in terms of the distinction between history and theory, or differently in terms of the distinction between nomothetic and ideographic studies); between studies of the economy, polity, and culture; between studies of the West and the rest; between studies of the true and the good; and between studies in two academic cultures, that is, between the sciences and the humanities.

It is interesting to note that absent from Wallerstein's list of distinctions to be erased was the distinction between the whole and its parts. Nor did he—and these may be variants of the latter—call for erasing the distinction between the macro and the micro, or the global and the personal. This is perhaps due to the fact that the holism of world-systems analysis has been a defining feature of this perspective. In the world-systems perspective, no part of the system can be understood (and thereby effectively transformed) without giving due consideration to the knowledge and transformative requirements of the world-system as a whole.

The problem is, however, that the adoption of such a macro-gravitating conceptual framework characterizing the world-systems analysis does not fit well with the requirements for developing a Millsian sociological imagination. Mills was not oblivious to the need for understanding the nature of the present society as a whole, nor did he fail to point out that the latter needs also to be studied in a world-history context. What Mills required was that the individuals' reflections on public issues at the macro level be undertaken in intimate conceptual conversation with their thoughts on inter/intrapersonal social reality on the micro level.

The positive irony behind Wallerstein's useful advice to sociologists in his 2000 essay is that, if one follows it, one would need to discard many of the a priori determinisms traditionally associated with the world-systems analysis. How can one erase the distinctions between economy, polity, and culture and not also dismantle the analytical primacy of the economy over politics and culture? How can one erase the distinction between the present and the past (and future, if we consider Wallerstein's *Utopistics* [1998]) and not consider how economy, polity, and culture may be differently implicated as primary causal factors across diverse past, present, and emerging world-systems? How can one erase the distinction between theory and history, between nomothetic and ideographic study, and not find a need to conceptualize broadly macro and intimately micro social processes in addition to concrete historical investigations? How can one erase the distinction between the West and the rest, between the true and the good, and between the sciences and the humanities and not pay equal attention to diverse forms of knowledge produced across multiple civilizational traditions, secular and religious alike, that have appeared in history and shaped the diverse regional trajectories of human development?

In the spirit of erasing the distinction between the world-systems analysis and the sociological imagination, in this chapter I aim to apply a mode of analysis informed by what Wallerstein has proposed in terms of the erasure of a variety of distinctions as noted above. If, as Wallerstein has repeatedly stressed, the world-systems perspective is not an already accomplished theory but an evolving and transient conceptual framework open to modification, it can perhaps also benefit from the adoption of imaginative sociological frameworks that would make it more truthful, and effective, in fostering the good in the self and the broader society in favor of utopistic outcomes.

Toward this end, I will draw upon my studies of a particular Asian esoteric tradition associated with the teachings of G. I. Gurdjieff (see Tamdgidi 2002b, 2004, 2006a, forthcoming [b] and more broadly 2005/2006 and 2007a), the twentieth century Transcaucasian mystic philosopher and teacher, as a heuristic device for the development of a microlevel conceptual framework critically complementing the macro conceptual apparatus of the world-systems perspective.

Gurdjieff's Conceptual Apparatus

Mysticism has traditionally been concerned with seeking direct knowledge or experience of the ultimate hidden meaning or truth of existence. Inspired by the Hermetic principle "As Above, So Below"—and in contrast to its extroversive Western counterpart—Eastern mysticism has generally pursued its aim introversively, through the attainment of personal self-knowledge and transformation in search of "perfect" inner states. Since such ideal inner states have often been associated with or are considered to be derived from the assumed perfect being of god(s), mysticism has frequently been associated with religious doctrines or experiences—even though, strictly speaking, mysticism does not have to be religious or introversive in orientation, such as in the cases of Western pantheistic and nature mysticisms (Bishop 1995).

Gurdjieff's teaching represents an effort at seriously grappling with the problem of habituation as a cardinal factor in human enslavement. Although his conceptual apparatus limits the scope of such a liberatory project to the inner and at most interpersonal dimensions—more or less taking for granted the objective conditions that may be responsible for the fragmented and alienated nature of the inner personal life—one can critically engage with his and similar spiritual traditions in a broader project involving the implications the human propensity to habituation may pose for the perpetuation and reproduction of inner and global world-systems.

George Ivanovitch Gurdjieff (1872?–1949) was an enigmatic Transcaucasian philosopher, mystic, and teacher of esoteric dances, exercises, and movements who has been widely acknowledged for having introduced to the West during the early twentieth century a rational synthesis of Eastern mysticism and, subsequently, for having significantly shaped the ideas and practices of the new religious movements. According to Jacob Needleman, "Gurdjieff gave shape to some of the key elements and directions found in contemporary spirituality" (Needleman 1996: xi). "In the half-century after Gurdjieff's death," writes Needleman,

> Tibetan lamas, Indian gurus, Zen roshis have become increasingly familiar figures in Western culture, and many of them have been struck by the traditional aspects of Gurdjieff's teaching. It is more difficult, however, for the Western scholar, theologian, or seeker to place a figure like Gurdjieff, who seems to fit no formula, wears no robes, recites no mantras, and demands no homage. He seems neither of East nor West. Possibly he is both. (1996: x)

What distinguishes Gurdjieff's ([1933] 1973, 1950, [1963] 1985, 1973, [1981] 1991) mysticism is its hybrid character drawing upon and moving beyond many of the mystical sources of his teaching. As a "seeker of truth," Gurdjieff distinguished three traditional ways of the fakir, the yogi, and the monk in Asian mysticism—ideal-types that may roughly, though not entirely, correspond with certain mystical practices in Islam, Hinduism, and Buddhism—depending on whether the physical, the intellectual, or the emotional center of human organism is one-sidedly exercised in retreat from social life as the initial launching ground for efforts toward the ultimate goal of all-rounded spiritual self perfection (Ouspensky 1949). Suggesting that these three one-sided "ways" to self-perfection are prone to failure since their trainings take longer (thus often unrealizable during a single lifetime) and their one-sidedly developed adepts become often vulnerable to habituating forces upon reentry into social life, Gurdjieff advocated an alternative "Fourth Way" school in mysticism. He characterized this approach as one concerned with the *parallel harmonious development* of the physical, the intellectual, and the emotional centers of the organism to be pursued not in retreat from, but *in the midst of*, everyday life. Such a three-fold task simultaneously taking place in the midst of life was, in his view, essential for awakening the human organism (via the radical attainment of personal self-knowledge) from sleep, mechanicalness, and spiritual imprisonment and for bringing about effective self-transformation in pursuit of harmonious human development in search for the ultimate truth of existence.

Gurdjieff treated the ordinary human "individual" as a multiplicity, fundamentally structured by his or her "three-brained" physical, intellectual, and emotional centers, to which he associates three primary forms of awareness—the instinctive (or unconscious), the waking conscious, and the subconscious.[1] For Gurdjieff the ordinary individual is actually a "legion" of I's acting independently from one another. Conditions of ordinary life prevent the automatic formation of an actual "individual," a master self, and ultimately a "soul," in the human being, making the attainment of these possible only as a result of conscious and intentional efforts on the part of the person him/herself. The journey of self-understanding and change must therefore begin with the conscious labor of self-knowledge. Through self-observation, self-remembering, and external considering of one's interactions with others in or outside school "work," the actual reality and the complex dynamics of one's inner multiplicity, fragmentation, sleep, mechanicalness, and slavery is increasingly revealed to oneself and brought under one's immediate attention. This leads to a deeply felt "shock" to the organism expressed in terms of experiencing the "terror of the situation," that is, of suddenly realizing one's being a machine, a slave, asleep.

Through discovering and then melting down, in the heat of intentional physical, intellectual, and emotional exercises and "sufferings," the chief and subsidiary forms of habituated "buffers" deeply entrenched within and across the three centers, it becomes possible to gradually dealienate and harmonize one's fragmented body, thoughts, and emotions. This—a second intentional shock to the organism—then leads to the more prolonged awakening of the innate sense of objective conscience already in existence but deeply buried in the subconscious. By means of this one can then unite one's inner essence and external personalities into a single, indivisible but consciously and intentionally adaptable, whole guided by a singular master, a truly "individual" "I." The organism, having died to its mechanicalness through experiencing the conscious and intentional shocks of self-knowledge and change, is now exposed to the possibility in time of achieving extraordinary levels of physical health, intellectual productivity, and emotional stability. These higher self-experiences of the organism, according to Gurdjieff, are prerequisites for conscious ascendance in the "cosmic food chain" in the path of fulfillment of duties towards possible understanding of, and union with, God.

According to Gurdjieff, the energies associated with the three inborn and relatively independently functioning centers in the human inner world are not automatically blended into one another by nature but require conscious and intentional effort on the part of the person throughout his or her lifetime to harmoniously develop the organism into an "individual" being. Human evolution and development, according to Gurdjieff, cannot be truly comprehended without an appreciation of the role played by the conscious and intentional human agency.[2] Gurdjieff used the analogy of a passenger's carriage driven by a horse and driver in order to illustrate the three-part architecture of the human organism. In an ideal state, the master "I" represented by the passenger can effectively communicate and direct the actions of the intellectual driver, carriage body, and the emotional horse, by a functioning mediation of the symbolic languages of words (between the passenger and the driver), motion/brake lever (between the driver and the carriage), shafts (between the carriage and the horse), and reins (between the driver and the horse). The ideally developed organism can act in conscious unison, as an indivisible whole, because the forms of consciousness corresponding to the carriage, the driver, and the horse—namely the physical instinctive, the intellectual waking conscious, and the emotional subconscious minds—are able to mutually blend into one another at the will of the master "I" represented by the passenger. In actual conditions found in reality, however, the organism is often alienated and fragmented within to such a degree that the body carriage is drastically out of shape and abused; the driver intellect is in a state of perpetual sleep, drunkenness, and false imagination; and the emotional horse is completely out of control. The supposed master "I" lacks the knowledge and ability to communicate with and guide the centers using their unique languages. Most often, he is simply not there—the organism takes any passerby as its "true self," submitting to it for a short while until the next wandering passenger comes along. The self that promises to get up at 6 a.m., Gurdjieff mused, is often not the self which actually gets up, turns off the alarm, and goes back to sleep. Consequently, depending on the situation of each organism, one or another lopsidedly developed and "fixated" center and its associated selves rob other centers (and their associated selves) of the energy needed for their development, leading to the crystallization of diverse forms of habituated and disharmonious personality types—physical, intellectual, emotional, and a variety of their blends—across human organisms.

The most fundamental challenge Gurdjieff's cosmology and anthropology poses for the sociological thought—including the world-systems analysis *and* that of the Millsian sociological imagination—is the problematization of the singularity of the "individual" considered as a singular acting unit. Gurdjieff turns the notion of "multiple personality disorder" onto its head and in effect tells us that it describes a general human condition responsible for the human propensity to habituation. For Gurdjieff, considering his focus on the microsocial everyday interactions, the working unit of analysis is not the individual, therefore, but the self, or the "I," legions of which occupy, under prevailing conditions, the inner and interpersonal landscapes of the disharmonized and fragmented person in everyday life. Gurdjieff takes the multiplicity of selves as a point of departure of his understanding of the nature of human behavior and troubles, and he regards the existence of individuality, that is, a conscious and intentional unity of diverse selves, to be the ultimate goal of a lifetime's effort rather than a presumed, inborn, and taken-for-granted attribute of the person.

What puts the person to sleep and makes him or her a prisoner of social circumstances, acting like a machine, is the separate functioning of the physical, intellectual, and emotional centers in the organism, which contributes to the presence of unconscious, waking conscious, and subconscious modes of awareness and behavioral patterns in the organism. It is this fragmentation of the organism, and the separate, unevenly developed, functioning of the centers that then set the ground for an inner landscape populated with separately acting and behaving selves.

Revisiting the Unit of World-Systems Analysis

The most defining concepts of the world-systems perspective are perhaps best expressed in its name, that is, the ideas of the "world" and the "system," implying spatial and temporal considerations to be employed in social analysis. On the one hand, a concretely existing society is to be analyzed spatially in the entirety, encompassing the totality, of social relations organically constituting it. On the other hand, temporally, the enduring and organically fundamental features of those relations are to be identified. The notion of the "world" in "world-system," in other words, does not necessarily imply a globally encompassing social organization, nor should the notion of "system" prevent the recognition of the transient and changing nature of a given society under consideration. The point of a unit of analysis thus considered, therefore, is to always keep the *relational totality* of the *structural features* of a social formation under constant attention and scrutiny when studying any of its respective parts. This interpretation of the "world-system" may be noted in the manner in which Hopkins and Wallerstein (1982) used the concept to identify a variety of social formations in history that were neither necessarily globe-encompassing nor transhistorically enduring. Ancient minisystems, world empires, and world economies have all been considered varieties of world-systems appearing in history.

The value of insisting on the world-system as a singular unit of analysis has therefore been in regard to adopting a holistic methodology that would aid the consideration of each part of the social system in relation to the workings of the system as a whole. In this regard, it is important to note the *relative* nature of what constitutes wholes and parts. For example, the existence and nature of an apple cannot be adequately understood without recourse to its position in the structural system of a tree that constitutes it. In this sense, the apple is considered a part of the tree. An apple, on its own, however, constitutes an organic whole for the parts constituting its own respective inner structure/system. Likewise, what we regarded as a whole previously, that is, the tree, is a whole only unto itself in a relative sense, and actually its existence cannot be adequately explained and understood without the consideration of it as a part of a broader whole, that is, the orchard, the land, the earth's biosphere, and even more broadly the solar system, and so on.

Therefore, it is important to consider that when we use the notion of the "world-system" as a research tool, it can be applied on a variety of spatiotemporal levels without losing its conceptual value. The application of the concept to the study of capitalism, therefore, should be seen as only one such application and should not be limited to it. In fact, failing to regard the capitalist world-system as only a part of broader social or historical wholes constituting it would limit the value of the concept to the point of arriving at misleading conclusions. For instance, if the primacy of economy in a capitalist social formation is overly generalized to an attribute of all human history as a whole (an approach that Marx, in my view wrongly, adopted via his "materialist conception of history"), this would lead to analytical practices and conclusions that ignore the specificity of other types of world-systemic structures in which, variously, politics or culture may predominate or, alternatively, social formations in which the distinction between the three spheres are not institutionalized or rigidly separated, as in ancient civilizational contexts, or as may perhaps be created in emergent or future social formations (cf. Tamdgidi 2006b, 2007b).

Drawing on the example of the apple and the tree, therefore, we could expand the notion of world-systems studies in such a way that would recognize the dialectics of global and inner world-systems. The inner life of the person, in other words, may be regarded as a whole at its own level, which is, from another vantage point a part of the global world-system as a broader whole. Undoubtedly, an adequate understanding of one's inner life cannot be arrived at without an understanding of the larger social world-system of which it is a part—as one would not expect to understand the existence of an apple apart from the tree, the orchard, and so on. It can also be argued, however, that an understanding of the tree as a whole may not yield an adequate understanding of the specific apple now in my hand with all its defects, an understanding of which requires a concrete study of that specific apple. As far as the working of the tree system is concerned, the apple's inner system is in its uniqueness an important part of what makes the tree what it is. I think it is this consideration that led Mills to stress so emphatically that we should practice sociology in both its macro and intimately micro and personal dimensions because the understanding and transformation of one cannot be adequately achieved without the understanding and transformation of the other. After all, how a world-system is conceived and transformed (or not) is always conditioned by the unique biographical circumstances of the person(s) engaging (or not) in such conceptualizations and transformations.

For the purpose of advancing the sociological imagination, and more specifically a sociology of self-knowledge, therefore, this manner of conceptualizing world-systems studies can be very fruitful, for it would expand the notion of the world-system as a unit of analysis into a dialectical consideration of macro- and microsociological twin units of analyses that can accommodate the exploration of nonreductive dialectics of personal troubles and broader public issues.

Moving from spatial to temporal considerations, fusing a simultaneously macro- and microsociological framework into the world-systems analysis must begin with the notion of "system," or more broadly, "structure." When we speak of system or structure, we usually mean to suggest that an enduring, patterned, and repetitive process of social interaction is at work. For instance, the set of concepts "core," "periphery," and "semiperiphery" are used in world-systems analysis to denote structurally enduring systemic zones in the capitalist world-system associated with the presence (or co-presence in the case of semiperiphery) of relatively low-wage and low-skilled labor and weak-state social features (as in the peripheral regions) versus relatively high-wage and high-skilled labor and strong-state social features (as in the core regions). The notion is that the modern world-system continually produces and reproduces a structural pattern of hierarchically organized zones associated with core, peripheral, and semiperipheral characteristics, even though concrete geographical regions constituting the world economy may, in one or another historical time, move up or down the hierarchical ladder.

But what does a patterned, repetitive social interaction *actually* consist of, and why is it treated, or referred to, as systemic or structural? It means that social actors continually, often subconsciously or habitually, engage in behaviors that continually produce and reproduce specific modes of economic, political, and cultural outcomes that maintain the world-systemic status quo. From a microsociological point of view, especially that envisioned in the work of the sociologist Herbert Blumer (1986), social structure is not one standing over and above the concrete conduct of individual social actors but is produced and reproduced *through* the personally conducted social interactions of everyday life at work, home, and street, actual or (nowadays) virtual. To the extent that one, consciously or subconsciously, engages in producing and reproducing patterns of social (economic, political, and cultural) interaction that sustain the perpetuation of the global world-system, one is contributing to its maintenance, and to the extent that one consciously (and perhaps at times unconsciously) disrupts such patterns of world-systemic behavior, one has disrupted the reproduction of the system. At the level of social movements, involving what Blumer calls "joint actions," the continuity of antisystemic and what Tamdgidi (2001) has called "othersystemic" behavior can perhaps lead to the transformation of the system as a whole. In *The Exercise of Influence in Small Groups,* based on his doctoral dissertation, T. K. Hopkins (1964) pointed to this tension and dialectics of the small group of acting participants and the larger social structures when he wrote:

> Any type of social system can tolerate a certain degree of deviance. For each type a characteristic range exists within which the activities of the participants may depart from the norms of the system without occasioning any basic changes in the structure of the system. Departures outside of this range do, however, occasion fundamental structural changes, even, possibly, the dissolution of the particular system. (Hopkins 1964:183)

If we regard the "world-system" not as a state, but as a *process* of "world-systemization," a unity of diverse, consciously and subconsciously/habitually, interacting behaviors (macro- or micro-oriented, economic, political, cultural, physical, intellectual, emotional, and so on), then we can consider personal human behaviors in everyday social interactions in terms of the extent to which they produce and reproduce or, differently, question, resist, and transform what are the constituent, conscious or subconscious, processes of the world-system. Similarly, one can also conceive of human behaviors that actually produce alternative types of social interactions that do not simply aim at resisting and transforming the prevalent "interaction rituals" (Goffman 1982) constituting the world-system, but construct and reconstruct alternative modes of social interaction that may be qualitatively different from those associated with the prevalent world-systemic status quo.

Imperial systems are by their very nature socially stratified systems, and the reproduction of such stratified social structures requires everyday social (personal as well as economic, political, and cultural) interaction rituals that produce and reproduce the stratified imperial social structures. As simplistic as it may seem at first, it may be of interest to consider the extent to which the inner life of the disharmonious person may be characterized, on the micro level, as being hierarchical, similar to the architecture of the hierarchical zones in an imperial world-system. Applying Gurdjieff's ideas, one may similarly identify core, peripheral, and semiperipheral regions in the landscape of multiple selves populating the inner and interpersonal lives of the individual. The consideration of a divided inner life and its population by alienated and stratified selves is not new and original in Gurdjieff, and other scholars have explored this view (cf. Deikman 1982, and Zurcher 1977, for instance). The works of the late cultural theorist Gloria Anzaldúa embody imaginative considerations of the multiplicity of selves in spiritual and self/social transformation (Anzaldúa 1987; see also Keating 2000; Anzaldúa and Keating 2002; Tamdgidi 2006a and forthcoming [a]). George Herbert Mead (1934) also recognized how the existence of multiple personalities can be regarded as a common affair. Even

Marx's reference, in his famous "preface" to *A Contribution to the Critique of Political Economy* ([1859] 1970), to the distinction between what social actors say and do in politics may be reinterpreted in terms of the significance of a divided geography of multiple selfhoods at work complicating the course of human political action. With Gurdjieff, however, this possibility is raised to a paradigmatic trouble afflicting the human race and regarded as a cardinal question to be dealt with in the pursuit of human liberation from inner slavery, mechanicalness, and existential anesthesia.

The consideration sought after here is to associate the continuity of hierarchically organized imperial world-systems with the continuity of hierarchically organized inner world-systems of selves at the personal level. The macro and micro conditions may then be regarded as being twin-born, making the workings of the hierarchical world-system as a whole possible. The distinction between the two spheres, thereby, is erased in such a consideration, since the perpetuation (and, therefore, disruption) of one is dependent upon the perpetuation (and disruption) of the other. It is the inner divisions of centers and the disparate workings of a multitude of alienated selves populating the inner and interpersonal lives of the individuals that allow for the perpetuation of behavioral patterns that un/subconsciously, and at times consciously, reproduce the structural attributes of the world-system that constitutes them in return. Mead's (1934) notion of twinborn-ness of the self and society is quite relevant here, one that Anzaldúa (1987) differently articulates in terms of the simultaneity of self- and world knowledge and transformation (cf. Tamdgidi forthcoming [a] for elaboration of this theme).

Gurdjieff's approach to the study of personal troubles is different from the Millsian in that the former does not take for granted the singularity of the person reflecting on his or her troubles. Besides, in Gurdjieff's view, such states of inner division make the organism vulnerable to habitual behavior that can most effectively be recognized and dealt with through conscious and intentional efforts on the part of the person him/herself. It is one thing to study others' personal troubles and how they are shaped by broader public issues, and another to study one's own.

Conclusion

The basic point here is that the continued operation of an imperial world-system fundamentally requires habituated behaviors on the part of those participating in and running it. Such a habituated functioning of human behavior is what makes possible the continued operation of the hierarchically organized and stratified world-system that also in turn constitutes, educates, and conditions such behavioral patterns on the part of the participants in the world-system. Disruptions of such automatic processes would effectively involve, to the extent they are undertaken, disruptions in the operation of the world-system hitherto constituting them. But the disruption of a personal behavior on the part of the person first requires becoming aware of the existence of the habitual behavior in the first place, and in particular the extent to which the particular behavior is a product, and in turn reproductive, of the workings of the world-system as a whole. As Gurdjieff put it, for one to set oneself free, one must first realize that one is in prison.

Here is where the significance of a sociological imagination—and of Gurdjieff's contributions in terms of his emphases on the paradigmatic significance of the human inner division and multiplicity, the resulting human propensity to habituation, and the subsequent need for seeking radical personal self-knowledge and change—becomes evident. In Gurdjieff's conceptual framework, the disruption of the person's habitual behavioral pattern does not come by itself without conscious and intentional effort on his or her own part. A teacher can only supply his pupils with leather, Gurdjieff advised; they should make their own shoes. Using the analogy of the carriage, driver, horse, and passenger as described above, Gurdjieff would maintain that the passenger I, the master self—often not even present in the inner world-system owing to long years of the system's malfunctioning—cannot emerge without a conscious and intentional decision and effort on the part of the person to turn his or her own life and organism into an object of his or her observation, autobiographical self-remembering and reexamination, and continual self-reflective study in ever broader contexts.

This conscious and intentional splitting of the self into a subject and an object of study would be the first and a most important step of taking charge of the process, but by no means is it sufficient. The various centers of the organism whose separate habitual functionings make possible the continuation of the habituated and mechanical functioning of the organism and its behaviors have their own languages, and their workings cannot be adequately understood, let alone transformed, without specific efforts and exercises—physical, intellectual, and emotional—that would enable the unique behavioral "inner world-system" of the person to be adequately comprehended and transformed in the desired direction. Here is another area in which Gurdjieff's "three-brained" approach to inner world knowledge and transformation becomes distinguished from Mills's merely intellectual approach. To understand and change oneself, it is not sufficient merely to "think" through one's personal troubles; it is necessary to partake in specific physical, intellectual, and emotional exercises that harmoniously develop one's knowledge of oneself and the world across the three physical, intellectual, and emotional dimensions.

Asian mystical traditions, their shortcomings notwithstanding in other regards, diversely provide highly developed and precise meditative techniques for cultivating such continual and many-sided modes of self-observation, self-remembering, external considering, and detachment regarding possessive attitudes to ideas, things, feelings, relations, and processes. Gurdjieff's "Fourth Way" school is notably different, given its aim to move beyond ascetic and world-escaping habits of traditional Asian mysticisms in its effort to cultivate detached attitudes toward social life while living *in its midst* rather than in retreat from it.

Significantly, what needs to be added to Gurdjieff's conceptual apparatus—and this is where he falls short in his teaching—is the effort on the part of the person to also seek an understanding of the extent to which his or her personal life and troubles are shaped by and reproductive of the life of the global world-system on the macro level. Such a two-fold understanding is what Mills characterizes as the sociological imagination, an imagination that the sociology of self-knowledge also seeks to foster by way of its more specific focus on achieving a simultaneity in the investigator's self- and world-historical reflexivity.

Studying Asia through the world-systems perspective is one thing. Another, is to appreciate how historical world-systems, and the world-systems perspective, can be more effectively comprehended and transformed in favor of utopystic outcomes through learning from the ideas and traditions diversely indigenous to the continent.

Notes

1. According to Gurdjieff these three forms of awareness are present in each of the three centers. In other words, the physical body is said to be constituted primarily of instinctive, but also of consciously, performed and subconsciously learned/habituated behaviors. Likewise, our intellectual activity is regarded as being predominantly conscious, but also accompanied by instinctive and habitually performed dimensions; and so our emotions are considered to involve mainly subconscious, but also conscious and instinctive dimensions.

2. According to Gurdjieff, "In speaking of evolution it is necessary to understand from the outset that no mechanical evolution is possible. The evolution of man is the evolution of his consciousness, and *'consciousness' cannot evolve unconsciously*. The evolution of man is the evolution of his will, and 'will' cannot evolve involuntarily. The evolution of man is the evolution of his power of doing, and 'doing' cannot be the result of things which 'happen.'" (quoted in Ouspensky 1949: 58

References

Anzaldúa, Gloria E. 1987. *Borderlands/La Frontera: The New Mestiza*. San Francisco: aunt lute books.
Anzaldúa, Gloria E., and AnaLouise Keating (eds.). 2002. *This Bridge We Call Home: Radical Visions for Transformation*. New York: Routledge.
Bishop, Donald H. 1995. *Mysticism and the Mystical Experience: East and West*. London: Susquehanna University Press.
Blumer, Herbert. 1986. *Symbolic Interactionism: Perspectives and Method*. Berkeley: University of California Press.

Deikman, Arthur J. 1982. *The Observing Self: Mysticism and Psychotherapy.* Boston: Beacon Press.
Goffman, Erving. 1982. *Interaction Ritual: Essays on Face-to-Face Behavior.* New York: Pantheon Books.
Gurdjieff, G. I. [1933] 1973. *Herald of Coming Good: First Appeal to Contemporary Humanity.* New York: Samuel Weiser.
———. 1950. *All and Everything: Beelzebub's Tales to His Grandson.* New York: Harcourt, Brace.
———. [1963] 1985. *Meetings with Remarkable Men.* New York: Viking Arkana.
———. 1973. *Views from the Real World: Early Talks of G. I. Gurdjieff.* New York: Arkana/Penguin Books.
———. [1981] 1991. *Life Is Real Only Then, When "I AM."* New York: Viking Arkana/Triangle Editions.
Hopkins, Terence K. 1964. *The Exercise of Influence in Small Groups.* Somerville, NJ: The Bedminister Press.
Hopkins, Terence K., Immanuel Wallerstein, and associates. 1982. *World-Systems Analysis: Theory and Methodology.* Beverly Hills, CA: Sage Publications.
Keating, AnaLouise (ed.). 2000. *Gloria E. Anzaldúa: Interviews/Entrevistas.* New York: Routledge.
Marx, Karl. [1859] 1970. *A Contribution to the Critique of Political Economy.* Ed.and with an introduction by Maurice Dobb. New York: International Publishers.
Mead, George Herbert. 1934. *Mind, Self, and Society.* Chicago: University of Chicago Press.
Mills, C. Wright. 1959. *The Sociological Imagination.* New York: Oxford University Press.
Needleman, Jacob. 1996. "Introduction." Pp. ix-xii in *Gurdjieff: Essays and Reflections on the Man and His Teaching,* ed. Jacob Needleman and George Baker. New York: Continuum.
Ouspensky, P. D. 1949. *In Search of the Miraculous: Fragments of an Unknown Teaching.* New York: Harcourt Brace Jovanovich.
Tamdgidi, Mohammad H., instructor, ed., and contributor. [1997] 2005. *'I' in the World-System: Stories from an Odd Sociology Class. Selected Student Writings, Soc. 280Z: Sociology of Knowledge: Mysticism, Utopia, and Science, Binghamton University, Spring 1997.* Medford, MA: Okcir Press.
———. 2001. "Open the Antisystemic Movements: The Book, the Concept, and the Reality." *Review* 24, no. 2: 299–336.
———. [1999] 2002a. "Ideology and Utopia in Mannheim: Toward the Sociology of Self- Knowledge." *Human Architecture: Journal of the Sociology of Self-Knowledge* 1, no. 1 (Spring): 120–140. [An earlier version of this article was presented to the "History of Sociology" Refereed Roundtable Session at the Ninety-Fourth Annual Meeting of the American Sociological Association, August 6–10, 1999, Chicago.]
———. 2002b. "Mysticism and Utopia: Towards the Sociology of Self-Knowledge and Human Architecture (A Study in Marx, Gurdjieff, and Mannheim)." Ph.D. diss., State University of New York at Binghamton.
———. 2004. "Freire Meets Gurdjieff and Rumi: Toward the Pedagogy of the Oppressed and Oppressive Selves." *The Discourse of Sociological Practice* 6, no. 2 (Fall): 165–185.

———. 2004/2005. "Working Outlines for the Sociology of Self-Knowledge." *Human Architecture: Journal of the Sociology of Self-Knowledge* 3, nos. 1 and 2 (Fall/Spring): 123–133.

———. 2005. "Orientalist and Liberating Discourses of East-West Difference: Revisiting Edward Said and the Rubaiyat of Omar Khayyam." *The Discourse of Sociological Practice* 7, nos. 1 and 2 (Spring/ Fall): 187–201.

———. 2005/2006. "Private Sociologies and Burawoy's Sociology Types: Reflections on Newtonian and Quantal Sociological Imaginations." *Human Architecture: Journal of the Sociology of Self-Knowledge* 4, nos. 1 and 2 (Fall/Spring): 179–195.

———. 2006a. "Anzaldúa's Sociological Imagination: Comparative Applied Insights into Utopystic and Quantal Sociology." *Human Architecture: Journal of the Sociology of Self-Knowledge* 4, Special Issue (Summer): 265–285.

———. 2006b. "Toward a Dialectical Conception of Imperiality: The Transitory (Heuristic) Nature of the Primacy of Analyses of Economies in World-Historical Social Science." *Review* (Journal of the Fernand Braudel Center) 24, no. 4: 291–328.

———. 2007a. "Abu Ghraib as a Microcosm: The Strange Face of Empire as a Lived Prison." *Sociological Spectrum* 27: 29–55.

———. 2007b. *Advancing Utopistics: The Three Component Parts and Errors of Marxism*. Boulder, Colo.: Paradigm.

———. 2008a. "From Utopistics to Utopystics: Integrative Reflections on Potential Contributions of Mysticism to World-Systems Analyses and Praxes of Historical Alternatives." Pp. 202–219 in *Islam and the Orientalist World-System*, ed. Khaldoun Samman and Mazhar Al-Zo'by. Boulder, Colo.: Paradigm.

———. 2008b. "Public Sociology and the Sociological Imagination: Revisiting Burawoy's Sociology Types." *Humanity & Society* 32, no. 1: 131–143.

———. Forthcoming (a). "'I Change Myself, I Change the World': Gloria Anzaldúa's Sociological Imagination in *Borderlands/La Frontera: The New Mestiza*." *Humanity & Society*.

———. Forthcoming (b). *Gurdjieff and Hypnosis: A Hermeneutic Study*. New York: Palgrave Macmillan.

Wallerstein, Immanuel. 1998. *Utopistics: Or, Historical Choices of the Twenty-First Century*. New York: New Press.

———. 2000. "Where Should Sociologists Be Heading?" *Contemporary Sociology* 29, no. 2:306–308.

Zurcher, Louis A., Jr. 1977. *The Mutable Self: A Self-Concept for Social Change*. Beverly Hills, CA: Sage Publications.

CONTRIBUTORS

Christopher Chase-Dunn is Distinguished Professor of Sociology and Director of the Institute for Research on World-Systems at the University of California—Riverside. He is the author of *Rise and Demise: Comparing World-Systems* (with Thomas D. Hall), *The Wintu and Their Neighbors: A Very Small World-System in Northern California* (with Kelly Mann). He is the founder and former editor of the *Journal of World-Systems Research*. Chase-Dunn is currently conducting research on global party formation and antisystem social movements as well as on the growth/decline phases and upward sweeps of cities and empires and future global state formation.

Wilma A. Dunaway is Professor in the School of Public and International Affairs at Virginia Tech. She is a specialist in world-system analysis, international political economy, international slavery studies, Native American Studies, and Appalachian Studies. She has won several awards for her four books about Appalachia and about slavery. Her interdisciplinary work has appeared in numerous history and social science journals.

Thomas D. Hall holds the Edward Myers Dolan Chair of Anthropology and is University Professor at DePauw University in the Department of Sociology and Anthropology in Greencastle, Indiana. He writes about indigenous peoples; pastoral nomads; ethnicity; world-systems analysis ancient and contemporary; and frontiers. His books include *Social Change in the Southwest, 1350–1880* and with Christopher Chase-Dunn, *Rise and Demise: Comparing World-Systems*. His teaching and research interests include globalization; comparative study of frontiers; and social, economic, political, and cultural changes taking place over thousands of years.

M. Cecilia Macabuac is Assistant Professor of Sociology and Director of the Kinaadman Research Center, Xavier University, Philippines.

Richard Niemeyer is a graduate student in the department of Sociology at the University of California–Riverside. His research in Political Economy focuses on synthesizing and expanding classical and contemporary theory through the utilization of empirical insights derived from fractal geometry, complex network analysis and dynamical systems.

Contributors

Robert J. S. Ross is Professor and former Chair of Sociology and Director of the International Studies Stream at Clark University where he was elected Faculty Chair of the University 2000–2006. He is an Adjunct Professor of Community Development and Planning. In 2005–2006 he was Chair of the American Sociological Association Section on the Political Economy of the World System. He has taught at Clark University since 1972 and has held visiting appointments at MIT, Michigan and Harvard Universities, and Wheaton College. His books include *Global Capitalism: The New Leviathan* (coauthored) and *Slaves to Fashion: Poverty and Abuse in the New Sweatshops*. His latest work, on labor rights and international trade, is published in *Foreign Affairs, Third World Quarterly, Labor Studies Journal,* and *Dissent* magazine. Ross's work has also appeared in *The Nation, In These Times,* and *Tikkun.* He is an Associate Editor of the *Journal of World-Systems Research.* He has been a consultant to the economic development agency of the city of Boston, the Massachusetts Department of Welfare, and a speechwriter and policy adviser in the Massachusetts State Senate.

Robert Schaeffer is Professor of Global Sociology at Kansas State University. He is coauthor with Torry Dickenson of *Fast Forward: Work, Gender, and Protest in a Changing World* and *Transformations: Feminist Pathways to Global Change*.

Steven Sherman is a scholar and activist with a doctorate in sociology from Binghamton University. His work has appeared in *Review, Journal of World-Systems Research,* and *Counterpunch.* He maintains the web site www.lefteyeonbooks.org.

Boris Stremlin is a comparative macrosociologist with interests in world history, the sociology of knowledge, and geopolitics. His dissertation is on "Constructing a Multiparadigm World History: Civilizations, Ecumenes and World-Systems in the Ancient Near East" at Binghamton University. He taught sociology at Wright State University in Dayton, Ohio. His publications have appeared in *Review* and in the Political Economy of the World-System series.

Mohammad H. Tamdgidi teaches sociology and social theory at the University of Massachusetts, Boston. He is the author of *Advancing Utopistics: The Three Component Parts and Errors of Marxism.* He has published in *Review, Sociological Spectrum,* and *Contemporary Sociology,* and his works have appeared in several edited collections. Tamdgidi is the founding editor of *Human Architecture: Journal of the Sociology of Self-Knowledge,* a publication of the Omar Khayyam Center for Integrative Research in Utopia, Mysticism, and Science.

Ganesh K. Trichur is Assistant Professor of Political Economy at St. Lawrence University. He has published in *Globalizations* and in the *Journal of World-Systems Research.* His recent publications are on the social effects of Hurricane Katrina (in *Racing the Storm: Implications and Lessons Learned from Katrina* edited by Hillary Potter), on political Islamism and political Hinduism *(Islam and the*

Orientalist World-System, edited by Khaldoun Samman and Mazhar Al-Zo'by), and internal migration in China.

Immanuel Wallerstein is Director of the Fernand Braudel Center for the Study of Economies, Historical Systems, and Civilizations, Binghamton University, and Senior Research Scholar at Yale University.

ACKNOWLEDGEMENTS

This volume grew out of the thirty-first meeting of the Political Economy of the World-System (PEWS) Section of the American Sociological Association, 10–11 May 2007, at St. Lawrence University in Canton, New York. I thank St. Lawrence University for offering the space and the financial support to convene the conference in the North Country. Dr. Eve Stoddard (Chair of the PEWS Committee) and Dr. John Collins (Associate Professor) from the Department of Global Studies, were the strongest supporters of the Conference—it was their involvement, encouragement, and help that enabled the Global Studies department to successfully organize the conference. Thanks to Professor Grant Cornwell, Academic Dean of St. Lawrence University, and to Margaret Bass and Liz Regosin, for their support and encouragement. As the chair of the PEWS Committee, Dr. Eve Stoddard provided invaluable direction. Many thanks also to the other members of the PEWS Committee for their involvement in the process—Anne Csete and Erin McCarthy (from the Asian Studies Program), Karl Schonberg, Assis Malaquias, Judith DeGroat, Evelyn Jennings, Florence Molk, Abye Asefa, Elun Gabriel, Donna Alvah, and Vernadette Gonzales. Joyce Sheridan was indispensable for logistical support and Juli Pomainville designed the flyer. Thanks to President Dan Sullivan and Anne Sullivan of St. Lawrence University for warmly welcoming all the participants. Thanks to all the students who attended the conference.

Political Economy of the World-System Annuals Series

Immanuel Wallerstein, Series Editor

I. Kaplan, Barbara Hockey, ed., *Social Change in the Capitalist World Economy.* Political Economy of the World-System Annuals, 01. Beverly Hills/London: Sage Publications, 1978.

II. Goldfrank, Walter L., ed., *The World-System of Capitalism: Past and Present.* Political Economy of the World-System Annuals, 02. Beverly Hills/London: Sage Publications, 1979.

III. Hopkins, Terence K. & Immanuel Wallerstein, eds., *Processes of the World-System.* Political Economy of the World-System Annuals, 03. Beverly Hills/London: Sage Publications, 1980.

IV. Rubinson, Richard, ed., *Dynamics of World Development.* Political Economy of the World-System Annuals, 04. Beverly Hills/London: Sage Publications, 1981.

V. Friedman, Edward, ed., *Ascent and Decline in the World-System.* Political Economy of the World-System Annuals, 05. Beverly Hills/London/New Delhi: Sage Publications, 1982.

VI. Bergesen, Albert, ed., *Crises in the World-System.* Political Economy of the World-System Annuals, 06. Beverly Hills/London/New Delhi: Sage Publications, 1983.

VII. Bergquist, Charles, ed., *Labor in the Capitalist World-Economy.* Political Economy of the World-System Annuals, 07. Beverly Hills/London/New Delhi: Sage Publications, 1984.

VIII. Evans, Peter, Dietrich Rueschemeyer & Evelyne Huber Stephens, eds., *States versus Markets in the World-System.* Political Economy of the World-System Annuals, 08. Beverly Hills/London/New Delhi: Sage Publications, 1985.

IX. Tardanico, Richard, ed., *Crises in the Caribbean Basin.* Political Economy of the World-System Annuals, 09. Newbury Park/Beverly Hills/London/New Delhi: Sage Publications, 1987.

X. Ramirez, Francisco O., ed., *Rethinking the Nineteenth Century: Contradictions and Movements.* Studies in the Political Economy of the World-System, 10. New York/Westport, CT/London: Greenwood Press, 1988.

XI. Smith, Joan, Jane Collins, Terence K. Hopkins & Akbar Muhammad, eds., *Racism, Sexism, and the World-System.* Studies in the Political Economy of the World-System, 11. New York/Westport, CT/London: Greenwood Press, 1988.

XII. (a) Boswell, Terry, ed., *Revolution in the World-System.* Studies in the Political Economy of the World-System, 12a. New York/Westport, CT/London: Greenwood Press, 1989.

XII. (b) Schaeffer, Robert K., ed., *War in the World-System*. Studies in the Political Economy of the World-System, 12b. New York/Westport, CT/London: Greenwood Press, 1989.

XIII. Martin, William G., ed., *Semiperipheral States in the World-Economy*. Studies in the Political Economy of the World-System, 13. New York/Westport, CT/London: Greenwood Press, 1990.

XIV. Kasaba, Resat, ed., *Cities in the World-System*. Studies in the Political Economy of the World-System, 14. New York/Westport, CT/London: Greenwood Press, 1991.

XV. Palat, Ravi Arvind, ed., *Pacific-Asia and the Future of the World-System*. Studies in the Political Economy of the World-System, 15. Westport, CT/London: Greenwood Press, 1993.

XVI. Gereffi, Gary & Miguel Korzeniewicz, eds., *Commodity Chains and Global Capitalism*. Studies in the Political Economy of the World-System, 16. Westport, CT: Greenwood Press, 1994.

XVII. McMichael, Philip, eds., *Food and Agrarian Orders in the World-Economy*. Studies in the Political Economy of the World-System, 17. Westport, CT: Greenwood Press, 1995.

XVIII. Smith, David A. & József Böröcz, eds., *A New World Order? Global Transformations in the Late Twentieth Century*. Studies in the Political Economy of the World-System, 18. Westport, CT: Greenwood Press, 1995.

XIX. Korzeniewicz, Roberto Patricio & William C. Smith, eds., *Latin America in the World-Economy*. Studies in the Political Economy of the World-System, 19. Westport, CT: Greenwood Press, 1996.

XX. Ciccantell, Paul S. & Stephen G. Bunker, eds., *Space and Transport in the World-System*. Studies in the Political Economy of the World-System, 20. Westport, CT: Greenwood Press, 1998.

XXI. Goldfrank, Walter L., David Goodman & Andrew Szasz, eds., *Ecology and the World-System*. Studies in the Political Economy of the World-System, 21. Westport, CT: Greenwood Press, 1999.

XXII. Derluguian, Georgi & Scott L. Greer, eds., *Questioning Geopolitics*. Studies in the Political Economy of the World-System, 22. Westport, CT: Greenwood Press, 2000.

XXIV. Grosfoguel, Ramón & Ana Margarita Cervantes-Rodriguez, eds., *The Modern/Colonial/Capitalist World-System in the Twentieth Century: Global Processes, Antisystemic Movements, and the Geopolitics of Knowledge*. Studies in the Political Economy of the World-System, 24. Westport, CT: Greenwood Press, 2002.

XXV. (a) Dunaway, Wilma A., ed., *Emerging Issues in the 21st Century World-System, Volume I: Crises and Resistance in the 21st Century World-System*. Studies in the Political Economy of the World-System, 25a. Westport, CT: Greenwood Press, 2003.

XXV. (b) Dunaway, Wilma A., ed., *Emerging Issues in the 21st Century World-System, Volume II: New Theoretical Directions for the 21st Century World-System*. Studies in the Political Economy of the World-System, 25b. Westport, CT: Greenwood Press, 2003.

XXVI. (a) Reifer, Thomas Ehrlich, ed. *Globalization, Hegemony & Power*. Political Economy of the World-System Annuals, 26a. Boulder, CO: Paradigm Publishers, 2004.

XXVI. (b) Friedman, Jonathan & Christopher Chase-Dunn, eds. *Hegemonic Decline: Present and Past*. Political Economy of the World-System Annuals. Boulder, CO: Paradigm Pubishers, 2005.

XXVII. Tabak, Faruk. *Allies as Rivals: The U.S., Europe and Japan in a Changing World-System*. Political Economy of the World-System Annuals, 27. Boulder, CO: Paradigm Publishers, 2005.

XXVIII. Grosfoguel, Ramón, Nelson Meldonado-Torres, and José David Saldívar. ed., *Latin@s in the World-System: Toward the Decolonization of the Twenty-first Century U.S. Empire*. Political Economy of the World-System Annuals, 28. Boulder, CO: Paradigm Publishers, 2005.

XXIX. Samman, Khaldoun, and Mazhor Al-Zo'by. eds., *Islam and the Orientalist World-System*. Political Economy of the World-System Annuals, 29. Boulder, CO: Paradigm Publishers, 2008.

XXX. Trichur, Ganesh K., ed., *The Rise of Asia and the Transformation of the World-System*. Political Economy of the World-System Annuals, 30. Boulder, CO: Paradigm Publishers, 2009.